THE GRAND NATIONAL

Anne Holland was a successful point-to-point rider and one of the first to compete (and win) under National Hunt rules once the law changed. She is the author of many books on horse-racing including *Steeplechasing: A Celebration of 250 Years; The Grand National: The Irish At Aintree; Arkle: the Legend of 'Himself'*; and *Festival Fever: the Irish at Cheltenham*. She lives near Marlborough in Wiltshire.

THE
GRAND NATIONAL

*A Celebration of the
World's Greatest Horse Race*

Anne Holland

WEIDENFELD & NICOLSON

First published in Great Britain in 2019 by Weidenfeld & Nicolson
This paperback edition published in 2021 by Weidenfeld & Nicolson
an imprint of The Orion Publishing Group Ltd
Carmelite House, 50 Victoria Embankment
London EC4Y 0DZ

An Hachette UK Company

3 5 7 9 10 8 6 4 2

ISBN (Mass Market Paperback) 978 1 4746 1199 2
ISBN (eBook) 978 1 4746 1200 5

Typeset by Input Data Services Ltd, Somerset

Printed and bound in Great Britain by Clays Ltd, Elcograf S.p.A.

www.weidenfeldandnicolson.co.uk
www.orionbooks.co.uk

Contents

Author's Note and Acknowledgements

The Grand National always delivers. This celebration of the world's greatest horse race is loosely based on various record holders – indisputable ones, like the youngest winning jockey Bruce Hobbs, for instance, along with those less defined but probably agreed by most, such as unluckiest loser, Devon Loch. It is surprising how few records have changed over the decades. One chapter from more than a century ago features the tiny dual grey winner The Lamb, another the five wins of jockey George Stevens (still more than any other rider). Fascinating tales and fantastic feats old and new including, in more recent times, jockeys like Richard Dunwoody and Leighton Aspell with their own special records in the great race and featuring some of the trainers and owners who supported them; the determination to run the bomb scare National; Mick Fitzgerald's account of surviving a Stewards' Enquiry (and a special thanks to him for writing the foreword); the huge Irish resurgence after enjoying only one win (L'Escargot) in forty years, from the memorable heyday of the 1950s to Bobbyjo on the cusp of the new century; the two Scottish winners and one from Wales; the great racing rivalry of A.P. McCoy and Richard Johnson; the National's legendary commentators from television and radio; horses who won at 100-1; and, of course, the rise of female jockeys – how much longer to wait until the first one emulates *National Velvet*?

I extend my heartfelt thanks to all the following for their time, help and co-operation freely given, and without whom this book could not have been written. I am especially indebted to Mick Fitzgerald for kindly writing the foreword and Rose Paterson, Chairman of Aintree Racecourse, for her warm words; also, in alphabetical order:

Aintree Racecourse; Marcus Armytage; Leighton Aspell; BHA; Kim Bailey; Tracey Bailey; John Baker; Charles Barnett; Vida Bingham; David Bridgwater; Charlotte Budd (née Brew); Joanne Burke; Frank Casey; Frank Casey Junior; Bob Champion; Bob Champion Cancer Trust; The Hon Mr Justice Frank Clarke, Chief Justice of Ireland; Richard Dunwoody; Gordon Elliott; Charlie Fenwick; Mick Fitzgerald; George Freeman, MP; Bryony Frost; Tim Gautrey; Lavinia Greacen; Martin Greenwood; John Hales; Trevor Hemmings; Leanne Holden; Griselda Houghton-Brown; Richard Johnson; John Kempton; John Leadbetter; Brian Lee; David Lort-Phillips; Martin Lynch; Jimmy Mangan; Belinda McClung; Sir Anthony McCoy; Louise Magee; Mouse Morris; Sir Nicholas Mostyn; Dr Richard Newland; Lady Oaksey; Michael O'Leary; Jonjo O'Neill; Lisa O'Neill; Rose Paterson; Nigel Payne; John Pinfold; David Pipe; Martin Pipe; Jenny Pitman; Chris Pitt; Geraldine Rees; Kathryn Revitt; Davy Russell; Lucinda Russell; Alan Samson, Orion Publishing; Peter Scudamore; Oliver Sherwood; Christopher Simpson (the Grand National Anorak); Deborah Thomson; Katie Walsh; Andrew Wates; Caroline White; Lucy Wilkinson; Evan Williams; Venetia Williams.

Foreword by Mick Fitzgerald

The first thing that hit me about this book is how enthusiastic Anne is about the world's greatest steeplechase. Anybody who has ever had 50p on a runner in the race or drawn one in a sweepstake will feel they know a bit about the Grand National, but the thing that shines through here is how much the writer has enjoyed the journey talking to the players in this great sport.

Some of the stories in here are ones that I am familiar with as I was part of them. Reading them again was a fantastic trip down memory lane and I enjoyed the journey. Lots of the other great stories of triumph are filled with personal snippets that made the read even more worthwhile.

In a strange way, reading this made me feel very proud of the fact that I am part of something that is so special on lots of levels. The Grand National is the world's greatest steeplechase and Anne's book only enhances this fact with some brilliant anecdotes.

I am sure you will enjoy the journey it takes you on.

Message from the Chairman

Reading Anne Holland's superb Grand National reminds me why it is such a privilege to be involved with the great race.

This encyclopaedic and lively book resonates with the author's passion and knowledge and, as she relates tales of triumph, tragedy, farce and sheer unexpectedness, gives us all the chance to re-live those glorious stories.

The National has overcome many vicissitudes in its long history and the stalwarts who saw it through its darkest hours are rightly acknowledged. But from Lottery to The Lamb and Manifesto, from Devon Loch to Foinavon and Red Rum, from Captain Becher to the Duke of Albuquerque, Ginger McCain and Trevor Hemmings, this is a race that forges hero horses, magnificent losers, unforgettable legends, huge characters and great public affection.

For me, the chapters on recent winners have brought the spine-tingling excitement of the last few years to life. Many Clouds, the bravest of the brave, Arthur, the big bay horse from Scotland and of course, Tiger Roll, the 'little rat', have given us memories to savour for ever.

I hope you will read this book and revel in it all, then come to Aintree, the home of the world's greatest race, and take part in racing history.

Rose Paterson
Chairman, Aintree Racecourse

Introduction

Saturday, 6 April 2019: 180 years since the first running of the Grand National. Much has changed – but so much more has remained the same: the excitement, the anticipation, the adrenaline. Those challenging fences, the long distance, the brave jockeys and most of all the magnificent horses.

The build-up is a time-honoured part of the race, no less so in 2019. From the anticipation of the announcement of the weights at a special lunch in the Cunard Building, close to the Liverpool docks and the larger-than-life statue of the four Beatles, to many press discussions as to the chances of the most fancied . . . and then along comes Tiger Roll. A second Cross-Country victory at the Cheltenham Festival was meant to be his big moment, but by winning so easily his price shortened sharply, bringing another record into debate: could he win the National as the shortest-priced winner ever, exactly one hundred years after the 11-4 winner Poethlyn? (Golden Miller started at 2-1 in 1935 the year after he won, but unseated.) Or can Richard Johnson finally win on his twenty-first attempt? And then the hopes of golden girl Bryony Frost are dashed with a broken collarbone at a minor meeting just days after her victory in the Cheltenham Festival's Grade 1 Ryanair Chase, ruling her out of Aintree.

The Grand National is spine-tingling and never fails to produce stories. It fired the public imagination right from the beginning, in 1839, and today there is more interest than ever, with a worldwide television audience of some 600 million in 140 countries.

Once, in the late 1970s, I savoured being a tiny part of the supporting cast, riding in the amateurs' hurdle race after the National and absorbing the whole intense atmosphere. Riding out among the stars early in the morning, away from the empty stands and pristine surroundings; breakfast in the lads' hostel, walking the course and seeing the crowds stream in, watching the race from close quarters; and later looking across to the stands, empty once more, but now engulfed in a sea of white litter.

Today there is increased safety, but one has only to look at the opening chapter to see that safety concerns were expressed from its founding. There have always been those dead set against it, claiming it to be dangerous. Much has been done over the years, and in the twenty-first century the famous fences have been modified, with the solid inner core being made more flexible, the drop at Becher's reduced, and the landing levelled (the ditch behind it had already been filled in, in 1989, and a safety factor of forty horses was introduced in 1984). Apart from the laudable result of drastically reduced injuries, modifications to the fences have also resulted in a better class of horse taking part, where previously owners would not risk running their best horses.

With a maximum top weight of 11 stone 10 pounds, the days of a winner carrying 12 stone 7 pounds have long since gone (my favourite National horse, Manifesto, once humped 12 stone 13 pounds into third place). The last horse to carry 12 stone to victory was the immortal Red Rum.

It is interesting but maybe not surprising with this greatest of all steeplechases to discover just how few records have been broken over the years. The most obvious is the number of consecutive rides, held for so long by Michael Scudamore (sixteen), and it is Richard Johnson who has ridden in it for twenty in a row, from a total of twenty-one rides, without winning yet. Sir

A.P. McCoy rode seventeen times consecutively, finally winning it in 2010, from a total of twenty rides.

It is no great revelation, either, that female jockeys have been quietly, steadily – and deservedly – rising to the fore. Three, all with reasonable chances, took part in 2018, with the first British-trained horse home ridden by one of them. Why, in these days of equality, when women have become an integral part of jump racing, have I included two chapters on them? The answer lies in history. Just look at the early difficulties, berated by press, pundits, male jockeys and trainers, and even their own sex, and then see how they have come into their own in the final chapter.

Let us salute all the awe-inspiring horses, heroes and heroines past and present – and future.

1

Lottery

First winner, 1839

If one quality is needed above all others to win the world's greatest steeplechase, the Grand National, it is 'heart', that intangible will to win; only then come luck and ability . . .

So it was with the very first winner, Lottery, and Jem Mason – a highly spirited pair with as much will as talent. There was nothing foppish about 'Dandy' Jem, as he became known, when, at the age of fourteen, he set off with his cob to travel eighty miles from Stilton, Leicestershire, to his parents' new home near Harrow. Having scorned a lift in the carriage, the lad completed the journey on horseback in one day.

His father was a horse jobber and it was natural that Jem and his brother, Newcombe, should grow up nagging and making horses, schooling them, and showing them off in the hunting field. Horses were in Jem's blood, and when he discovered that a dealer called Mr Tilbury had about two hundred horses near their new home, and that Mr John Elmore, a great steeplechasing figure of the time, had horses only four miles away, he was soon to be found 'rough-riding' for them – if it happened that Jem found his way more frequently to Elmore's, it might just have been that the owner's pretty daughter had something to do with it.

Soon Jem had but two ambitions: to be a famous jockey and to win the hand of the fair Miss Elmore. Being a determined sort of chap, with the inherent will to win, he succeeded in both.

Jem learned much about horse coping from Mr Elmore, who

had an old-fashioned manner but knew how to win races, often working his horses in hand. When Mr Elmore acquired Lottery, Jem set about training him in a fashion that would be considered cruel today but raised few eyebrows at the time. Back then, before the birth of the Grand National, he was not considered a likely top horse. No one could have foreseen that he would still rank among the immortals 180 years later.

Bred in Yorkshire on the Jackson farm near Thirsk, the mealy-mouthed colt, who was originally called Chance, was by another horse called Lottery out of an unregistered mare, Parthenia. He was unfurnished, narrow and rather long-backed but showed modest promise by winning a flat race at the Holderness Hunt meeting of 1834 as a five-year-old. He was then sent to Horn-castle Fair and offered for sale as a hunter.

John Elmore was the only dealer to take much interest in the leggy horse; he had him trotted up, then got Newcombe Mason to jump him over some rails. He was a bit green, but Newcombe reported, 'The 'orse can jump from 'ell to 'ackney,' and a deal was done for £120.

Not that Lottery's jumping lived up to much when he arrived back at the Harrow stables: in his first schooling session he fell over a gate and was out of action for some months.

It was about this time that Jem Mason set out on a path towards his first ambition: to be a famous jockey. At the St Albans meeting of 1834, he was offered the ride on a rogue reject from the flat, a hard puller called The Poet, owned by Lord Frederick Beauclerk, the hunting vicar of St Albans. The ground was a quagmire, and it was all Jem could do to carry his saddle and the 4 stone of lead needed to build his weight up to the required 12 stone. Things went badly for him at the start, for the horse was slowly away and refused the first fence. Lord Beauclerk, wanting to do well on his local track, wrung his hands in despair, probably wondering why he had put up such an inexperienced young jockey. But suddenly everything changed, for 'Mason had magic in his hands and quicksilver in his heels and few horses would not run sweetly for him.' The Poet won by twenty lengths.

No wonder, after such a debut, everyone in racing was talking about Jem Mason. His name was made. There was not a big race he did not go on to win in his career, and he even went to France, where he won the big steeplechase in Paris on St Leger.

With fame came Jem's love of clothes and of a gentlemanly image. He found tailors in Savile Row who were only too happy to cut him fine suits for nothing, knowing he would be a walking advertisement for them. As for his boots (free, of course), he had the feet made by Messrs Wren in Knightsbridge and the legs by Messrs Bartley in Oxford Street; history does not record which maker stitched the two together. On his hands he wore white kid gloves.

None of this finery prevented Jem from getting on with his job of schooling young horses, and with Lottery he had plenty of wrangles. The jockey always made sure he won the battles,* but he took many falls in the process. The first thing he did when Lottery arrived was dispense with the severe curb bit, using instead a double-reined snaffle. He then set about converting the 'uncouth brute' into a 'balanced, cracking hunter', regularly following Mr Anderson's fast-running staghounds. If Lottery fell at a fence, Jem would give him such a hard knock that the horse made sure he jumped it clean next time. Should he refuse, Jem kept at him until he jumped, even if it ended in a fall. He made him jump the garden table – set for a meal, complete with chairs, which became quite a party piece – and anything else he could find to school over.

Soon Lottery detested the sight of Jem so much that, when they went racing, Jem had to hide his racing silks under his jacket until the last minute before mounting, lest he should be savaged. But then the horseman kidded him into tractability,

* As told by Ivor Herbert and Patricia Smyly in *Winter Kings*.

Lottery responding to what were described in *Winter Kings* as Jem's 'magic hands and the hypnotic power in the soul of all great jockeys'.

Lottery's early racing career was inauspicious: he raced round little local tracks, today mostly covered by London suburbs, and indoors at the Bayswater Hippodrome; he dead-heated in a steeplechase at Kensal New Town; but it was when he bolted off the course at Finchley and leaped right across a lane that Jem told John Elmore this was no ordinary hunter.

In 1837 he ran in the St Albans Steeplechase, the precursor of the Grand National, but his saddle slipped. Before the 1838 race he was 'amiss' and, as was the custom of the day (for both humans and equines), he was 'bled'. Even with this drastic treatment he finished third (and was placed second after an objection). When fully recovered, he won a big steeplechase at Barnet 'in a common canter', and then caused a minor sensation by beating Captain Becher on his great Vivian at Daventry, more famous today for its radio mast than any trace of a racecourse.

So John Elmore's sights were firmly set on the big new steeple-chase that was to be run at Aintree the following year, a similar race having taken place at nearby Maghull for the past three years. He sent Lottery to the Epsom yard of George Dockeray, who had won the Derby with Lapdog. There, none of the speedy flat-racers could get away from the raw-boned half-bred chaser called Lottery.

The new race was all the rage and over fifty of the best steeple-chasers in the land were entered, including some from Ireland. Called the Grand Liverpool Steeplechase (in 1843 the Liverpool and National Steeplechase), it was a sweepstake of 20 sover-eigns, forfeit 5 sovereigns, with 100 sovereigns added; weights 12 stone each for gentlemen riders; four miles across country; the second to save his stake, the winner to pay 10 sovereigns towards expenses; no rider to open a gate or ride through a gateway or more than 100 yards along any road, footpath or driftway.

Long before the time of radio and television, cars or planes, sponsorship or mass media, and certainly mobile phones or internet, the whole racing fraternity was talking about the race. On the day, Aintree was a veritable Mecca. From north, south, east and west, Scotland, Ireland and Wales they came; by railway, steamer, coach, gig and wagon; the gentry arriving in 'swell turn-outs' and staying in fine mansions.

The Liverpool hotels and boarding houses were overbooked to the extent that some slept four to a bed; the Waterloo and Adelphi Hotels each let 100 beds. Omnibuses and horse-drawn cabs were so full that even offers of half a guinea for a 2/6d seat failed – with the result that, on Tuesday, 26 February 1839, droves of people walked the three miles from Liverpool to Aintree in the bright early morning sunshine, ready for a scheduled 1 p.m. start. All roads led to Aintree and were jammed solid, piemen mixing with chimney sweeps, cigar sellers with thimble-riggers. Scuffles broke out in brimful taverns along the way, and pickpockets had a field day.

The fashionable wore tall hats with curved brims and short boots with loose 'trowsers'; some were dressed in frock coats, while others were kitted out in knee breeches and hessian boots. Women – and there were a fair few – wore large, fan-shaped bonnets, shawls across their shoulders and 'skirts of majestic volume'.

Soon the crowds had filled the stands to overflowing, paying 7 shillings (35 pence) each for the privilege. Most were unable to find more than oranges and hot gingerbread to eat as other provisions soon ran out. Everyone was abuzz. Would the Irish horse Rust beat the English favourite Lottery, who could be backed at 5-1? Or would the fancied mare The Nun prove good enough on the day? Surely the best bet to clear the 5-foot stone wall in front of the stands would be another well-backed mare, Charity, for she was trained over stone walls in Gloucestershire. Would

Tom Ferguson's three Irish horses – Rust, Daxon (which he was to ride himself) and Barkston – cope with the fly fences after their native banks and ditches?

There were only three really formidable fences on the course. Besides the wall, there was a dammed brook making 8 feet of water, faced by a 3 foot 6 inch timber paling out of plough; this was called Brook no. 1 (but not for long). Brook no. 2 had a small bank guarding a deep wide ditch and stout post and rails, with an overall spread of 9 feet and a considerable drop. The rest – a total of fifteen on the first circuit, with fourteen jumped again on the second round – were mostly little banks barely 2 feet high, gorsed on top and faced with small ditches. The last two fences were ordinary, upright sheep hurdles.

The ground was as testing as the most difficult fences; it had been a fill-dyke February and there was plough and wheat to cross as well as turf, very tiring over a distance of four miles. Then, as now, it was not a course for the unfit or the faint-hearted.

The runners and riders had spent the morning getting themselves sorted out – The Nun, found to be 'too fat', was reputedly given a severe pre-race gallop – and as one o'clock approached Lord Sefton called the seventeen horses into line. With a mighty roar from the crowd, he dropped his flag and they were off, skipping over the first small fences.

Daxon was the first to show, followed by Captain Becher on Conrad, but when they came to the first brook Captain Becher fell and, with sixteen other horses thundering towards it, he took the only evasive action he could think of: he crawled into the deepest part of the brook to escape the flying hooves. Thus the fence entered history, and ever since has been known as 'Becher's Brook'. As for the captain, who is purported to have said that he never knew water tasted so foul without whisky in it, he scrambled out, remounted and chased the remainder so hard that he soon regained the lead – only to fall again, after which Conrad galloped off loose, avoiding recapture and a possible further fall.

Meanwhile, Tom Ferguson and Daxon were setting a great pace, the Irishman unaware that another of his runners, Rust, had been trapped in a lane by a mob who, not wanting him to win, had virtually kidnapped him.

There was another surprise at the end of the first circuit when the Cotswold horse Charity fell at the wall, which Lottery jumped superbly. The Nun seemed to fade at the second brook, and Dictator caught his knees in a fence, fell and was remounted, but he fell dead at the next fence. The race's first fatality caused the sort of outcry in the press which has occurred repeatedly up until the present time.

It was now becoming obvious that Lottery was going the best and, when Daxon fell, with The Nun and Paulina tiring, Lottery and Jem Mason sailed into the lead. They put in a mighty 33-foot leap at the last hurdle and won, as they liked, in a canter.

Only Sir George Mostyn's Seventy Four, whose rider was the great 'Black Tom' Olliver, got anywhere near the winner; while the Irish, ignoring the fact that it was the same for everyone, belligerently claimed that the fences had been unfair. Paulina was a poor third, True Blue fourth, The Nun fifth, Railroad sixth, and Pioneer seventh and last. Of the remainder, poor Rust, who had been abducted, was recorded as pulled up, while Dictator, Conrad, Cramp, Rambler, Daxon, Barkston, Cannon Ball, Jack and Charity all fell.

Lottery's time of 14 minutes 52 seconds is the slowest on record (although in a couple of early years no time was recorded), but the race had included heavy plough and there is no doubt that he was a great horse. So great, in fact, that, in future races, conditions were stipulated specifically against him, the like of which were not to be seen until the mighty Arkle almost a century and a quarter later. There was one race 'open to all horses except Lottery' and another for which the entry fees were: '£40 Lottery, £5 maidens, £10 all others'.

*

After that historic first Grand National win, Lottery swept all before him: he won at Cheltenham, Stratford-on-Avon, Maidstone and Dunchurch, after which it was said he could trot faster than most could gallop.

Lottery uncharacteristically fell at the stone wall in the 1840 Grand National, possibly through trying to take on Mr Power on Valentine, who had laid a bet that he would be first over that obstacle. Lottery took a terrible fall, bringing down Columbine and The Nun, who landed in a heap on top of him. Yet his reputation was such that the following year, after he had won the Cheltenham Steeplechase, the Grand National conditions stipulated that a winner of the Cheltenham race must carry an 18-pound penalty. (The weight for the National was a level 12 stone for the race's first four runnings; thereafter it became a handicap.) So in 1841, when the wall was temporarily replaced by an artificial brook, the great Lottery was burdened with 13 stone 4 pounds – which remains a record – and Jem Mason, with good sense ahead of his time, pulled the horse up.

In the next National, the organisers again insisted that Lottery should shoulder the 18-pound penalty for his Cheltenham win two years earlier. Refusing to forsake their hero, the public backed him down to 5-1, but the weight proved too much and he was again pulled up. It seems poetic justice that the winner was another horse of John Elmore's, Gay Lad.

In 1843, when the race became a handicap and the stone wall was revived for one more year before being banned for ever, Lottery ran once more. Now carrying 12 stone 6 pounds, on fast ground in contrast to the first year's deep, he was backed to 4-1 second favourite and was not disgraced in finishing seventh.

Lottery is known to have won his last race at Windsor in 1844, but accounts of his retirement vary: either he became a hack at Epsom then pulled a cart at Neasden, or he pulled a plough, or he retired to the hunting field.

For Jem Mason there was to be a painful illness, cancer of

the throat, from which he died in 1866. The esteem in which he was held was such that Tattersalls organised a Jem Mason subscription, to which many people felt honoured to contribute. He had numerous glowing obituaries, none more sincere than that of his long-time friend and rival, Tom Olliver, who had ridden hundreds of miles with him both racing and schooling across country: 'I can say without fear of contradiction that he was the finest horseman in England – I have never ridden with him without envying the perfection of his style.'

Meanwhile, the most successful National-winning rider of all time was making his mark on the great race . . .

2

George Stevens

Rode most winners, 1856–70

If there was ever a fine judge of pace and master of the tactical waiting race it was George Stevens, record five-time winner of the Grand National, the instigator of the maxim 'hunt round on the first circuit'.

A jockey of unusual caution – whose approach was the reverse of the devil-may-care attitude that typifies many intrepid riders – he was rewarded with almost no injuries in a career spanning twenty years, only to be killed while riding his cob at home.

Born in 1833 on Cleeve Hill, overlooking what is now the premier National Hunt track at Cheltenham, it was at Aintree, home of the world's most famous steeplechase, that Stevens left his indelible mark.

His was a feat of horsemanship and jockey-craft unparalleled. Between 1856 and 1870 he won the National on Free Trader, on the sisters Emblem and Emblematic, and twice on The Colonel; and he unselfishly passed on his knowledge and advice to many budding young riders.

About the rashest thing Stevens ever did was run away from home to become a jockey. Although he was light and small enough to ride on the flat, it was the sight of steeplechasers in action in the natural amphitheatre of Cheltenham race-course below his home that stirred the lad. He grew up at a time when the sport was having to withstand pressures from such as Dean Close, founder of the school which still bears his name in Cheltenham, who opposed racing on moral grounds.

In Tom Olliver, one of steeplechasing's first riding cracks, George found the best possible mentor, and he gleaned much valuable advice from him.

George Stevens calculated his riding to the last degree in order to avoid interference. To see his frail form shivering with nerves before a race, one might have thought his career doomed, but in fact he was simply concentrating intensely on the task ahead. Once in the saddle he displayed nothing but cool confidence. He would invariably lay off the leaders on the first circuit and at Aintree would frequently drop himself out in last place.

In race after race those in the stands thought he must have left it too late. Time and again he would catch hold of his horse's head and come with a rattle to pass runners tired by the pace and distance; his timing seldom let him down.

George was eighteen years old when he achieved his first major success, winning the Grand Annual Steeplechase at Wolverhampton; and that year, 1852, he had his first ride in the Grand National, without success. The title 'Grand' had been prefixed to the National five years earlier in 1847, when its precise title became The Grand National Handicap Steeplechase.

From the start his style caused considerable comment. Never one to bustle a horse going into a fence, he remarked, 'More races are lost through a horse being interfered with than by falling of their own accord.'

George's home town of Cheltenham took the small, delicate-looking man to their hearts. After his first National win on Free Trader in 1856, at the age of twenty-two, they lit a bonfire on Cleeve Hill and presented him with a watch. The horse's owner, Mr W. Barnett, also gave him £500. Free Trader, a brown stallion by The Sea, carried only 9 stone 8 pounds and started at 25-1, in spite of having finished second the previous year, only two lengths behind Wanderer. It was the year Mr Topham was criticised for cutting the size of the fences.

George Stevens should really have won six Grand Nationals. He rode in the race without success in each of the four years after Free Trader, including 1858, when poor weather postponed it for three days and only five hundred people attended. In 1861 he turned down no fewer than thirteen rides in order to take the mount on Jealousy, whom he was sure would win. Then at the last minute an owner who paid George a retainer vetoed it, even though he did not offer an alternative ride. Stevens had to watch Jealousy win from the stands.

His 1862 mount was unplaced, but then came his splendid double on full sisters, the chestnuts Emblem and Emblematic, both of them rather weedy-looking flat-race cast-offs. Lord Coventry had bought the mares from Mr Halford, paying 300 guineas for Emblem as a three-year-old after thirteen runs on the flat with one win, and 250 guineas for Emblematic. They were not bred to be staying chasers; their class came from their sire, the 1851 Derby winner, Teddington. Emblem was sent hunting in the Cotswolds to learn her new job, but she appeared to be decidedly lacking in aptitude. The plough which was still much in evidence round Aintree would surely sap her of what little stamina she had. But that was without taking her jockey into the reckoning; for, over the first four miles of the 1863 National, she did not race at all.

Stevens simply hacked her quietly at the back, going the short-est way, while all sorts of disasters took place ahead of them, and did not produce her on the scene until the last hurdle. The crowds held their breath then as she jumped sideways, but the consummate horseman Stevens sat tight and the mare drew away for a twenty-length victory. The residents of Cleeve Hill lit an-other bonfire that night.

They were to do so again the following year, when Stevens rode Emblematic. The popular press had been full of criticism about the small size of the course and the state of the Grand National in general, and had especially expressed surprise that a flat racehorse should be able to compete in a race intended for staying chasers.

In fact, Emblematic was more robustly made than her sister, with good shoulders and quarters, although also somewhat lacking in bone, and she relished the perfect ground and bright weather.

It was another race with plenty of mishaps among the twenty-five runners, and it climaxed in another masterly Stevens-produced win. What's more, the jockey won £300 from having backed her; Lord Coventry won £500 from his bet, which he gave to Stevens. On the proceeds, George built a new home on Cleeve Hill, calling it Emblem Cottage.

Both mares ran in 1865, Lord Coventry 'declaring to win' with Emblematic, as was the custom of the time when two or more runners were in the same ownership. Emblematic started favourite but she was carrying 18 pounds more than before and Stevens for once overplayed the waiting game, finishing third to Alcibiade. Emblem, burdened with 12 stone 4 pounds on her slender back, was pulled up.

If the mares' breeding had been in the purple, the case with Stevens' next National was just the reverse, for The Colonel was supposed to have Exmoor pony blood on his sire's side and his dam was half-bred. Nevertheless, he also had Stockwell blood in him. Stockwell had won two Classics, the 2000 Guineas and the St Leger, suggesting he possessed both speed and stamina, and was a champion sire for over a decade.

The Colonel was bred near Ludlow by John Weyman, who co-owned him with Matthew Evans, an uncle of George Stevens' wife. Stevens helped to break in The Colonel, who was big and had powerful limbs – far more strongly built than the mares. Just thirteen mares have ever won the National; the last two were Sheila's Cottage in 1948 and Nickel Coin in 1951. These days mares rarely run in it. Gentle Moya (second) and Tiberetta (third and second) ran in the 1950s; the 1970s saw Miss Hunter and Eyecatcher (twice) come third; and in the 1990s Auntie Dot (third), Ebony Jane and Dubacilla, both fourth. It then took from 1995 until 2019 for a mare to place again (Liberthine was fifth for Sam Waley-Cohen in 2007). In 2019 the Jessie Harrington-trained Magic Of Light under National debutante Paddy Kennedy ran a cracker to finish just over two lengths behind Tiger Roll.

The Colonel ran one year in Mr Weyman's name and the next in Mr Evans'.

As usual, Stevens had been offered several mounts in the 1869 National, and again he made the right choice in The Colonel. The race was almost a carbon copy of his previous wins: plenty of trouble up front as horses fell or refused or were brought down; behind them, riding a copybook waiting race, the incomparable Stevens, like a cat poised to pounce. The cheers for his cool riding, which had taken him into the winner's enclosure for a fourth time, were deafening. Again, his home town cheered to the echo, sang his praises, drank his health – and lit another victory bonfire.

When George Stevens, then thirty-six, set out on The Colonel in 1870, he already had a record number of National wins under his belt, but of all his rides in the race this was to prove the most exciting. For, that year, there was one rider out to emulate him, to take a leaf out of his book. As Stevens and The Colonel lobbed quietly round in the rear on the first circuit, for once they were not alone: George Holman and The Doctor were there too. And when Stevens made his forward move, Holman followed suit, finding, as Stevens had so often before, a mount fresh and full of running beneath him.

The consequence was one of the greatest finishes in the history of the race, as the pair, closely attended by the mare Primrose, raced neck and neck towards the last flight. There, Primrose pecked,* but The Colonel and The Doctor, both as gallant as their names, fought it out stride for stride with the crowd roaring. In the end it was only Stevens' superior strength and experience which prevailed; riding like a man inspired, he coaxed The Colonel home by a neck, with Primrose only a length away in third.

When George Stevens rode his retirement race on The Colonel the next year, unplaced, the crowds broke into spontaneous applause for their hero as he returned. The man who looked as if a puff of wind would blow him over had ridden nearly a hundred winners in the toughest sport of all, five of them in the Grand National itself. The toast of the town wherever he went, he could look forward to a well-earned retirement, coaching young riders and probably horses, too.

It was not to be. As he hacked home towards Emblem Cottage after meeting a few friends in the Rising Sun on 2 June, a gust of wind blew off his hat and, as a lad lifted it back to him, Stevens' horse took fright and bolted down Cleeve Hill. Nearing the foot of the steep hill, the horse stumbled over a drainpipe and Stevens was thrown into the gutter, crashing his head against a stone. Aghast local people gingerly carried him into a nearby farmhouse, but his skull was fractured and he died the next day without recovering consciousness.

A plaque marks the spot where he fell:

IN MEMORY OF GEORGE STEVENS, THE RIDER OF THE
WINNERS OF FIVE GRAND NATIONAL STEEPLECHASES
WHO, AFTER RIDING FOR TWENTY YEARS WITH NO
SERIOUS ACCIDENT WAS HERE KILLED BY A FALL FROM
HIS HACK ONLY THREE MONTHS AFTER RIDING 'THE
COLONEL' IN THE GRAND NATIONAL OF 1871.

---

* When a horse makes a mistake and almost touches its nose on the ground on landing, it is said to have 'pecked' or 'nodded'.

It was in that year that one of the most endearing horses in National history recorded his second win.

3

The Lamb

First grey winner, 1868 and 1871

Only three greys – The Lamb, Nicolaus Silver and Neptune Collonges – have won the Grand National, one each in the nineteenth, twentieth and twenty-first centuries.

The Lamb, a stallion who won in 1868 and 1871, was literally a pony, standing only 14.3 hh. when first broken, and although he grew a little more he was most probably the smallest winner.

Foaled in 1862 by Mr Henchy, a farmer in County Clare, The Lamb was by Zouave out of an unnamed mare by Arthur, who was himself second in the 1840 Grand National; Zouave was bred by Mr Courtenay, owner of Mathew, the first Irish winner of the National in 1847.

The Lamb had features similar to an Arab horse: an almost dish face; big, dark, liquid, wide-apart eyes; and a marked daintiness. Certainly he looked too frail and small to be a racehorse to the first person to whom he was offered, one Edward Studd, who had just won the 1866 Grand National with his Salamander. 'He's not fit to carry a man's boots,' the owner declared. (Mr Studd had to swallow his words some five years later when his horse Despatch led over the last in the National, only to be beaten on the run-in by The Lamb.) The very prettiness of the horse earned him his name. Mr Henchy's son was a delicate lad and he liked the gentle foal so much that he named him The Lamb.

It was for a sickly child that The Lamb was finally bought, as a pony, by Dublin veterinary surgeon Joe Doyle for £30. It is believed that Doyle passed a half-share on to a William Long for £300. Mr Doyle's daughter suffered from consumption and it was considered necessary for her to pursue an activity in the fresh air.

Being a top vet, Joe Doyle had an eye for a horse and could see at once that the grey pony was a smart little number – too much for his weak daughter, as it turned out, for he was constantly jumping out of his paddock. This was quite likely the result of too much food and not enough exercise, but anyway it was discovered he had a turn of foot and so he was leased to Lord Poulett to go into training.

The sixth earl, Lord Poulett had served in three regiments before settling in Waterloo, Hampshire, where he was Master of the Hambledon Hunt for nine seasons and became a founder member of the National Hunt Committee and a steward. He was also a keen yachtsman and a notable whip.

The Lamb's first runs were in Ireland, where he started well by winning the Kildare Hunt Plate at Punchestown by four lengths for the £285 prize. But he failed in his next two runs at Louth and he was sent to England where he was trained for the National.

Helping Lord Poulett was his great friend, the gentleman rider George Ede, alias 'Mr Edwards', who lived with him and who rode 306 winners in fourteen years before his untimely death in the Grand Sefton of 1870 on a chance ride. Ede's other great passion was cricket and he was a joint founder of Hampshire Cricket Club and a renowned batsman.

By the time the 1868 National came round, it was clear that The Lamb was one of those little horses with a big heart, that intangible quality that can make all the difference between winning and losing on the racecourse. He had agility, too, and was soon vying for favouritism with Chimney Sweep and Moose.

With challengers from France and Germany as well as Ireland, 1868 was very much an international year, but the meeting did not get off to an auspicious start, for on the opening day there was one walk-over and one race in which all three runners

refused the first fence! Nevertheless, Liverpool was bursting at
the seams. The National was not thirty years old and, then as
now, held tremendous sway with the public. A fierce wind blew
down the elite's gambling tent and the police faced hard work to
move the crowd who swarmed round.

The Lamb was trained by Ben Land, who had transformed the
pretty pony into a hard, fit, well-muscled racehorse. Land had
formerly been a farmer in Norfolk, where he kept his own pack
of staghounds, and was an amateur rider, but he had turned to
training, both of horses and riders, with great success. George Ede
had been under his wing when still an Eton schoolboy; George
would leave his school lessons for coaching in steeplechasing.

The success of that coaching was never more apparent than
in the National of 1868. The race itself was full of incident, with
several horses refusing and falling. One unfortunate casualty on
the flat was Lord Poulett's Chimney Sweep, who struck a stone as
he crossed the Melling Road, shattered a pastern (the equivalent
of an ankle or wrist) and had to be destroyed.

The Lamb, meanwhile, was in the front rank and led Pearl
Diver by half a length approaching the water. Here, Ede's prowess, quick thinking and cool head came into their own, for he was
being harried by two loose horses, one on either side. He calmly
smacked one with his whip, changed hands, and also hit the other
out of the way before jumping the water perfectly. It was an operation executed smoothly, quickly, neatly and efficiently – to the
delight of those spectators sharp-eyed enough to have spotted it.

Going out into the country for the second time it was the
1865 winner, Alcibiade, who took over from The Lamb, Pearl
Diver, Moose and Colonel Crosstree, and this quintet drew some
hundred yards clear of the remainder. The Pearl Diver and The
Lamb broke clear, going into the last together. 'Now you'll see
what the Diver will do with the pony,' said one watcher, but it
was the gallant grey who squelched through the mud best for a
victory, quoted variously as by a head or by two lengths.

The National is full of 'might have beens' . . . The Lamb was entered again the following year but, by one of those irritating mistakes, his age was incorrectly supplied and his entry refused. So, while The Colonel won the 1869 National, The Lamb was fourth in the Grand Sefton, a race patently too short for him.

That was to be his last race for two years; The Lamb suffered a wasting disease in his hindquarters, his muscles shrank to nothing, and in the end it was only rest and a heat treatment known as blistering which cured him.

Lord Poulett had a habit of getting the best connections for his horses. In the 1870–71 season, with George Ede having been killed in the 1870 Sefton, he had to find a new jockey. Chris Green, who rode two National winners on Abd El Kader and Half Caste, had taken over the training, although in fact Lord Poulett did much of it himself. After a dream, three months before the race, Lord Poulett dashed off a letter post-haste to Tommy Pickernell, who rode as 'Mr Thomas', saying:

Let me know for certain whether you can ride for me at Liverpool on The Lamb. I dreamt twice last night . . . the first dream he was last and finished among the carriages. The second . . . he won by four lengths and you rode him. I saw the cerise and blue sleeves and you as plain as I write this. Now, let me know as soon as you can and say nothing to anyone.

As race day drew nearer, the enthusiastic earl had found it impossible to say nothing himself, so when trainloads of passengers disembarked at Liverpool and saw a lamb escape from a wagon in a siding and run down the platform, they all knew on which horse they would be placing their shillings! The incident added to the spirit of rejoicing that was already in the air following the wedding of Princess Louise to the Marquis of Lorne at a time when it was unheard of for a princess to be allowed to marry a subject of the crown.

It was The Lamb's first appearance of the season but that was nothing unusual in those days and reports of his well-being were so encouraging that money was heaped on him to the extent that he came out favourite, in spite of his two-year absence and the presence of other previous winners Alcibiade and The Colonel.

At the parade it was clear that The Lamb had thickened out and grown and, unusually for a grey, his coat shone. His appearance was a great credit to his new trainer and to the son of his former trainer,* Ben Land Junior, who found that it was all he could do to hold the horse as he led him round. The crowds pressed round as 'Mr Thomas' prepared to mount, watched by a relaxed Lord Poulett and his friend Tom Townley. Tommy Pickernell's experience was to stand him in good stead. Born in Cheltenham, he had ridden in Tasmania with such success that the natives there eventually got up a petition asking him to stop! He returned to England, where he was coached by 'Black Tom' Olliver and William Holdman, and rode under both rules all over Europe.

On a perfect spring day, the horses paraded before a crowd of about 45,000, some of them enjoying the privilege of private boxes for the first time. The Colonel was burdened with 12 stone 13 pounds following his wins of the previous two years, and The Lamb carried 11 stone 4 pounds. Even so, many expected The Colonel to become the first-ever triple winner – a record that, in the event, was not to be set for another 106 years.

The twenty-five runners set off at a scorching pace on ground described officially as 'perfect' and charged through a crowd of local boys who had failed to clear the course in time, scattering them in every direction and injuring not a few. The Lamb was close up and a pocket handkerchief could have covered fifteen at the water. There was still plough in two places, approaching Becher's and at the Canal Turn, where The Lamb lost his place

* Ben Land Senior was to die by cutting his own throat a year later.

both times. As he approached the Canal Turn for the second time he found two fallen horses in front of him, but neither he nor his jockey panicked and he jumped over them both with the agility of a cat.

Back on turf The Lamb regained his position after being vigorously ridden and as they came back on to the racecourse the contest clearly lay between him and Mr Studd's Despatch. The two horses were absolutely together at the last hurdle but The Lamb met it in his stride and cleared it in splendid style to deafening cheers from the crowd. Despatch threatened briefly on the flat, but it was The Lamb who found the faster turn of foot to run out a two-length winner in the very fast time, bearing in mind the plough, of 9 minutes 35¾ seconds.

The crowd fever and hero hailing for such as Red Rum and Aldaniti, and Don't Push It for champion A.P. McCoy on his fifteenth attempt in modern times, is nothing new. For those extra-special winners, it has always been part of the National scene: Cloister, for example, with his big weight of 12 stone 7 pounds, and Manifesto, who shared in the cheers for the future king's winner, Ambush II, when defeated by him in 1900 while carrying 12 stone 12 pounds at the age of thirteen.

And so it was before any of these for The Lamb. It was a fantastically popular result. The Irish went wild and, it is said, horse, jockey and owner were 'carried bodily' into the winner's enclosure, where amid the excited reception most of The Lamb's tail hairs were pulled out by souvenir hunters and Lord Poulett had his gold watch pinched from his pocket (it was later retrieved). Tommy Pickernell, who rode in a total of eighteen Grand Nationals, said in later years that The Lamb was 'the finest fencer' and best horse he ever rode in his life.

Before the next year's National, Lord Poulett's lease on The Lamb ran out and the horse's original owner, Joe Doyle, sold him to a German, Baron Oppenheim, for the then huge sum of 1,200 sovereigns. He was made to carry 12 stone 7 pounds in the race, which, despite his boundless courage, was simply too much for such a small horse to cope with. Still he ran his heart out; yet again he avoided heaps of trouble, but close to home the weight proved too much and on the flat he relinquished third place to his old rival Despatch behind Casse Tete and Scarrington.

The National had again been The Lamb's first run of the season, but he was kept busy after it, running at two hunt meetings. In the first, at Abergavenny, only two weeks later and carrying 12 stone 10 pounds, he was unplaced but he then won at South Hampshire by thirty lengths.

His new owner took him to Germany and in September ran him in the Grosser Preis von Baden-Baden, when he was ridden by Count Nicholas Esterhazy. It was a race of nearly three miles and sixteen fences, including a six-foot-high 'bullfinch'. The gallant 'pony' was winning easily when, just a hundred yards from the winning post, he hit a patch of bog-like ground and, in trying to extricate himself, broke a foreleg and later had to be destroyed.

The little grey with a heart like a lion had won four of his fifteen races and was undoubtedly one of the National's all-time greats.

Nicolaus Silver

Nearly one hundred years later, the next grey to win was Nicolaus Silver in 1961, ridden by Irishman Bobby Beasley, whose father Harry 'HH' Beasley had won two Irish Derbies. His grandfather had won the National on Come Away and his great-uncle had won it three times (the Beasleys are featured in the next chapter). Nicolaus Silver was bred in Ireland and trained by Dan Kirwan of Gowran, who died suddenly in 1960. This led to the grey being sold, and moved to Fred Rimell at Kinnersley in Worcestershire.

Nicolaus Silver was lucky to run at all: doping was rife in the 1960s, with nothing like the security measures there are today, such as CCTV. Fred Rimell moved Nicolaus Silver to a different stable and put another grey in his usual stable; unfortunately, this horse was 'got at' and never ran again.

When Bobby Beasley was offered the 1961 ride on Nicolaus Silver it was because the grey's regular rider, Tim Brookshaw, considered him too careful for Liverpool and chose to ride Wyndburgh, who was sixth. Bobby Beasley had won the 1960 Champion Hurdle on Another Flash, and the racing world was at his feet.

In 1961 the Russians brought over three contenders, of which two ran but both failed to get round. Bobby heeded his idol Bryan Marshall's advice to 'let down your jerks, go round the inside, and take your time' and he enjoyed a nearly trouble-free ride on Nicolaus Silver.

'His only mistake was when I asked him too far off Becher's,' Bobby told me in the 1980s. 'I can still feel the reverberation now, and the horse's effort to get up – his nose was on the ground.'

The stunning grey was a well-balanced athlete; he attacked his fences with enthusiasm, made no further mistake and, with two fences to go, took over the lead from the previous year's winner, Merryman, and saw off the attentions of Wyndburgh and the horse who was to win the next year, Kilmore. He ran out a de-serving five-length winner at 28-1.

Sadly, Nicolaus Silver – the only grey to win the National throughout the twentieth century – broke a leg in retirement when hunting in Sussex and had to be put down. He was the second of four Grand National winners trained by Fred Rimell, along with E.S.B. (Devon Loch's rival) in 1956, Gay Trip in 1970 and Rag Trade in 1976. The only other trainer to achieve that in modern times was Ginger McCain, who won three times with Red Rum and once with Amberleigh House; his son, Donald, won with Ballabriggs. Back in time, George Dockeray also trained four winners, including three of the first four: Lottery and Jerry in 1839 and 1840, Gay Lad in 1842, followed ten years later by Miss Mowbray in 1852.

Bobby Beasley lost his way after winning the National on Nicolaus Silver. A non-drinker until he won the Galway Plate, he celebrated his National win in style – and went on drinking and drinking. Alcoholism cost him his marriage, his prized job with Fred Winter (who promised to hold open the position for him once recovered), his religion, and nearly his life.

At fourteen, Bobby – surprisingly, given the family background – had never ridden a horse. In 1957, at nineteen, he rode in his first National on a tiny mare called Sandy Jane.

Bobby completed the course on Nicolaus Silver in the next two years, finishing seventh and tenth. He also rode Lizawake in 1964, the year when Paddy Farrell fell and was paralysed, leading to the foundation of the Injured Jockeys Fund; he also rode Anglo the year after that horse's 1966 victory in the race.

An even greater achievement than winning the National came for Bobby Beasley thirteen years later when, having quit the bottle, he won the Cheltenham Gold Cup at the age of thirty-eight on the novice Captain Christy. He went on to train near Marlborough, Wiltshire, remarried, and died in January 2008, aged seventy-two.

Neptune Collonges

It was to be more than half a century (fifty-one years) after Nicolaus Silver before the next grey winner, Neptune Collonges, in 2012 – and that was by the skin of his teeth, or rather 'a nose'. Turning for home, any of half a dozen or so horses looked to be in with a chance: Sunnyhillboy was close; Welsh trainer Evan Williams' pair, Cappa Bleu and Planet Of Sound, ran cracking races, as did the joint favourites Shakalakaboomboom and Seabass. Over the last Seabass looked as if he might give a female rider, Katie Walsh, a first victory in the race but his stamina did not quite hold out and it was Neptune Collonges who went off in hot pursuit of Sunnyhillboy. One hundred yards from home Sunnyhillboy, ridden by Richie McLernon, was a length to the good but Neptune Collonges – Nipper to his stable – dug deep for Daryl Jacob. The two horses passed the post locked together, and neither jockey knew who had won. A dead-heat would have been the perfect outcome. Before anyone shouts that a nose is a nose and therefore the winner, the physiology of a horse galloping means that its head bobs up and down; when it is up, it is closer to its chest, when it is down it is more extended, hence the term for a victory being 'on the nod'. It is pure luck as to whether a horse has its head up or down as it passes the post.

After the race, owner John 'Teletubby' Hales, founder of Golden Bears toy company which produces the Teletubbies, Peppa Pig and Thomas the Tank Engine toys, immediately announced the retirement from racing of his hero. Neptune Collonges' career had begun in France where he won five of his six starts before moving to Paul Nicholls' Somerset yard, where he was trained for the rest of his racing life. Before the National he had run in the Cheltenham Gold Cup four times, finishing third to Denman and fourth to Kauto Star. He also won big races in Ireland.

Neptune Collonges has been the only Grand National winner to date for ten-time British champion trainer Paul Nicholls; the trainer was originally a professional jockey whose best horse was Playschool, on whom he won the Hennessy Gold Cup at Newbury, the Welsh National at Chepstow and the Grade 1 Irish Gold Cup at Leopardstown. Paul Nicholls started out training with just eight horses but from the start had an innate will to win, to achieve; and achieve he has, having topped 3,000 British winners, four victors of the Cheltenham Gold Cup, an astonishing ten King Georges – and one Grand National winner. In 2019 he was crowned champion trainer for the eleventh time.

In retirement, John Hales' daughter Lisa trained Neptune Collonges for dressage with considerable success from her show-jumping stud in Shropshire, but now the horse only makes special visits, such as to parade at Aintree or to visit Alder Hey Children's Hospital in Liverpool. He loves nothing more than to be surrounded by fans and eating polos out of the hand of Tim Wilkins who leads him up.

Other greys to have gone close include Suny Bay who was runner-up in consecutive years, to Lord Gyllene in 1997 and behind Earth Summit the following year. What's Up Boys, who chased home Bindaree in 2002, is another memorable Grand National grey horse. King Johns Castle, trained in Ireland by Arthur Moore, was second in 2008, but in 2010 resolutely refused to start.

Now we come to probably the greatest family of Grand National jockeys who added their own colour to its history.

4

The Beasley Family

Four brothers, 1877–92

Of all the distinguished families who have been connected with the National over the years, few can be more remarkable than the Beasleys. They can be traced back to the sixteenth century, originating from the west of Ireland, were reared on the Curragh, and have always been involved in racing.

Four amateur brothers, Tommy, Harry, Willie and Johnny, rode in the 1879 Grand National. Over fifteen years, from 1877 to 1892, they rode four winners, six seconds and two thirds from thirty-four rides; in 1961 Harry's grandson, Bobby, rode another winner, the grey Nicolaus Silver. The brothers were all involved in what were then the only two objections in the race.

Of all the Beasley brothers, Harry was perhaps the most outstanding: after winning the National on Come Away in 1891, he continued steeplechasing until he was seventy-three years old, when he rode at Punchestown. Even that was not the end of his race-riding career, for he rode on the flat for the last time when he was eighty-two. It is said that he once booed his own son, Willie, for beating him by a short head in a four-and-a-half-mile chase at Punchestown; Harry was a mere seventy-two at the time.

As for Harry's training methods, they were unorthodox in the extreme. Come Away, who finally gave him a winning National ride, had very bad legs. It was said that, to avoid galloping him on ground hardened by frost, he used to take him out on the Curragh at night, and gallop him by the light of storm lanterns before the frost had got into the ground. His usual mode of reaching the Curragh from his stables was to jump the rails dividing them.

His brother Tommy had a better National record but was un-luckier in the end. He won the big race three times, was second twice, third once and fourth once. But eventually he was killed at the double of banks at Punchestown, and was buried beside it.

Willie was second once, but Johnny was never placed in the National and rode in the race less often than his brothers.

The Beasley National story began in 1877, when Sultana, ridden by 'Mr Beasley', was pulled up. The next year Tommy was second on Captain Grotton's Martha – and he was to win or place for six years in succession. In 1878 Tom lodged an objection, alleg-ing foul riding by Jack Jones on the winner, Shifnal. But it was quickly overruled and left a bad taste in the mouth.

Tom rode Martha again in 1879, the year when all four broth-ers rode, repeating his front-running tactics of the previous year, but the mare could give no more when challenged by Jackal and the winner, The Liberator, finishing third. None of the brothers fell. Willie, on Mr P.M.V. Savrin's Lord Marcus, and Harry, on Mr R. Stackpoole's Turco, both got round, to finish eighth and ninth respectively, and John pulled up on Victor II. Of eight-een starters on ground described as 'average', ten completed the course and only four fell.

Victor II, the only Beasley mount not to complete, was the shortest price of the four, at 100-8. Turco was 100-6, while Martha was on 50-1 in spite of her good run the previous year, and Lord Marcus was unquoted. (Jackal, who finished second, started at the unusual price of 1000-65.)

There was at the time a trainer called Harry Eyre Linde who made winning the Grand National his prime objective in life and built replica Aintree fences on his Curragh training grounds; it was to be around a century later that this became more universally practised among trainers of National horses; in between times, the majority went to Aintree with only park-course experience behind them.

Certainly the practice was successful for Mr Linde, a sergeant in the Royal Irish Constabulary, and for the five-year-old Empress, named after the Empress of Austria, who used to hunt in Ireland. The public not unnaturally assumed that the big chestnut with just a little flat-racing experience would be a complete novice. But Mr Linde had schooled her so thoroughly, and the Irish backed her so heavily, that she started at 8-1 in the 1880 National. With Tommy Beasley in the saddle, she came through beaten horses after the second Valentine's to tackle The Liberator. She was flying at the finish, jumped the last superbly and won by two lengths. The race was watched by a record crowd, the Prince of Wales among them, and both Harry Beasley on Woodbrook and Johnny on Victoria were among the ten to finish from just fourteen starters.

It was thought that the mare would go on to more victories, but the one apparent disadvantage of Linde's continual schooling was that it had a weakening effect on horses' legs and many broke down. So it was with Empress, and she never ran again, retiring instead to stud.

The ground was bottomless the next year; it had snowed all week and the going was so heavy that the thirteen runners could only trot through the mangold fields. Not surprisingly, a very slow time was recorded. It proved an easy win for Tom Beasley on Woodbrook. Only The Liberator, humping 12 stone 7 pounds, could live with him until falling at Valentine's, when the 1876 winner Regal took up the challenge, but it was a short-lived one, Tom's horse winning in a canter. Woodbrook was sold to a German for £1,300 but died at Newmarket within a year.

Tom was again on a Linde-trained horse the next year, but they were beaten by a Linde cast-off. Seaman had been sold to Lord

Manners for £2,000 and it seemed most of Ireland was laughing, for they knew the horse was unsound. Back at Newmarket, the local wags, seeing the horse's legs, also feared that his lordship had been outsmarted.

Lord Manners was a genuine amateur who had never ridden in the National before. In 1882 it was again snowing, the ground was heavy and several horses fell, including the favourite, Mohican, another Linde horse. Tom brought Cyrus through with a seemingly invincible, devastating run and, even as Lord Manners and Seaman appeared on the scene at the last hurdle, the race looked a foregone conclusion.

Seaman was a length behind; he was not fluent and twisted like a corkscrew over the hurdle, but the amateur picked up the reins, held him together, and drove him on. From the bustle with which Tom Beasley set about Cyrus as Seaman appeared at his quarters, it would appear that he was well and truly caught napping. He was beaten by a short head.

So Lord Manners became the first peer to win the National and, like Dick Saunders exactly 100 years later, was successful in his only ride in the race. As for Seaman, his hind leg had broken down irreparably and he never raced again – the third Linde or ex-Linde winner in a row never to do so, and none of them over seven years old.

In 1883 Tom was favourite on the Linde horse Zitella and Harry was riding Mohican. A number of small, trappy fences had been improved but there was still some plough (it was to be 1952 before plough had gone permanently). Ten runners made it the smallest field in the National's history. It was Zoedone's turn for victory, for the horse appreciated the bigger fences which slowed down some of the faster runners, especially in the ground made heavy by rain. Zitella faded to finish fourth and Mohican fell.

The 1884 winner, Voluptuary, was bred at Hampton Court Stud by Queen Victoria, was sold for less than £700 as a yearling, and reputedly ended his days on a revolving stage in Drury Lane, appearing nightly in *The Prodigal Daughter.* The six-year-old was ridden to victory by Mr E.P. Wilson, an outstanding amateur who rode in seventeen Grand Nationals in all.

It was a three-horse race going into the final flight, between Harry Beasley on Frigate, Roquefort and Voluptuary; Frigate led but stumbled and was outpaced by the classically bred Voluptuary, who ran very well.

Roquefort, an impressive third, had supposedly pulled a dog cart in the past, but he won the race the next year, 1885, giving Mr Wilson a second successive win, when the course was all grass and railed in for the first time; Frigate and Harry were second again. Poor Zoedone had evidently been poisoned; she fell at the practice hurdle with blood pouring from her nose, then ran lifelessly until taking a vertical dive at the second Becher's and falling in terrible pain. She recovered but never ran again; her owner, Count Kinsky, was heartbroken.

The only good thing to come out of Zoedone's misfortune was that, from then on, security was considerably improved and a number of highly undesirable characters were weeded out of stables. It was a time of general improvement, and in 1888 the course was altered to its present shape and finished over two small fences within the flat racecourse.

When Willie Beasley was second on Frigate in 1888, after Harry had filled the same place on her in 1884 and 1885, the mare looked destined to be always the bridesmaid. But in 1889, this time with Tommy up, and having fallen at the first in 1886 and unseated in 1887, she finally came back the blushing bride – only to fall again in 1890. It certainly was a very popular win for Frigate and a real case of try, try, try again . . .

Harry Beasley was the only jockey ever to ride the 1891 winner Come Away, and the Irish backed the powerful seven-year-old down to 4-1 favourite.

Come Away, owned by Mr W.G. Jameson, trained as well as

ridden by Harry Beasley, was a tall horse with strong quarters, a long, narrow neck and fine head. He was a high-class individual by Cambusland out of Larkaway and had won two Conyngham Cups at Punchestown and a Valentine Chase, but he was difficult to keep sound. As part of his rehabilitation he was 'fired', i.e. thermocauterised, a more severe form of heat (or ice) treatment than blistering, which is said to stimulate the healing process of pulled tendons; though not banned, it is rarely used today. There are records that it was first used in AD 500 but there has never been absolute proof of its effectiveness; a year off is necessary for recovery and this amount of rest on its own can prove equally beneficial.

The 1891 National proved a contentious ride as well as a winning one for Harry. No fewer than four previous winners were in the twenty-one-strong field and when three of them, Ilex, the second favourite, Roquefort and Gamecock, jumped the water in line at halfway it looked like being a vintage National. The pace proved too much for the other previous winner, Voluptuary, while two future winners were also in the race: Why Not, who fell carrying joint-top weight of 12 stone 4 pounds, and Cloister. Ilex was a spent force, as was the Linde-trained Cruiser, giving Tom Beasley his last ride in the race (they finished sixth). Going to the last it was a close-fought battle between Cloister and Come Away. Captain Roddy Owen tried to squeeze Cloister through on the inside halfway up the run-in but, as he reached Come Away's quarters, Beasley edged his mount inwards and closed the gap. It was a rousing finish and, as Come Away lived up to his name to score by a length, he clocked the fastest time since The Lamb twenty years earlier.

But it was not over yet. Against trainer Richard Marsh's wishes, Captain Owen lodged an objection. Marsh warned him that he might come off second-best again, and so it proved, the stewards taking the view that Beasley had acted within his rights and over-ruling the objection. Come Away's dodgy legs had finally given

way and, although he was fired all round, he was another horse
who never ran again.

Harry Beasley's last ride in the National the next year was a
complete contrast, for Major Kearsley's Billee Taylor bolted with
him, careering right off the racecourse. But that was not the sort
of performance Harry would be remembered for. He loved life
and lived it to the full, dying peacefully in his sleep at the age of
ninety-one. The portrait of Harry and Come Away was to hang in
pride of place in the sitting room of his grandson, Bobby.

The Beasley brothers certainly enlivened the scene; but possibly the most impressive individual winner of all came just one
year after the last of the brothers retired . . .

5

Cloister

Of all the winners in the Grand National's 180-year history, Cloister can lay claim to being the most dazzling. On a sweltering hot March day in 1893 he led from start to finish in an unbelievable display of boldness, jumping and weight-carrying.

There were both past and future winners in the line-up but Cloister made it look a one-horse race as he powered to a record forty-length victory, carrying a record 12 stone 7 pounds, and in a time of 9 minutes $32\frac{2}{5}$ seconds – a record that stood for forty years.

Three records in one go – which was all the more remarkable because Cloister was born at decidedly the bottom end of the scale, with a sire and dam both described as 'useless'. Bred in Ireland by Lord Fingall, Cloister's sire, Ascetic, later proved himself beyond doubt by also getting the 1903 and 1906 winners, Drumcree and Ascetic's Silver. But in mid-career he earned his keep by being taken to collect the post each day from the village after failing as a racehorse. Cloister's dam, Grace II, not only failed on the racecourse but was described as a hopeless hunter as well.

Their dark bay offspring, however, grew into a grand model of a horse, big with good conformation, epitomising all that is best in the staying chaser. One has only to look at W.A. Rouch's portrait of Cloister to visualise his devouring stride and great jumping power, for he stood well 'over the ground' and possessed good bone, splendid sloping shoulders, sensible head carriage and big quarters with a 'jumping bump' from which he held a well-sprung tail. By maturity, he stood 16.3 hh., and given his size it is not surprising that when he was sold by Irish dealer James Daley he was still somewhat backward; a big, developing horse generally needs more time to grow into his frame and mature (a bit like some teenagers, really). The kind, well-mannered, intelligent horse changed hands several times as a youngster, so that by the time he ran in his first National in 1891 he was listed as 'aged'. He was in fact seven years old, which today is the minimum age for runners; up until 1887 no horse *over* seven is listed in the admittedly somewhat scanty records as having won.

When Cloister made his first National appearance he was owned by Lord Dudley and trained by Richard Marsh, who was later to train for two kings, Edward VII and George V. On that clear day, there were no great expectations of him, his recently sidelined stable companion Royal Meath being reputedly far superior. Come Away, the Irish horse, started favourite in a field of twenty-one, and Cloister, his stable's second string, was unconsidered at 20-1. He must have had some assessable form, however, for he carried 11 stone 7 pounds.

It proved a remarkable race between two of the era's finest jockeys, Harry Beasley on Come Away and Captain Roddy Owen on Cloister. It is too simplistic to say that Captain Owen was outjockeyed, for he was described as a 'fearless and peerless' horseman and 'the finest of all soldier riders'. Towards the end of Harry Beasley's long and distinguished career, he earned himself another win, by a length.

Against trainer Richard Marsh's advice, the furious Captain Owen insisted on objecting, and the two jockeys came perilously close to a punch-up, while the Irish looked like lynching Captain Owen should he be awarded the race. But the stewards ruled that the winner's manoeuvre had been fair play and overruled the objection.

Come Away had broken down badly, and the winning

margin was a narrow one. *If* Captain Owen had taken Cloister round Come Away's outside for a clear run, he surely might have won . . . But how many 'ifs' are there in the history of the great race?

By the following year Cloister had matured considerably and had also changed hands. He was now trained by Arthur Yates and owned by Mr Charles Duff – later to become Sir Charles Assheton-Smith and to own two more winners, Jerry M and Covercoat in 1912 and 1913. Before him, James Machell owned three winners in the nineteenth century: Disturbance, Reugny and Regal. Only two other owners have won three times: Noel Le Mare with Red Rum in the 1970s, and Trevor Hemmings with Hedgehunter, Ballabriggs and Many Clouds, all in the twenty-first century.

Roddy Owen would have given anything to ride Cloister again in the 1892 Grand National. The horse had run well all season and even with a weight of 12 stone 3 pounds he was favourite – although no horse carrying over 12 stone had ever won. But with the new stable came a new jockey for Cloister, another amateur, Mr J.C. Dormer. Captain Owen had to make do with the scrawny Father O'Flynn, a 470-guinea purchase with a reputation for refusing. Five years earlier the horse had won a lowly two-year-old selling race at Aintree – which is exactly what Red Rum was to do sixty years later.

However, the thirty-six-year-old Owen was determined to win a National before going off to fight abroad. (He was to die of cholera or food poisoning serving with Kitchener four years later.) Using all his strength on Father O'Flynn, and taking full advantage of his 26-pound weight pull with the front-running Cloister, he emerged from the fog which shrouded much of the course that year to kick on for a surprising twenty-length victory.

So Cloister had now been runner-up twice. Could he make it

third time lucky, even carrying 12 stone 7 pounds, having failed under less weight the previous year? His supporters thought so, and in 1893, at nine years old and in his prime, he again started favourite.

Cloister's amateur rider, Mr Dormer, was now out of action, having had the misfortune to lose an eye in a horrible fall at Sandown, and so the horse had yet another pilot, stable jockey William Dollery.

The race was on 24 March that year, during a freak spring heatwave. The ground at Aintree, always well drained and fast drying, was officially described as 'very hard and dry'. As the crowds began to pour into the course, on foot from Liverpool, in horse-drawn conveyances or by steam train, they could sense they were in for a hot day.

There was a keen sense of anticipation in the packed stands, while Cloister's owner, Charles Duff, strutted about proudly in his suit and bowler hat, sporting a handlebar moustache and monocle, a pair of binoculars slung over his shoulder. The runners jumped the practice flight of hurdles in front of the stands and cantered on down to the start.

At first, William Dollery, the professional, tried to be master of Cloister's performance, attempting to hold him up and present him at the first couple of fences, but the jockey quickly let the horse settle in his own inimitable style: head low, as he devoured the ground with his long stride, gripped hold of the bit and surged forward – a packed powerhouse doing what he loved best, galloping and jumping.

There may have been other runners alongside or fractionally ahead of Cloister at the first fence; after that, he never saw another horse. He flicked over the fences as if they were toys, his long, lolloping stride devouring the ground effortlessly for every yard of the four and a half miles.

There were fifteen runners in the race, but fourteen of them might as well not have been there. Cloister pounded rhythmically on, dust flying behind his heels, the rest well strung out behind him by the end of the first circuit. He took the water in his stride, flicked over the hurdles and set out on a glorious second circuit: a procession led by the king, his minions trailing.

For those watching, victory, barring a fall, looked certain, but by how far? Down the daunting stretch towards Becher's Cloister galloped; the big drop fence and brook might just as well have been another hurdle and he swept on, increasing his lead all the time.

All Dollery could hear was the beat of his magnificent partner's hooves and, as they headed back towards the racecourse proper, the rising crescendo of the ecstatic crowd. Two fences from home Cloister was still gaining on his rivals, good winners many of them, but outclassed, outgalloped, outjumped and totally eclipsed now.

When the post came, Cloister's nearest rival, Aesop, was a full forty lengths adrift; Cloister had had no other horse to spur him on for over four miles but on the fast, dry ground he had clocked an astonishing record time. And he had shouldered his 12 stone 7 pounds burden as if it were a featherweight.

It was the greatest single Aintree performance up to that time, if not of all time. Those fortunate enough to witness it talked about it for the rest of their lives – and the memory brought tears to their eyes.

Nothing like Cloister's achievement had been seen before, nor has been since. The great era of Manifesto was shortly to follow; Golden Miller, five-time winner of steeplechasing's blue riband, the Cheltenham Gold Cup, added the 1934 National to that class sequence; Crisp came the closest to a Cloister-like victory but tired on the run-in; Red Rum became a legend and was as clever as they come; and the little grey hero The Lamb had already stamped his name in the National record book: any of these might have been judged better than Cloister, but none won quite like him.

Strictly speaking, there have been three other horses that have won by a distance: Covercoat in 1913 (left in the lead at the last fence after the leading horse fell there), Tipperary Tim likewise fifteen years later, and Red Marauder, one of only two to finish in 2001. However in those three cases it was due to the rates of attrition among their rivals rather than through their own merits, for all that they did indeed put in clear rounds.

Shortly after Cloister's heart-pounding win came the era of the National's most frequent player, a record eight appearances with two wins and several placings . . .

6

Manifesto

Most runs, 1895–1904

Before Red Rum devotees suffer apoplexy – and bearing in mind that statistics can be interpreted differently – consider the following. Red Rum: five runs, three wins, two seconds from the age of eight to twelve years. Manifesto: eight runs, two wins, three thirds, one fourth, one fall, one unplaced, from the age of seven to sixteen years.

Red Rum held the course speed record until Mr Frisk in 1990, and is the only horse to have won the race three times. Manifesto jointly holds the record winning weight (12 stone 7 pounds), and the record weight for a place (12 stone 13 pounds); and was joint oldest runner with Peter Simple, at sixteen years – even then he had to carry 12 stone 1 pound.

Comparisons done, let's look at Manifesto himself. He was a well-made, beautifully proportioned bright bay with black points, a class head, with intelligent eyes set off by a white star and broken white snip (not a full blaze), a good shoulder and powerful quarters, which were to help him carry the big weights he was allotted.

By Man O'War, supposedly a savage stallion, Manifesto was bred in Ireland by solicitor and hobby farmer Mr Harry Dyas, out of his appropriately named mare Vae Victis (Latin for 'woe to the vanquished') at Navan in County Meath.

Although many early National winners, where recorded, were young (five-year-olds won four times up to 1880 and few were over seven years old until the end of the 1880s), Mr Dyas was, to his credit, content to be patient with his horses. Manifesto was a gawky, unfurnished youngster and, after falling in a chase and winning a hurdle in England at the age of four, he returned to Ireland to be given more time to fill out. He ran only twice as a five-year-old, winning a race at Derby, and again only twice at six.

When Manifesto was seven, Mr Dyas deemed him mature enough for a fuller programme. The horse won the Lancashire Chase and from then on the public began to sit up and take notice of him. Even in his first National, and despite his inexperience, he was set to carry 11 stone 2 pounds.

Fog hung so densely over the flat expanse of Aintree on National day in 1895 that spectators could hardly see anything of the race, and the nineteen jockeys themselves could see each fence – by now all upright furze ones as opposed to the mix of fences described at the start – only as it loomed eerily, black and large, out of the mist.

Manifesto took to the mighty fences like a natural and, under Terry Kavanagh, made much of the running until tiring and finishing fourth to Wild Man From Borneo.

That promise came to nought the next year. Some records state that Manifesto fell at the first and brought down Redhill; others that it was Redhill who brought down Manifesto; another, perhaps more likely, has it that the pair collided. Certainly there was confusion at the first fence as jockeys jostled for position.

Whatever the truth of it, Manifesto and his jockey, Gourley, were out of the race. Twenty-eight runners made it the biggest field for twenty-three years; the bottom weight had been reduced to 9 stone 7 pounds; and the prize money had jumped dramatically from £1,500 to £2,500 plus entrance stakes. It was won by amateur David Campbell on The Soarer.

The following year, 1897, saw a record attendance, and a bit of style had been added to proceedings by the introduction of paddock name-cloths for each horse. The Prince of Wales's emblem had been embroidered on the corner of the cloth carried by his horse, Ambush II. It was the year of Queen Victoria's Golden Jubilee, and the spectators were in buoyant mood.

Mr Dyas, whose gambling prowess was such that bookies apparently feared his approach when they saw him arrive with his loaded satchel, had put Manifesto in training with Willie McAuliffe at Everleigh on Salisbury Plain and engaged Terry Kavanagh to ride again. It was said that Kavanagh, if told to make a certain weight, would do so by whatever means, even if it meant humping sacks of potatoes by day and sleeping in a manure heap at night! There was no need for such drastic action in order for him to ride Manifesto, who, having run before Christmas for the first time – on which occasion, unquoted by the bookmakers (i.e. he did not feature in the betting), he finished unplaced – had been allotted 12 stone 7 pounds.

The same stable's Gentle Ida, a 'slashing great mare', was fancied even more, but she was withdrawn at the last minute, which meant Manifesto and Terry Kavanagh started 6-1 favourites.

The Soarer was in the race again but he fell and fractured his skull at Valentine's and when Timon, leader for much of the way, fell at the penultimate, Manifesto, up with the leaders throughout, was left clear and stormed away to a twenty-length victory.

He ran twice more that season, falling in the Lancashire Chase but winning the three-and-a-half-mile Grand International at Sandown, the forerunner of the Whitbread Gold Cup (now the Bet365), carrying 12 stone 5 pounds. After a winning reappearance at Gatwick the following February, carrying 12 stone 10 pounds and giving *37 pounds* to the runner-up, he looked the closest thing to a certainty for Liverpool.

Manifesto was then sold to Mr Bulteel, who had made a fortune on the Stock Exchange and was anxious to own a National winner. The price was the then huge sum of £4,000 (the same figure was exchanged in a similar bid nearly thirty years later, in 1927, for

Jack Horner, winner in 1926). Mr Bulteel, however, suffered the sort of bad luck familiar to many owners before and since when his magnificent new purchase was injured after getting loose. His stable lad, in a careless moment, had left Manifesto's box insecurely latched. The horse pushed it open and – freedom! With a week to go before the big race, fit, blooming and raring to go, he galloped off across the surrounding countryside, misjudged a five-foot gate and rapped a fetlock so badly that he was out of action for several months. The erring stable lad was so afraid of the consequences of his actions that he ran away and went to work for another stable under an assumed name.

It was not until the following January, happily fully recovered, that Manifesto ran again. He was unplaced in a hurdle race carrying 13 stone, then came second in another hurdle on 12 stone 7 pounds.

That winter was exceptionally harsh. Everywhere there was frozen or snow-covered ground over such a long period that even Aintree itself looked threatened. When National day finally came, conditions remained so difficult that hay was placed both sides of each fence, and this nearly proved Manifesto's undoing.

All the hay was supposed to have been cleared away before the race, but a patch was left by mistake at the Canal Turn. Manifesto slipped on it, and his pilot, George Williamson, saw 'one of his legs sticking straight up over my head; the toe of my boot was on the ground and both irons gone. I left everything to the horse and he recovered himself and I picked up the reins and went on.' In such calm and modest words, Williamson described (in *Winter Kings*) his fine feat of horsemanship and Manifesto's ability to find a 'fifth leg'.

Manifesto was carrying 12 stone 7 pounds – 19 pounds more than when he had won previously – and, this time, stable connections thought that Gentle Ida, who had meanwhile been sold for an even bigger sum than Manifesto himself, would have the beating of him, being in receipt of 14 pounds. Mr Dyas did not think it possible for any horse, even Manifesto, to give her a stone, and she started favourite, with her stable companion 5-1 second favourite. But Gentle Ida fell heavily at Valentine's, the leader Pistache fell at the Chair, and Manifesto made his brilliant recovery at the Canal. Manifesto was pulling Williamson's arms out and there beside him, matching him at the fences, was the riderless Gentle Ida, as if out to prove herself. To all but Williamson himself, it looked a frightening duel as Manifesto responded with bolder and bolder jumping. After Valentine's for the second time, Williamson made his move, hitting the front shortly before the home turn, which started the enthusiastic crowds cheering, and came home to a fine five-length victory with his ears pricked, over Ford Of Fyne, receiving 25 pounds, and Elliman, receiving 24 pounds. It was to be Manifesto's last win.

Of all the gallant failures in the history of the race, few can rank greater than Manifesto's in 1900 and 1902. His performances then could be described as even braver than those which brought him his two wins.

By the turn of the century Manifesto was the undisputed champion chaser of his day and excelled nowhere more than at Liverpool. He had the cocky stature of a king who knows he reigns over all, and Aintree was his kingdom, as it was to be over seventy years later for Red Rum. In 1900 the handicapper allotted him a weight of 12 stone 13 pounds, forcing him to give 48 pounds to some horses. Only once has a horse had to give more weight and that was Arkle who once had to give 49 pounds, but not in the National.

Covert Hack, the only faller on the first circuit, brought down the favourite Hidden Mystery at the water when loose. Turning for home, the Prince of Wales's Ambush II led from Barsac – yet who should be stealthily creeping up on them but Manifesto. The crowd drew breath: their hero *could* do it. He drew alongside the royal horse at the second last and stride for stride, neck for neck, they galloped towards the last fence. It was a battle royal indeed and the roar of the spectators rose to an unprecedented crescendo – its like not to be heard again until just before Devon Loch's debacle in 1956. Ambush touched down first, but here was Manifesto, fighting his way back; for a moment he appeared to be in front – or was he? It had been a final all-out effort and, with barely a hundred yards to go, the people's hero conceded to youth and crippling weight. As Williamson eased him, Barsac stole second place and hats came off for a royal victory.

For an age of strict etiquette and formality the scenes that followed were astonishing. Grown men cried at the defeat of Manifesto. A scribe of the time commented, 'There are some things about which it appears sacrilege to write in commonplace black and white.'

In 1902 Manifesto was fourteen years old; heavy rain had turned the ground to a quagmire; the veteran was set to carry 12 stone 8 pounds through it.

Ridden by Ernie Piggott, Lester's grandfather, Manifesto made a supreme effort. Shannon Lass's forward move three out was matched by Manifesto; but it was a 50-1 six-year-old called Matthew, carrying only 9 stone 12 pounds, who jumped the last with her. Then suddenly the crowd was looking at a potential miracle: Manifesto was coming up from behind with a stupendous run. Fifty yards from the line, the impossible still looked possible, but again that gruelling run-in proved just too long; the mud was just too deep; the weight was just too much; the courage was still there, but it was not enough. He was beaten three lengths by Shannon Lass, receiving 35 pounds, with Matthew in second, receiving 38 pounds, another three lengths in front of Manifesto.

Still it was not the end of the line. In 1903 the fifteen-year-old Manifesto was no longer top weight – Ambush bearing that with 12 stone 7 pounds – but the veteran nonetheless carried 12 stone 3 pounds. Williamson was in the saddle again, and he started at 25-1.

Manifesto was never going to win it, but in an incident-packed race he showed all his old resolution to hold off Kirkland by a head and secure third place. There were greater cheers for him than for the winner, Drumcree, Ambush having fallen at the last.

There had been a fifteen-year-old winner of the National in 1853, a record, when Peter Simple won for the second time, carrying 10 stone 10 pounds; his first win came four years earlier. Incredibly, in 1904, at sixteen years old, Manifesto received weight from only one horse, Ambush (who fell at the third). Now the aged hero of chasing, he was treated as a star by spectators, who crowded round him during his early morning work and admired his vigour, sprightliness and unblemished legs. A leading flat jockey of the time even asked to be allowed to sit on him. There was no one who seriously thought Manifesto could win, but many believed he might place and backed him to do so. He started at 20-1 and was this time ridden by H. Piggott. But the advancing years had caught up with the gallant horse and Manifesto, sure-footed to the end, was outpaced, to finish unplaced behind Moifaa.

What a truly amazing horse Manifesto was, as tough and courageous, sound and genuine as they come. But for an accident at home in the year between his two wins he is surely the most likely candidate for emulating Red Rum's three. His Grand National record reads: fourth, fell or brought down, first, first, third, third, third, unplaced.

By now, the Grand National was known worldwide and for the first time there was a winner from the other side of the world: Moifaa.

7

Moifaa

New Zealand winner, 1904

The most romantic of all Grand National stories belongs to Moifaa, the New Zealand horse reputedly shipwrecked and marooned on his journey over. In 1904 Moifaa may have looked to English eyes a horse of 'incredible ugliness', with the head and shoulders 'of a camel', but he powered his way to the front and there he stayed; nothing could live with him and he left a litter of fallen idols in his wake.

New Zealand is ideally suited for producing the thoroughbred. It has a temperate climate and lush, fertile grass rich in minerals, with the optimum amount of rainfall and warmth.

Horses were almost certainly not indigenous to the Antipodes but imported from both England and South Africa, the first recorded shipment into Australia being in 1788.

The Australian Race Committee was set up in 1840 with the objectives of breeding for strength, endurance and maximum speed. When New Zealand acquired its own racing organisation fifty years later it followed the same maxim, with the result that both countries successfully bred horses with these qualities not only for flat racing and steeplechasing but also for the immensely popular sports of trotting and pacing.

It was easy for the British and Irish to dismiss horses from Down Under out of hand as insignificant, although they were to gain popularity from the 1970s.

If the rumour that went the rounds in America after his victory is true, Moifaa was lucky to have reached Aintree at all. The story went that en route to England he was shipwrecked off the Irish coast; at first he was given up for lost but then some fishermen found him pacing up and down the strand of a small island and brought him ashore to the mainland.

This story should perhaps rank in the 'truth is stranger than fiction' category and be given at least some credence. What is true is that his sire was called Natator (swimmer).

Another source believes it was two racehorses on a different ship, also en route from New Zealand for England, that hit a reef off South Africa, and one of those, Kiora, also ran in the 1904 National but fell.

When Moifaa arrived in England, by whatever means, he had already conquered all comers in his native country. As the 1904 National approached, his connections, like those of the American horses Battleship, Jay Trump and Ben Nevis in years to come, had decided that the moment was ripe for him to take on the ultimate against the world's best steeplechasers. They had nothing left to prove in their home country. Moifaa had won nine of his thirteen New Zealand races, including a £500 three-and-a-half-mile race in June 1901 in which he carried 13 stone, giving 3 stone to his nearest rival. He was probably the Antipodes' first star chaser, for racing had only begun in any organised fashion in New Zealand in the 1890s, barely ten years before Moifaa's departure for England. Indeed, the very first racing in New Zealand is said to have taken place on the beach of Wellington Harbour in January 1840, organised by a group of British settlers.

A brown gelding, Moifaa was eight years old when he arrived in England. He was not immediately impressive. It must have taken time for horses to acclimatise, to say nothing of coping with the disadvantage of the six months' calendar difference.

Moifaa was the third New Zealand horse in the space of six years to sail to England for a crack at the National. All three,

Levanter, Liberator and Moifaa, had won the principal steeple-chase in New Zealand, the Great Northern Steeplechase at Ellerslie, North Island, founded in 1885.

Liberator was a top-class horse on both sides of the world but failed to reach Aintree. Then Levanter paved the way for Moifaa by running fifth in the 1900 National and fourth in 1901.

Moifaa himself won the Great Northern in 1901, after which he was bought from Alfred and Emily Ellingham of Hastings, Hawke's Bay, by wealthy pioneer, jump-racing enthusiast and all-round athlete Spencer Gollan, expressly to aim at Aintree. (Gollan died in 1934 after being hit by a bus in London; Moifaa's jockey, Arthur Birch, was badly injured in a fall at Gatwick two years after his National, confining him to a wheelchair, and he died in 1911.)

Ellerslie, flanked by a motorway these days, boasts modern facilities and has two flat courses and a particularly testing steeplechase course which showed Moifaa's stamina. The chase course slopes away from the oval flat track up the steep Ellerslie Hill which is climbed three times in the Great Northern, a race almost four miles long. It was also essential for Moifaa to jump well because in those days the fences included posts and rails, and an unusual double in front of the stands.

Moifaa failed in his first three races in England, and one can imagine cynics muttering disparagingly about their 'poor relations' on the other side of the world not being up to standard. But, when it came to Aintree, the big fences, heightened in 1904 as if on cue, suited the massive New Zealander.

Moifaa, trained by Mr O. 'Jim' Hickey at Epsom and ridden by Arthur Birch, was a 25-1 shot and carried 10 stone 7 pounds. The twenty-six runners included past winners Manifesto, now sixteen years old, and King Edward VII's horse Ambush II, as well as future winner Kirkland, fourth the previous year.

In all the preliminaries, Moifaa towered above everything else, and it was impossible not to notice him, with his giant head and high withers; everything about him was big.

Moifaa's domination in the paddock continued in the race. Birch was little more than a helmsman from about the fifth, able to steer but incapable of holding back the big horse as he bulldozed his way through his fences. Behind him horse after horse fell like novices; Kirkland was the only one able to stay anywhere near him, briefly heading him once, the only time he was overtaken.

Railoff was the first to go, falling at the first; Ambush and Deerslayer fell at the third; Cushendon and Inquisitor at the fourth. The thorn fence before Becher's saw the worst carnage: Patlander, Hill Of Bree, Comfit, Kiora and Loch Lomond all fell, Loch Lomond breaking his neck. At Becher's itself, Biology came down; Honeymoon fell two fences before the water, May King and Old Town having dropped out of proceedings somewhere along the way.

Moifaa was in command as the survivors stormed past the grandstand. Midway through the race, half of the twenty-six runners were out of it. The riderless Ambush knocked out Detail at the Canal Turn, and Pride Of Mabestown fell two from home. It was left to Kirkland to follow Moifaa to the post, a respectful eight lengths behind the black colours with white sleeves and red cap.

The victory was so impressive that the King, looking for a replacement for the ageing Ambush II, who did not run in the race again, arranged for Lord Marcus Beresford to buy the winner on his behalf. Lord Beresford described Moifaa as 'a great machine at high pressure over fences who would jump any fence he saw'.

Moifaa duly ran in the King's colours the following year and started favourite, but 1905 proved to be Kirkland's turn and Moifaa himself fell at Becher's. It was his last attempt in the race for, like many another big horse, he went wrong in his wind (a bit like COPD) and was given away as a hunter. Today, numerous horses are given small wind operations known as tie-back, hobday and soft palate and, because the procedure is likely to improve their form, it now has to be declared (so that punters can take that into account). One of the oldest forms of wind operations was tubing, where a hole was made in the horse's neck and it gained extra breath through that.

It is believed that Moifaa led the cortège at the King's funeral in 1910, carrying an empty saddle.

Which brings us from a horse of exceptional size to a record-breaking field . . .

8

Gregalach

Biggest field, 1929

The victory of a ten-year-old tubed maiden called Tipperary Tim in 1928, after thirty-five of the record forty-two runners fell, led to changes in conditions the following year to try and ensure a smaller and better-qualified field.

The starting fee for each horse was increased to £100, and two forfeit stages at which the horses could be withdrawn were introduced in an effort to deter owners of 'no-hopers' from taking part. But two other factors influenced matters: the very fact that a 'no-hoper' had won the previous year encouraged owners of such horses to believe that there was always a chance; and the prize money had been increased out of all proportion with previous years.

The race was worth some £13,000 to the winner, of which £5,000 was put up by the executive and the rest came from the sweepstake on the entrance fees. Ten years earlier, just after the First World War, the race had been worth £3,590, and ten years before that it was worth £2,500, having been £510 in its inaugural year back in 1839. In 1929 there were still many races worth only £150 to the winner, but a horse could earn that amount by finishing fourth in the National. Sponsorship began in 1983 with the *Sun*, followed the next year by Seagrams (in 1991 a horse called Seagram won). Martell, John Smith's and Crabbies followed. Under the present sponsor, Randox Health, prize money reached £1 million, going right down to £3,500 for tenth place.

Thus in 1929, instead of the desired reduction in the field, the reverse occurred. A staggering sixty-six horses went to post, some of them barely able to raise a canter.

In fact, much of the 1928 race's debacle had been caused not by the number of runners (they were fully aware of the unusual situation and went so steadily that all of them safely negotiated the first fence), but by one runner bringing down virtually the whole field (as was to happen again in Foinavon's year, 1967). Ironically, it was the classiest horse in the field who was responsible. Easter Hero, who was to win the next two Cheltenham Gold Cups, swerved and ran along the ditch in front of the Canal Turn before being straddled on top of the fence. It is believed that thirty-five horses were knocked out of the race in one fell swoop.

Easter Hero was again in the mammoth field of 1929, carrying 12 stone 7 pounds. Since his mishap the previous year, the open ditch at the Canal Turn had been done away with. Nevertheless its 90-degree angle ensured that it still offered a unique test in the steeplechasing world.

Among Easter Hero's sixty-five opponents was a seven-year-old gelding called Gregalach, the third string of Tom Leader, whose Sprig had won two years previously and was in the race again along with Mount Etna, Sandy Hook and Bright's Bay.

But, although Gregalach's price was 100-1, he was not a complete no-hoper like Tipperary Tim, as his future record would prove. His form was good enough already for him to be handicapped at 11 stone 4 pounds. That was partly why, with so many other runners to consider, his claims had not struck a chord with punters looking for their annual flutter.

Gregalach was fashionably bred; like Easter Hero he was by My Prince, and had the looks to match. A bright chestnut with a white star, he was a fine, upstanding horse, powerfully built, rangy, with good bone and plenty of scope. Mrs M.A. Gemmell had bought him for 5,000 guineas from Mr T.K. Laidlaw, who in turn had bought him from his Irish breeder, Michael Finlay.

Gregalach's long price could also be attributed to the fact that his stable was known to prefer at least two of their four other runners to him, and that his jockey, Australian Bob Everett, a former naval officer, was comparatively inexperienced, having begun race-riding quite recently as an amateur.

The day of the race dawned dry and sunny and there was an influx of enthusiastic American supporters who had crossed the Atlantic to cheer on their representative, Billy Barton, who they felt sure would make amends for his bad luck the previous year. Then owned by Mr Howard Bruce, grandfather of Charles Fenwick, who was successful in 1980 on Ben Nevis, Billy Barton had been in the lead at the last fence but had fallen, leaving Tipperary Tim to come home alone.

In his native America, Billy Barton had been a rogue on the track and was eventually banned for repeated misbehaviour at the start. He went hunting with the Elkridge Hunt, which he took to with enthusiasm, and began timber racing, winning his first, which led to him being entered for the Maryland Hunt Cup. He set off at a fast and furious pace, clearing the high timber and leaving his rivals in his wake, until he fell at the nineteenth. Horses went by but jockey Albert Ober, whipper-in, unpaid assistant to the Elkridge Hunt, vaulted back on and stormed to victory in record time in spite of his fall.

At Aintree, the American supporters, joined the huge number of runners and their attendants packed into the paddock, praying none would be kicked, while ringside spectators could barely wade through all the names on their race-cards. Most of them had eyes for only one, their Easter Hero, and it looked like being a one-horse race, too, as he set off at the head of the pack from flagfall. Mercifully, all sixty-six horses safely negotiated the first fence. Easter Hero's rider, Jack Moloney, was attempting to keep out of the way of no-hopers, but he was mindful of what had happened the previous year, for, as he approached the Canal Turn, he eased back to let others give Easter Hero a lead at his bogey fence, fearing that the horse would remember his last experience there.

Not a bit of it. Easter Hero jumped it with ease and soon resumed his rightful place at the head of affairs, like a general leading his troops to battle. Following him at a respectful distance in about seventh place, like Easter Hero with his ears pricked, was Gregalach, whose tangerine colours almost matched his bright chestnut coat.

Others fell by the wayside, including Tipperary Tim, and as Easter Hero led over the water the packed stands responded with spontaneous applause; just nineteen of the sixty-six runners were left, with a complete circuit still to go.

Again, Moloney took a safety precaution at the Canal Turn, allowing Richmond II and Shady Hook to lead him over it briefly, then on he swept majestically. It looked like being Easter Hero first and the rest nowhere.

Suddenly there was an ominous shortening of the favourite's stride. Easter Hero was in trouble. The glowing chestnut Gregalach was upsides and gaining on him. To the disbelief of the watching crowd, it became clear that the favourite could not shake off the outsider. A few moments later Gregalach had swept by and he drew away to win by six lengths.

Moloney, to his eternal credit, did not pick up his whip. 'If he slowed down, you knew he had given all,' he said later. He set a fine example to others in his profession.

Richmond II stayed on to finish third, with Melleray's Belle fourth. Altogether, fifty-six horses failed to finish, tenth and last place going to remounter Camperdown.

Easter Hero's defeat was one of the Grand National's hard-luck stories, for it turned out that he had spread a front plate, which had twisted into an S shape and was cutting into the protective boot of his other foreleg with every stride from the moment he suddenly faltered.

It was the sort of outcome to set tongues wagging. The 'who would have won if . . .' brigade were in full voice. But it was a meritorious win for Gregalach, his rider Bob Everett, trainer Tom Leader and owner Mrs Gemmell; just because the crowds had been unable to recognise the combination from the massive card should not detract from their achievement. They were the ones who got things right on the day.

Jockey Bob Everett became a Royal Navy Volunteer Reserve pilot during the Second World War. In 1941, as a Fleet Air Arm pilot, he achieved the first 'kill' by a rocket-launched fighter, shooting down a long-range Focke-Wulf Fw 200 Condor over the Atlantic, a feat which earned him the DSO.

The following year, 1930, Gregalach was up with the leaders when he baulked and was put out of the race at the Canal Turn, but in 1931 he confirmed that his win had been no fluke. Carrying 12 stone, he led at the water and set off foot-perfect for the second circuit. His jumping was almost too good, and his extravagant leap at the second Canal Turn probably cost him the race, for it landed him so far out that he was forced to run wide round the right-angled turn, while three horses passed him on the inside, with Grakle close behind them.

Going to the last, it was a battle royal between these two. Grakle led by half a length; Gregalach's jockey, this time Jack Moloney, picked up his whip and his mount responded; they drew alongside; but Grakle had the inside and 7 pounds less weight and drew away to win by one and a half lengths in one of the fastest recorded times.

Gregalach didn't quite manage two wins in the National but we move on less than a decade to one who did . . .

9

Reynoldstown

Dual winner in the twentieth century, 1935 and 1936

When Major Noel Furlong travelled to Ireland in the early 1930s it was with the specific intention of buying himself a future Grand National winner. The horse he procured was an excitable, jet-black youngster named after his birthplace, Reynoldstown, in County Dublin near Naul, close to the County Meath border. The horse was to fulfil the major's ambition not once but twice.

Noel Furlong had left his native Ireland a decade earlier because of the Troubles. Protestants' houses were being set on fire and there were fears that his son would be kidnapped. The fact that Noel had married a Roman Catholic was an added problem. His son, Frank, aged about eight, was sent ahead to London by boat and train with the coachman and told to wait at the Cavalry Club until his father arrived.

Shortly afterwards, in 1920, Noel Furlong paid his first visit to the Grand National, travelling by train. He found himself next to father and son Algernon and Jack Anthony, trainer and amateur rider, who won that year's race with Troytown. Always a keen hunting and point-to-pointing man in Leicestershire, and before that in Fermoy, County Cork, this chance meeting fired Noel Furlong's enthusiasm for racing, and he wondered if he could achieve the same distinction with his own son in due course.

Frank himself did not show much interest in horses until, at eighteen, on the spur of the moment, he followed hounds on a carthorse. His interest was furthered in the army, when he became great friends with Fulke Walwyn (the pair set up training together before the war) and Frank caught the racing bug. His grandmother relinquished her home-bred side-saddle hunter Robin O'Tiptoe for him to point-to-point and he went on to win the four-mile National Hunt Chase at the Cheltenham Festival of 1932. The following year he made a successful first foray into the Grand National, finishing second on Robin O'Tiptoe's half-brother, Really True.

The exploits of his son further fostered the racing ambitions of Major Furlong, who set off on a horse-hunting trail that led to Ireland and Reynoldstown. The youngster was sired by My Prince, the 'in' stallion of the day, having already sired the Grand National and Cheltenham Gold Cup winners Gregalach and Easter Hero. The breeder, Dick Ball, had also bred the Classic winner Ballymoss.

Reynoldstown was very highly strung and wild, but his breeding was right (though only in the half-bred non-thoroughbred book) and Major Furlong bought him for £1,500 and arranged for transport home. Major Furlong's granddaughter, Griselda Houghton-Brown, kept Dick Ball's account:

> The man's fare and travelling expenses, £4; transport to boat, 43 miles, £2.3/-; insurance for £1,000, £3./15/-; freight to Tilton, Leics, £6.19/-; total £16.17/-.

In addition, there was a contingency of £200 to be paid for the first race valued at £400 or more that Reynoldstown won. In a letter, Mr Ball said, 'He has eaten three years of good oats,' and added, 'I have found it more satisfactory to work him without a noseband, I cannot say why.' He was still without a noseband four years later, when he won the Grand National.

*

It was not all plain sailing for Reynoldstown on the path to Grand National fame. In many ways, his exceptionally nervous temperament made him his own worst enemy, and at times his jumping left a lot to be desired. He 'buried' Frank Furlong in a novice chase at Cheltenham and, once in England, he was only ever ridden by Noel and Frank Furlong and Fulke Walwyn. Even during the horse's retirement, the young Griselda would not venture into his box.

But the occasion and atmosphere of the Grand National brought out the best in Reynoldstown and he 'took on' the fences, tackling them with both enthusiasm and respect.

The 1935 National was a splendid family affair, for Major Furlong both owned and trained his black horse, and his son, Frank, rode him. This was in the heady day of Golden Miller, who, until then, had done nothing wrong – the reverse, in fact. He had won the Cheltenham Gold Cup in the preceding four years in a row, and had won the Grand National the previous year. With such form, there appeared no reason why he should not win again, even with 12 stone 7 pounds on his back, and he started at 2-1, still the shortest-priced National favourite.

Golden Miller unseated his rider, and it was his great Gold Cup rival, Thomond II, who took on Reynoldstown. On the second circuit the pair drew clear from Becher's, where Reynoldstown and Frank Furlong survived a bad peck. The two horses rose as one at the last, Reynoldstown distinctive with his workmanlike face and no noseband, Thomond with his white star and the striped sleeves of his jockey, Billy Speck. But the amateur Frank Furlong, already with a second in the race on his only previous ride, found himself drawing clear on the run-in, and Thomond, who had had a hard race against Golden Miller at Cheltenham, faded into third place.

For the Furlongs, it was a fantastic family achievement – and a remarkably quick return on their investment in a potential Grand National winner. They left the course in high spirits on their way to the traditional revelries in Liverpool – and Frank promptly bumped into a car in front of him in the queue to get out. The irate driver jumped out and confronted him. 'Who do you think you are – have you won the bloody Grand National or something?' he stormed. 'Well, yes, actually I have,' came Frank's reply.

There was a tremendous party at the Adelphi Hotel, with Fulke Walwyn in the high-spirited form he was known for, and one way or another a certain amount of damage was done by the revellers, including to a painting, for which Frank was obliged to pay the repair bill.

The following year, when they were again celebrating victory, Frank spotted the same picture, and said, 'That's mine!' – and threw a bottle at it.

There are those who claim Reynoldstown's second Grand National was due to luck.

Golden Miller was again in the field and once more he started as favourite, jointly with Avenger, but it was a rank outsider, the tubed Davy Jones, who stole most of the limelight.

Golden Miller went at the first and, although he remounted, he refused persistently at the ditch after Valentine's, hating the whole experience. Two fallers left Davy Jones, ridden by Anthony Mildmay, in the lead with over a circuit to go. At the Chair he landed a length ahead of Double Crossed, with Avenger, Emancipator, Reynoldstown and Blue Prince all in the air together. Poor Avenger broke his neck at the next fence, and at Becher's second time round Davy Jones had a half-a-length advantage over Reynoldstown (who was carrying 12 stone 2 pounds).

His jockey Fulke Walwyn, later to become a five-time champion trainer, with horses for the Queen Mother in his care, takes up the story:

'Reynoldstown was always going well. We were just behind the leader at the Chair then drew upsides with Davy Jones, and we jumped Becher's and the Canal Turn together. Reynoldstown made a terrible mistake at Valentine's. He was nearly on the floor and that cost him ten lengths.'

No one else was in the reckoning and Fulke was steadily making up the lost ground on that long sweeping turn towards the second last: 'I was nearly upsides again and, when Anthony Mildmay's reins broke, I had to check Reynoldstown to let him out. I saw the reins on the ground and I saw Anthony hit him on the head but he couldn't stop him running out. Then all I had to do was jump the last. I think we would have won anyway.' Most books record that Anthony Mildmay and Davy Jones were heading for certain victory.

And who is to dispute the man on top? It was something Fulke, ever the gentleman, said little about at the time, not wishing to compound Mildmay's disappointment. Reynoldstown nevertheless went down in the records as a dual Grand National winner with plenty of honour. Strictly speaking, there was also another dual winner that century, with Poethlyn in 1918 and 1919, but some records do not count the 1918 wartime substitute at Gatwick. Red Rum was to win three times (see Chapter 14).

Fulke Walwyn rode Reynoldstown in 1936 because Frank Furlong had put on considerable weight in the intervening year; he had also accepted a gift of £1,000 from his father for the 1935 race and, as an honourable gentleman, immediately said that his acceptance of the money made him a professional, so he gave up his amateur status. Fulke did exactly the same thing a year later, in consequence of his win on Reynoldstown.

After the 1936 victory, the Furlongs received a telegram from Edward, Prince of Wales, whom they knew from the hunting fields of Leicestershire. It read: 'Hearty congratulations once more and I backed Reynoldstown again. Edward RI.' (Apparently, the prince used to drive round Hyde Park during the race, so that he could listen to it on the car radio, evidently needing privacy to do so.)

*

While a long and luxurious retirement lay ahead for Reynolds-town, and for Noel Furlong too, Frank's life was all too short. War was looming, and he joined the Fleet Air Arm as a pilot. It was he who located the *Bismarck* and repeatedly radioed its position until he ran out of fuel and was forced to ditch in thick fog. Remarkably, as he paddled in his life raft, Frank was picked up by an off-course Allied boat, but that was the end of his good luck, for he was killed later in the war. He left behind a widow, who went her own way, and a baby daughter, Griselda, who was brought up by her paternal grandparents, Major and Mrs Furlong. When she was a year old, they moved from Leicester-shire to Marston St Lawrence near Banbury. Not long before his death, Major Furlong at the age of eighty-five was able to give her away when she married farmer Peter Houghton-Brown. Fulke Walwyn's sister, Jane, was her bridesmaid.

At Marston, Reynoldstown, ever excitable and highly strung, was cared for as if he was still a racehorse by his devoted groom, Mac – two pensioners together. It was quite impossible to turn out Reynoldstown in a paddock, for he would simply jump out; instead, he was led out daily for a buck and a kick at the end of a lead rope, and groomed, rugged and generally made a fuss of. To the young Griselda, he was ferocious, gnashing his teeth and 'ready to eat' her.

At the age of twenty-four, Reynoldstown cut his foot on an old bottle, contracted tetanus and had to be put down. He was buried in the grounds near the stables, and by coincidence was to be joined there in later years by the 1972 winner, Well To Do. Marston House was by that time owned by Mr John Sumner, and Well To Do was buried there after he was put down in 1985 at the age of twenty-three.

Apart from the general horrors of the Second World War, the conflict was also to affect a second Grand National-winning rider, the young man who won the great race at the tender age of seventeen.

10

Bruce Hobbs

Youngest winning rider, 1938

For Bruce Hobbs there was only one day in the year: Grand National day. It is more than eighty years since he became the youngest ever jockey, at seventeen, to win the National, by the closest of margins, on one of the smallest horses to achieve victory in the race, Battleship, who was also the last stallion to win.

Despite a highly successful career as one of Newmarket's leading flat trainers it was for winning the Grand National that Bruce Hobbs, a tall, well-preserved sixty-seven when I met him fifty years after his win, was best remembered, and he didn't wish it any other way. 'The National's the greatest spectacle in the world,' he said. 'If they alter the fences they might just as well run it at Sandown. There is no other atmosphere like it and since being saved and under the present management it has had its vitality renewed.'

Descended from four generations of Leicestershire hunting stock, with up to fifty thoroughbred hunters stabled at a time at his father's Melton Mowbray yard, Bruce grew up in the cream of hunting country; he was given his hunt buttons at the young age of nine. He was not only a fearless rider across country but had the showman's knack too, as he demonstrated with the virtually unbeaten 14.2 hh. show pony Lady Marvel. He was also one of the original members of the Quorn branch of the Pony Club.

*

Bruce Hobbs was born in America, where his father, Reginald, was for a time master of the horse to Singer Sewing Machine heir Ambrose Clark, but when he was two years old his family came to England in order for his father to set up the Melton yard for Mr Clark.

When Ambrose Clark found he had less time for commuting from America for his English hunting, he transferred his interest to racing, installing Reg Hobbs in Lambourn. He also introduced several American owners to the yard, one of whom was the 'dowager' of the American racing scene, Mrs Marion Du Pont Scott, wife of film actor Randolph, who donated the original trophy for the Carolina Cup in 1930.

For the young Bruce, racing was a natural progression from the world of ponies and hunting and he had his first ride in a hurdle race at the age of fourteen, and first win at fifteen in a hurdle at Wolverhampton.

At the end of 1936, on his sixteenth birthday, Bruce turned professional, and at the age of seventeen he finished third in the jockeys' table, as well as becoming the youngest ever rider to win the National.

Bruce did not achieve victory at the first attempt. In 1937 he rode Flying Minutes for Mrs Ambrose Clark. He was going well enough to think that he might place when the horse made a mistake at the last ditch four from home – 'And I fell off,' said Bruce. 'I was sixteen and full of enthusiasm without too many nerves. I was a hunting man and the loose horses were the biggest trouble.' He also rode Flying Minutes in the Sefton Chase over the National course and was beaten by a short head.

The next year, when Bruce was well established and making his name as a professional, there was a choice of four Grand National horses in the home yard: Flying Minutes, Bagatelle, What Have You and Battleship. Bruce, not surprisingly, chose Flying Minutes but at the eleventh hour the horse broke down.

The chance of riding the second favourite, the George Beeby-trained Delachance, then emerged, for his usual jockey, Fulke Walwyn, was injured. But a week before the race Fulke had recovered sufficiently to take the ride after all. So the diminutive American stallion Battleship became Bruce's third choice, and that only for financial reasons. 'Purely because I was offered more money to ride him – although he was also the best of the remainder,' he commented with a wry smile.

Battleship, a bay, stood only 15.1½ hh., but was a 'big little horse' to ride and 'a charming character, you could do anything with him', in spite of his full-horse status. By Man O'War, America's legendary 'racing machine', winner of twenty of his twenty-one races, out of Quarantaine, who won the French Oaks, he had the class to help him overcome his small size. He had had a successful career in America, winning from four and a half furlongs to four and a half miles, thus taking in a slightly broader width than Red Rum, whose shortest race distance was the English minimum of five furlongs.

Battleship won the American Grand National of 1934 at Belmont Park but broke down, and when he arrived in England in 1936 he had been fired. His owner, Mrs Scott, who lived in Montpelier, Virginia, once the home of President Madison, fourth president of the United States, was nevertheless keen for him to run in the 1937 Grand National – something Reg Hobbs managed to forestall.

Mrs Scott had her way the following year, however, by which time Battleship had won several English races and had been beaten by only three quarters of a length in the National Hunt Chase at the Cheltenham Festival, wearing blinkers for the first time. Bruce had been unable to ride him at Cheltenham, having broken his nose in the Champion Hurdle and therefore being out of commission.

Battleship was eleven years old when he ran at Aintree that sunny but cold day in March 1938 when overnight rain had made the going good. The only attribute that gained him a mention in previews was his size; dubbed the 'American pony', he started at odds of 40-1 and again wore blinkers.

Bruce Hobbs enjoyed a superb ride on the little horse. 'He jumped those big fences beautifully although he landed very steeply over Becher's; remember, he was a stallion and didn't want to hurt himself,' recalled Bruce, who wisely had had his reins lengthened by six inches so that he could slip to the buckle in true hunting style over the big drop fences.

As the leaders cleared Becher's for the second time and began to race in earnest, it was clearly a four-horse race between Royal Danieli, Workman, Delachance and Battleship, with the previous year's winner, Royal Mail, unable to cope on 12 stone 7 pounds.

Battleship just led and had the inside, four horses stretched out perfectly in the air together, yet from the stands it still looked as if the race lay between the other three. Instead, it turned into something of a David and Goliath contest on the long journey home as the big, long-striding, impressive Irish horse Royal Danieli led little Battleship.

At the third last fence, just before they crossed the Melling Road to come back onto the racecourse proper, Battleship made a major mistake and all but crumpled on landing. 'It won me the race, I'm sure,' said Bruce. 'He had to come from behind and he was running too freely at that stage; if he'd gone clear he would have given up, thinking his task was done, but the mistake stopped him in his tracks.'

To the watching crowds it looked as though Battleship's chance had gone, and that Workman (who was to win the next year) would follow the big-striding Royal Danieli home. But young Bruce, who had learned to sit tight in the hunting field, held the little stallion together, rallied him, passed Workman, who hit the second last hard, and set off after the big horse.

At the last fence he still had three lengths to make up and, when a loose horse carried him wide over to the stands side, the task indeed looked forlorn. But Battleship had plenty of battle in him and just got up.

I've won the National! was Bruce's first thought as he flashed past the line.

It was in the days before the photo finish, but the jockeys concerned usually have a good idea of who has won, although Dan Moore on Royal Danieli was also convinced he had won . . . After agonising minutes, the judge's verdict was announced: Battleship by a head. It was a great result for the bookmakers and the band of American supporters, but not for the majority of punters, especially the Irish, who were stunned into silence. As for Mrs Scott, she was too overcome with excitement to lead her horse in.

Battleship returned to America to a hero's welcome as the first American-bred and -owned winner of the Grand National. He returned to Montpelier to stand at stud and sired fifty-eight foals, including War Battle and Shipboard, steeplechase champions in 1947 and 1956 respectively, plus Sea Legs, winner of the 1952 American Grand National; he lived until a ripe old age, blind in one eye but in good heart at thirty.

Bruce Hobbs' promising career was to be cut brutally short. The following season, 1938–39, he broke his back in a selling hurdle at Cheltenham, at a flight by the winning post which was permanently removed after the accident. He was out of action for six months and had just returned with a winner at Buckfastleigh on his initial ride, giving Fulke Walwyn his first as a trainer, when war broke out.

So Bruce, the youngest Grand National hero, joined up at Bath on 3 September 1939 and became simply Trooper Hobbs 327184. He joined the North Somerset Yeomanry, because one of the stable's owners was in it and it meant he could be with horses. In March 1940 he went to Palestine with the horses and was commissioned into the Queen's Own Yorkshire Dragoons

– 'a marvellous bunch who I still keep in touch with', he told me in the 1980s.

Bruce saw much active service and was awarded the Military Cross for his part in the assault on a strongly defended German position near Tunis in May 1943.[*]

But, like other good jockeys, when Bruce returned he had put on too much weight and, after a short battle with the scales, he gave it up, put an advert in the *Racing Calendar* – and began a valuable five-year period as private National Hunt trainer to Mr and Mrs John Rogerson, whose daughter Valda Embiricos owned the 1981 National winner, Aldaniti, and is a cousin of Jim Joel, whose Maori Venture put him into the Grand National records as the oldest winning owner in 1987.

From there Bruce moved on to become assistant trainer to George Beeby at Compton, Berkshire. Then, through an introduction by royal jockey Harry Carr, he began his long association with Newmarket, joining Captain Sir Cecil Boyd-Rochfort as assistant for eight educational years.

A short spell at Gibsons, the Newmarket saddlers, was followed by another as assistant to Jack Clayton, after which he became private trainer to Radio Rentals and racehorse magnate Sir David Robinson. Although that job ended after two years, Bruce had nothing but admiration for the man: 'I am a horseman and he was a businessman and the two just didn't gel, but the experience stood me in good stead and was a stepping stone for me.'

Subsequently a consortium of owners, Sir David Wills, Jocelyn

---

[*] The full citation read: 'This officer crawled to the top of a hill occupied on the reverse side by the enemy in order to direct mortar fire and observe for tanks . . . He had to go so close to the enemy that it was not safe to speak on a telephone. He therefore climbed up and down all day to pass messages over his wireless at the bottom of the hill. Through his efforts and skill, effective fire was brought to bear on a party of enemy tanks which could not be seen from any other position.'

Hambro and Mr T.F. Blackwell and Major Jim Phillips, formed Palace House Stables (now the National Heritage Centre for Horseracing & Sporting Art which incorporates the Newmarket Racing Museum), and installed Bruce Hobbs as trainer: 'They put me on my feet and it was the start of a very rewarding twenty years.'

Bruce retired in 1985 but soon found himself as involved as ever in new challenges within the racing world he loved. He was made a member of the Jockey Club in 1986 and became a member of the disciplinary committee, work which took up some three days a week. He was also a director of the National Stud, along with chairman Chris Collins, David Gibson and Peter Willett. He loved shooting and cricket, umpired for the Newmarket Racing XI, and delighted in his three grandchildren.

Although Bruce Hobbs trained the winner of the Irish Derby, Tyrnavos, had eleven places in Classics, and trained horses such as Hotfoot, Jacinth, City Of Truth and Catherine Wheel, there was one thrill in his life to beat them all: that day in 1938 when he and Battleship got up on the line to win the National. 'I relive it every year,' he confessed.

Bruce Hobbs died in Newmarket, aged eighty-four, in November 2005.

With the advent of reliable photo finish cameras, it is easier to judge for sure which horse has won in a close finish. In 1882, the victory of Seaman was judged a short-head over Cyrus.

The photo finish as we know it today was first used on a British racecourse, Epsom, in 1947, although there was a less dependable type first used in America in the early 1880s.

It has played an important part in the Grand Nationals of 2012 and 2018. We have seen in Chapter 3 that Neptune Collonges won in 2012 by the shortest ever margin of a nose (a measurement that was not in use in Battleship's day). In 2018, the photographic evidence was that Tiger Roll beat Pleasant Company by a head.

To be beaten by a whisker can be described as bad luck, but the unluckiest of all was certainly 'the horse who didn't win the Grand National' . . .

11

Devon Loch

Unluckiest loser, 1956

The Pony Club members looked suitably awed as the kind bay horse turned his handsome head inquisitively towards his young visitors. This was the high spot of the Pony Club's visit to Mr Peter Cazalet's famous stables at Fairlawne, Shipbourne, near Tonbridge in Kent, for they had all heard of Devon Loch, 'the horse who didn't win the Grand National'.

In later years, my sister particularly remembered the horse being swathed in bandages; for me, it was the lovely old-fashioned stable, with its brick floor and curved iron railings atop the wooden partitions.

The whole place left a lasting impression: the magnificent William and Mary house set back from the road, surrounded by daffodils in spring, a ha-ha dividing it from the field in front; the spotless Victorian square yard well away to one side, with its clock tower, and tack-room reeking of newly polished leather, the saddles and bridles hanging line upon line. Everywhere there was an aura of smartness and pride in the work – no casual manners or sloppy jeans in sight. In those days dress for work was more formal, which included wearing jodhpurs or breeches.

This was the stable whence Devon Loch set off to become the most famous Grand National loser of all time – the royal horse owned by the most popular National Hunt supporter in the land, HM Queen Elizabeth the Queen Mother. He was the horse who sailed round 4 miles 806 yards of the Grand National with the race at his mercy, the thirty fences safely behind him, only to sprawl suddenly for no apparent reason just 50 yards from the winning post.

Various theories have been put forward as to what caused the dramatic, baffling collapse on that fine March day in 1956. The only thing that is certain is that the cause will never be established beyond doubt. On that bittersweet day, when so many hopes and dreams were shattered, and so many of the nation's people came to feel somehow cheated, the Queen Mother remained a shining example to all. She showed concern only for her horse, for the lads who looked after him, for her trainer Peter Cazalet, thwarted for a third time through sheer bad luck, and most of all for her jockey, Dick Francis.

'The Queen Mother's first thought was for the misfortune of both Peter Cazalet and Dick Francis,' her private secretary Sir Martin Gilliat told me in the 1980s. And when Fred Rimell and Dave Dick, whose E.S.B. had been left victorious, were taken to meet the Queen Mother, they were 'practically in tears, they were so sad for her'. Sir Martin added, 'It is impossible to know what happened; the Queen Mother is open to ideas, but the general consensus seems to be that it was the volume of noise from the cheering, this comes over and over again.'

It was fitting that the Queen Mother should have chosen Peter Cazalet* to train her horses, for it would have been hard to find a more immaculate yard than Fairlawne, with training standards to match.

Cazalet was a perfectionist and in his head lad, Scottish-born Jim Fairgrieve, a strict disciplinarian, he had the ideal man in charge. The stable that began with two horses and Jim ended with forty-nine horses and twenty lads, and was run like a regimental

* Cazalet also played first-class cricket for Kent and for the MCC.

barracks, firmly but fairly. At Fairlawne some lads, hearing of more lenient yards when away at the races, would leave, but it was surprising how often they returned, and those with any trace of ability were given every help to further their careers. Jim would often boast that he had the best lads in the country.

When the Queen Mother visited, she wouldn't see so much as a hayseed out of place. Once, on a pre-royal-visit inspection, Peter Cazalet found the horses duly polished, the stables scrubbed, the yard washed down. 'Jim,' he called, 'there are some cobwebs behind that piece of gutterpipe.' By the time the Queen Mother called, the cobwebs were gone.

Jim Fairgrieve had served with the Royal Army Veterinary Corps in the East in the Second World War but was invalided out with recurrent malaria. He worked with stallions in Newmarket and then moved to Burroughs and Wellcome, who had taken over Fairlawne during the war and were developing various equine vaccines.

One day at Fairlawne Jim saw young Edward Cazalet riding his pony. 'How can I stop my pony being so fat?' Edward enquired. Jim inspected the animal for a moment, then replied, 'She's in foal.' Not long afterwards, on a cold and frosty morning, the foal was born; Jim picked it up and carried it in his arms to a box. Peter Cazalet was home on leave from the Guards Armoured Division and the two men met for the first time.

When Peter Cazalet started training after the war, Jim Fairgrieve remained in situ. And he stayed there to the end, from the first day in 1946 when they had two unbroken horses and went on to end their first season with fifteen winners to the sad day twenty-seven years later when Peter Cazalet died and the stable was dispersed.

It was in 1951 that Peter Cazalet bought Devon Loch, as a five-year-old, in Ireland. By Devonian (by Hyperion) out of Coolaleen (who was bred by clergyman Charles Daly), Devon Loch himself was bred by Willie Moloney in County Cork. Moloney usually bred for the flat, but it was clear that this immature colt was more of a chaser type, so he sold him to Colonel Stephen Hill-Dillon in Navan for 550 guineas as a yearling.

Colonel Hill-Dillon was patient with the horse, first running him in a flat race at Leopardstown for five-year-old maidens, then winning a 'bumper'.* After that he sold him to Cazalet with a £1,000 contingency should he win the Cheltenham Gold Cup, or £2,000 for the Grand National.

Devon Loch's arrival at Fairlawne nearly ended in disaster, for he broke loose when Jim was lunging† him one day. He galloped flat out across the field, jumped a set of rails into the next one, luckily in the opposite direction from the road – and was caught without a scratch on him.

After a promising start in England, in which he was twice second over hurdles and second on his chasing debut behind the next Gold Cup winner Mont Tremblant, Devon Loch sustained a touch of leg trouble, was fired, and was then rested for two years. It was clear that he was a high-class chaser in the making and was worth waiting for. He also had the ideal temperament, and was much loved by all who came into contact with him, being quiet and a good 'doer'.

Jim Fairgrieve remembered that the horse's hindquarters did not match up to his front, for he had a poor 'second thigh'. Alex King, who was a lad at the Cazalet stables at the time, remembered that there was nearly always a bandage on his near hind

* Bumpers are National Hunt flat races designed to introduce young future steeplechasers and hurdlers to racing environs without having to take on more precocious and faster flat-bred progeny. In the past, only amateur riders were allowed to compete and the term 'bumper' was a derogatory one for amateur riders who sometimes bumped up and down in the saddle in ungainly fashion. Today, most professional jockeys 'bump' a horse along when it comes off the bit (i.e. is tiring). The difference is probably that professionals and good amateurs do it in a rhythmic way and therefore do not unbalance their horse.
† Schooling him in a circle on the end of a long rope.

joint when Marshall 'Mick' Taylor was schooling him. He believes that a weakness there made him slightly lopsided and could have affected his balance at the crucial moment of his collapse.

When Devon Loch returned to racing, Dick Francis was stable jockey, and Bryan Marshall was also riding some of the stable's horses regularly; Bryan predicted quite early in the horse's career that he would win the National.

Devon Loch won good races at Hurst Park and Sandown, was third at Cheltenham and fell in the Mildmay. The following season, 1955–56, he won his first race over three miles at Lingfield, won again at Sandown, was fifth in the King George at Kempton on Boxing Day, and was third in the Mildmay Memorial at Sandown. Significantly, perhaps, Bryan Marshall twice felt him falter in a race before finding a second wind. A hard winter caused some hold-up in work, but Devon Loch was second in the National Hunt Chase at Cheltenham, and then all sights were set on Aintree, the stable by this time full of hope.

Jim Fairgrieve, for one, had been backing him steadily through the winter, a couple of pounds a week at ever-reducing prices. Stable lad John Hole accompanied Devon Loch to Aintree and Alex King was in charge of the Queen Mother's other runner, M'as-tu-vu. They even planned how they would celebrate that evening, so sure were they that Devon Loch would win.

Jim spent the night before the race in the Cumberland Hotel, London, ready to catch the race train to Liverpool early the next morning. He was telling everyone that Devon Loch would win – he coupled him with every runner in the second leg of the Tote double, which was a flat race – but something kept nagging at the back of his mind. It was, he said, like a premonition, and it gave him a sleepless night.

The royal party also travelled by train, a special one. The race was held on a Saturday, as it had been ever since 1949, having been changed from a Friday at the request of the Labour Government.

The number of runners – twenty-nine – was not as large as on some occasions but the crowd was enormous. Two previous winners, Early Mist and Royal Tan, were in the field, as well as a future one, Sundew, but Must was favourite. Others who were well-fancied were Carey's Cottage, E.S.B., Gentle Moya and Devon Loch. M'as-tu-vu, well backed the previous year when he fell on the final circuit after disputing the lead, was out at 40-1 this time.

Four runners fell at the first fence amid groans from the watching punters, as both Must and Early Mist had gone. M'as-tu-vu was in the lead and Devon Loch, middle placed to begin with, was jumping so well that he gained lengths at every fence.

For his jockey, Dick Francis, it was literally a dream ride. His only really anxious moment came two fences after the Canal Turn, when Domata and Derek Ancil came to grief and Devon Loch had to twist in mid-air like a cat to sidestep him. From then on his jumping got better and better, making those massive fences look like hurdles. He treated the Chair as if it were a brush fence and when the water flicked beneath him he was lying sixth or seventh, still gaining in the air each time.

Sundew, lying second, fell at the second Becher's; Armorial III was leading, closely attended by Royal Tan, E.S.B., Eagle Lodge, Key Royal and Devon Loch. Gentle Moya blundered his way out of it, but Devon Loch avoided mishap and as he went into the Canal Turn for the second time he had only Armorial in front of him.

Dick Francis was in the incredible and enviable position of having actually to steady his mount in the Grand National with a mile to go. 'Never had I felt such power in reserve, such confidence in my mount, such calm in my mind,' he wrote later in his autobiography *Sport of Queens*. To be in that position in any race is a marvellous feeling; for it to happen in the Grand National a matchless experience.

Armorial fell at the fence after Valentine's and Eagle Lodge took over briefly until Devon Loch went on three from home, Dick Francis having time to note that those around him were already being hard-ridden – and he was still sitting with a double handful!

They galloped back onto the racecourse, strong and powerful, only two fences left, and those Devon Loch jumped as freshly as the first. E.S.B. was close by, but he was a beaten horse; Devon Loch was only toying with him and, as they landed safely over the last, the royal horse moved up a gear and Dave Dick, seeing his chance gone, settled for second place.

The crowds were well and truly cheering in anticipation of one of the most popular wins in the history of the race, as Devon Loch opened up more of a gap and reached the elbow. The roar of the crowd was deafening, a tumultuous crescendo reaching far down the course to that bay horse who was winning for the Queen Mother. And then he was down, sprawled flat on the ground; it had not been a fall in the normal sense, but he was lying there spread-eagled like a floppy puppy. One moment he was winning the race, the next he was on the ground; there was nothing in between, no fleeting image of danger lurking, no stumble before the fall, no indication of imminent disaster – just collapse, as total as it was unforewarned.

At that moment a graphic photograph was taken of the royal party and other spectators on top of the County Stand. Some are cheering delightedly; others have their mouths open in a big 'Oh', their eyes full of disbelief. Three quarters of the men have already raised their hats from their heads in salute of a royal victory.

Devon Loch got up again after his collapse more or less in one movement (it wasn't a fall that sent him right over on to his side) and with his rider still in the plate; Dick Francis's first instinct was to get going again and still be first past the post. But Devon Loch stood there stock-still, as if incapable of engaging his hind legs into gear. It lasted only a few moments, but that was enough. Dick Francis dismounted, the most miserably disconsolate man in England.

John Hole led Devon Loch back to the stables. The St John Ambulance Brigade came to Dick Francis's rescue; although unhurt physically, he readily accepted their lift back, thereby avoiding the crowd's enquiring gaze. After the race, he disappeared to his brother's at Bangor-on-Dee for the night to be out of the limelight.*

Everywhere there was incredulity. Jim Fairgrieve had started pushing his way down from his part of the stand when he heard 'this awful gasp' and looked up to see the disaster occur. Alex King and John Hole, already planning how they would celebrate that night, just could not believe what their eyes were telling them. John, prepared moments before for the proudest moment of his life, leading in the winner of the Grand National, took him instead to the stables.

Within ten minutes, the Queen Mother herself was at the stables. The horse was thoroughly examined by a vet, who could find nothing wrong. His heart, lungs, legs and back were all sound and the horse was not unduly distressed after his exertions.

The sad demise was to open up a floodgate of conjecture. The only person convinced he knows what happened is the man who was riding him at the time: Dick Francis. He believed that it was the noise from, as he put it, 249,999 people out there cheering for Devon Loch. In his autobiography, Dick Francis wrote:

> I have never in my life heard such a noise. It rolled and lapped around us, buffeting and glorious, the enthusiastic expression of

---

* Dick Francis went on to become a world-famous best-selling author of more than forty racing thrillers, as if inspired by what the fates had doled out to him. In time, he moved to Florida, having taken with him memories of a remarkable ride, a bizarre ending, and his most treasured memento, an inscribed silver ashtray from the Queen Mother. Dick Francis died in 2010, aged eighty-nine.

love for the Royal Family and delight in seeing the Royal horse win. The tremendous noise was growing in volume with every second, and was being almost funnelled down from the stands on to the course.

I remember how startled I was when I first heard the cheers for M'as-tu-vu at Lingfield, and they were a whisper compared with the enveloping roar at Liverpool.

He concludes that the noise which was uplifting and magnificent to him may have been exceedingly frightening to Devon Loch.

Some in the press speculated that Devon Loch saw the wing of the water jump to one side, thought he was going to be jumping it again, and took off in a 'phantom' leap. But slow-motion study of the film of the race would appear to refute this.

Jim Fairgrieve believed that a hind leg touched the ground toe-first, instead of the full foot, causing the leg to slip backwards – a bit like slipping backwards when walking up a steep, muddy hill. 'But I've seen the film so many times, stopped and started, and I still don't really know,' he admitted.

A police officer said there was a dark patch on the course which on inspection proved to be wet caused by a leaking stop cock near the water jump: could Devon Loch's fall have been caused by this patch of false ground?

Other theories centred on the state of Devon Loch's health: he had a weak hind leg which gave way at the crucial moment; one vet suggested that an infestation of red worms in early life might have caused bad circulation in his hindquarters. Some thought he'd had a heart attack, but if it was a heart condition, why didn't it show up afterwards?

Alex King believed the collapse could have been caused by cramp resulting from a surfeit of glucose: 'We used to buy glucose for the horses from Boots, but the late Professor Pugh had had some problems with athletes getting cramp from excess glucose. I don't know for sure what he discovered, but there was never a barrel of glucose at Fairlawne again after Devon Loch.'

Dave Dick was convinced that the cause was lack of oxygen. He had seen the horse's tongue hanging out almost black as he galloped alongside him on E.S.B. He believes that, as the horse recovered, and regained his supply of oxygen and normal breathing, so no ill effects remained to be seen on examination.

Another possibly significant point is the time of the race. E.S.B. finished only one second outside Golden Miller's record, so Devon Loch must have been easily on target to beat the course record himself.

Devon Loch never again showed any sign of abnormality and in fact went on to win again twice, a hurdle and a match against Early Mist. But one can imagine Peter Cazalet venting his pent-up frustration when a photographer, paying a rare visit to the stables, asked him to arrange for Devon Loch 'to repeat what he did at Liverpool' for him to capture on film! 'My father had taken it all extremely well until then,' says Edward Cazalet, 'but that man had to leave fairly quickly!'

Eventually Devon Loch suffered a recurrence of tendon trouble and was given away to Sir Noel Murless as his hack, although it was Murless's daughter Julie, later to become Mrs Henry Cecil, who mostly rode him, for he could be a 'bit of a monkey' and whip round on Newmarket Heath. 'He was a marvellous old character,' she reveals, 'and rather fun to ride.'

In time Devon Loch returned to Sandringham where, in 1962, he was put down.

While the Queen Mother, in the 1980s, would still have liked to win the Grand National if the right horse had come along, it was no longer a burning ambition. Of all the many incidents in the history of the Grand National, none has been debated more than the disaster that befell Devon Loch. What irony it would be should the noise theory be true, that the very popularity of the horse who was winning should have caused it not to win.

As the Queen Mother said of the incident, speaking on a television programme about her horses in April 1987, 'That's racing.'

The Queen Mother died in March 2002, aged 101. She had come so close to winning the Grand National.

The unluckiest loser takes us on a decade to the luckiest winner.

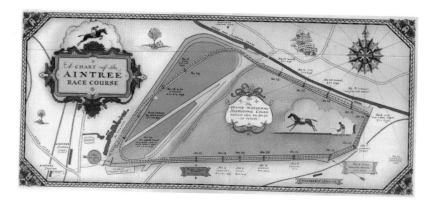

An early map of the course.

Lottery was the winner of the first Grand National in 1839.

An artist's image of the swells watching one of the first Grand Nationals as published nearly 100 years later in *Vogue* magazine in 1930.

George Stevens on The Colonel and Emblem, two of his five winning rides, still a record.

Top Dual grey winner, The Lamb jumps over two loose horses on his way to victory in 1871.

Above In 1961 Nicolaus Silver became the second grey to win, ridden by Bob Beasley.

Right Neptune Collonges (left) was only the third grey to win in the first 180 years of the Grand National. In 2012 he beat Sunnyhillboy (right) by a nose, with Seabass (Katie Walsh) close behind in third, the first female rider to place in the race.

Opposite page top Cloister was an impressive winner of the 1893 National.

Opposite page middle Manifesto, who ran in the National eight times, won twice and was third three times, is seen here jumping the practice hurdle on the way to the start, as was usual in those days.

Opposite page left Moifaa, the 1904 winner, was rumoured to have been shipwrecked on his way over from New Zealand.

Top The mayhem at the 23rd fence in 1967 when only Foinavon cleared it at the first attempt.

Left Devon Loch, 'the horse who didn't win the Grand National' in 1956 when sprawling on the flat on the run in. The Queen Mother's horse is seen here jumping the last fence perfectly, in the hands of jockey Dick Francis.

Above Red Rum cools off after exercise on Southport Beach.

Aldaniti and Bob Champion soar to a fairytale victory in 1981.

Mr Frisk put up the record time in 1990 for amateur Marcus Armytage.

Richard Dunwoody and trainer Martin Pipe with the trophy after Miinnehoma's victory in 1994.

Below
Miinnehoma (right), the first winner for Richard Dunwoody, alongside runner-up Moorcroft Boy (Adrian Maguire).

Top Rough Quest clears the last for Mick Fitzgerald and then survives a Stewards' Enquiry to keep the race.

Above Trainer Terry Casey on board Rough Quest at home.

Right Mick Fitzgerald and Richard Dunwoody showing the camaraderie between jockeys, embracing here at the end of Rough Quest's race.

12

Foinavon

Luckiest winner, 1967

There have been lucky winners of the Grand National but, of them all, Foinavon must rank supreme – and may also have been indirectly responsible for saving the race.

Sole contender to get over the twenty-third fence at the first attempt in a huge pile-up, the moderate, blinkered Foinavon held on to his unexpected lead all the way to the winning post, seven lonely fences later.

Yet, while Foinavon was indisputably lucky, bravery and, yes, skill also came into the reckoning. That day in 1967 twenty horses were put out of the race at the smallest fence on the course. All of them had safely negotiated Becher's for the second time. The commentator remarked on the fact that the two loose horses leading had caused no hindrance. They jumped straight and true, as if guided by jockeys. All that changed at the next, as the loose horses stopped and swerved broadside to the take-off side of the fence. The havoc they wreaked was total. Most horses baulked and refused. Some jockeys reached the landing side without their partners. A few combinations scrambled over only to fall apart on landing.

Into this melee came the backmarkers, Foinavon among them. Much credit is due to the quick thinking of his jockey, John Buckingham, riding in his first Grand National, in steering him over to the wide outside and popping him through a gap; and an equal amount to the horse himself, who had every excuse to stop on the take-off side along with most of his comrades. From a virtual standstill he jumped over. And entirely alone he faced the remaining seven fences: a situation not for the faint of heart, for it is in company that horses race best, their adrenaline stimulated by the competition at their heels or around them.

Foinavon's win may have been due, at least in part, to the some-what unorthodox, individual training of his young handler, John Kempton. Although his win brought amazed gasps on the day, and returned odds of 444-1 on the Tote, in fact Foinavon had been bought specifically with the Grand National in mind.

John Kempton had a small yard at Compton in Berkshire, and some loyal but unwealthy owners. Originally a Londoner, he studied to be a vet in Epsom but lack of finances forced him to quit and he became a blacksmith. He took out a permit, then, mustering a few owners, he was granted a licence to train and moved to Compton.

First owned by Anne, Duchess of Westminster, Foinavon – named, like Arkle and Ben Stack, after a Scottish mountain – had won three chases for Tom Dreaper in Ireland but had a tendency to fall, and the duchess decided to sell him. One of his wins had qualified him for the National so, when he came up for sale at Doncaster, Kempton secured him for 2,000 guineas on behalf of two of his owners who were keen to have a runner in the race.

John's prime aim was to improve the horse's jumping. He took him hunting with the Old Berkshire, where he jumped all sorts of obstacles and had to learn to look after himself in tricky situ-ations, and he found a new enthusiasm for life. He was lunged a 'fantastic amount' over jumps and popping over little schooling fences became a daily routine exercise.

A fine, upstanding sort, standing 16.3 hh., with a bright eye and plenty of heart room, Foinavon was 'one hell of a charac-ter' who 'could really talk', and he loved nothing more than the companionship of his great pal, Susie the goat. Foinavon got very upset if for any reason Susie was taken out of his box for a while, and he looked forward twice daily to her being milked. He looked on virtually drooling, just waiting for his drink, and as soon as she was milked he drank it like lightning, licking his lips with pleasure. Susie even used to accompany Foinavon to race meetings, as usual sharing his quarters.

Foinavon's form had not been as moderate as all those who wrote him off as a freak National winner claimed. He finished fourth in the King George VI Chase at Kempton on Boxing Day, though he came seventh (last) in the Cheltenham Gold Cup of 1967. He was usually ridden by John Kempton himself, and many times ran in a bitless bridle. Kempton had tried this unusual equipment before on a horse called Seasend with startling results. Anxious not to get into trouble, Kempton had asked the stewards' permission; there was nothing in the rule book to prevent it so it was allowed, with the proviso that, should the horse cause interference, Kempton would find himself in trouble. Far from that, Seasend won by twenty lengths, went on to win several more, and even finished second in the Becher Chase at Liverpool.

A bit of a psychoanalyst with his horses, John theorised that in a bitless bridle a poor jumper would no longer fear being jobbed in the mouth at a fence. The horses responded to his methods, and performances improved dramatically.

Foinavon ran sixteen times during the season in which he won the National but, once fit, was not trained hard between races, so he stood his racing well. Indeed, he hardly had a saddle on him during the fortnight before the National. He was mostly lunged and got used to jumping on his own – something that was to prove an advantage that even the most clairvoyant could barely have foretold.

John Kempton would have liked to ride Foinavon in the National himself but displayed loyalty to his owners on two counts: his minimum riding weight of 10 stone 10 pounds would have put him 10 pounds overweight; and he had another horse running at

Worcester – 'I had just as much responsibility to the owners of that as to those of a horse in a big race'.

So on Grand National day he went to Worcester, where he rode Three Dons in a novice hurdle race – and won. An hour or so later, he settled in the jockeys' changing room to watch the National on one of several television sets, his father having travelled to Aintree to saddle Foinavon, and John Buckingham having been booked to ride.

'As the pile-up happened, and before the commentator spotted him, I saw Foinavon pop over the fence; he was wearing distinctive yellow blinkers which I had had specially widened for the race to prevent mud blocking his eyes.' John Kempton, normally a cool customer, went 'just sort of loopy': 'I had bought the horse for the Grand National, and here it was coming off. I don't think the implication of it all penetrated my mind terribly quickly, that it was more than just an ordinary race . . .'

The splash all over the next day's papers soon brought it home.

Foinavon's dramatic victory came at a time when public interest in the race was waning and its very future was in doubt. Almost since its inception the course had been run by the Topham family, and in 1936 Mirabel Topham, a former actress and Gaiety girl, had taken over as chairman and managing director, making her the all-controlling matriarch of Aintree. By 1967 Topham had entered into negotiations to sell the site,* but the headlines generated by the sensational pile-up, and the fact that no horse or jockey was hurt in it, sparked the race once more into life. Suddenly everyone was talking about the National, the element of luck involved, the belief that 'anything can happen' which gives hope to thousands of the general public who place their ten bobs each year.

* The course was eventually sold in 1973 to Bill Davies, who tripled admission prices for the 1975 race, resulting in the lowest attendance on record.

'It was the era of constant "last" Grand Nationals and I believe this happening made people fight for it,' John Kempton said. 'It's possible there would be no National now but an estate of houses, had Foinavon's year not happened.'

Foinavon himself ran in the Grand National again but was brought down at the water when in much closer contention. He eventually died of old age and is buried at Compton.

Life took a change of course for John Kempton. For family reasons he had to give up training a few years later and, when David Barons offered him a job as assistant trainer, he jumped at the chance, having got to like Devon in annual summer forays round Newton Abbot, Exeter and the now-defunct Buckfastleigh. Once in his new job, he made many friends and was persuaded to take up sub-aqua diving as a hobby, his wife, Trish, joining in too. He began to get itchy feet to work for himself again, however, and after about five seasons with David Barons he set up a yacht-chartering business from Salcombe. He and Trish began taking groups of about ten throughout the summer on their 'floating hotel', sometimes nicknamed 'booze cruises', with Trish cooking and John teaching sub-aqua diving and navigating. Throughout the summer it was a seven-day-a-week job, and in the winter Trish was cooking for the freezer, John painting and maintaining the yacht, and there was little time left for racing . . . Now retired, John remains active and enjoys flying himself and Trish around Europe in his vintage Jodel aeroplane.

If racing's loss was sailing's gain in the case of John Kempton, racing was the winner with John Buckingham. As a fifteen-year-old school leaver, having never sat on a horse, he was faced with the choice of becoming shepherd, gamekeeper or stable boy for Mr Edward Courage. John's mother was a dairymaid on Mr Courage's Edgcote estate in south Northamptonshire, home of great Grand National horses such as Tiberetta and her son Spanish Steps, and it was to the stables that Buckingham went. He never regretted that decision. For him, racing became all-consuming. Although the Grand National victory inevitably changed his life, it did not alter him as a man; he remained modest and cheerful, in love with racing and only too happy to reminisce – for barely a day went by without some stranger recalling that great event in 1967.

John had ridden Foinavon once, a year before their win, at Cheltenham and in the bitless bridle, but when the offer came to ride the horse in the National it was at such short notice that all the Aintree accommodation was fully booked. John and his brother Tom had to stay in the sitting room of a nearby boarding house, Tom on a sofa and John sleeping on two armchairs pulled together – hardly ideal big-race preparation!

Although Foinavon's connections fully expected him to get round, victory was so unconsidered that the owner, Mr Cyril Watkins, did not even attend. He was watching at home in Berkshire with his wife, but after the pile-up he could not bear to continue and his wife had to call him in from the garden to tell him he had won! As for Foinavon's previous co-owner, Mac Bennellick, he had found his funds stretched in the autumn and failed to sell his half-share in the horse – so he had given it to Cyril Watkins!

In the race, Foinavon took a fair hold early on; he was in the leading flight over the first fence but the pace increased so much that he quickly dropped back. In fact, the pace was so fast that the race time was three seconds faster than that achieved by Anglo the previous year when there had been no mid-race hold-up. Only five horses were behind Foinavon when they jumped Becher's for the second time, but just ahead of him was the fancied Honey End, ridden by that good judge of pace, Josh Gifford.

As they approached the next fence, the twenty-third, mayhem was breaking loose, and when Foinavon drew closer there were horses and jockeys running about all over the place, doing everything except jumping the fence. They were literally piled up on top of each other, bits of broom and gorse everywhere, the fence almost demolished.

John Buckingham could hardly believe his eyes. He had Honey End ahead and to the inside of him; he was roughly central, when he pulled Foinavon over to the outside and, weaving his way as two loose horses trotted back towards him, Foinavon popped over from little more than a trot and set sail the other side.

For a few moments John did not realise he had been the only one to get over at the first attempt, but by the Canal Turn he knew, and by Valentine's he realised that all he had to do was stand up to win.

'It is to Foinavon's eternal credit that he did not refuse, either at the melee, when he had every excuse to, or when he was out on his own and especially when he was tiring,' said John twenty years later. 'When I saw Honey End and Greek Scholar coming, I didn't think they could catch me, but I gave him one slap after the last, just in case. I must admit I was nearly unconscious at the end of it.'

As for Foinavon, he passed the post with his ears pricked – and ate up as well as ever that night, in the company, as usual, of Susie the goat. Altogether, seventeen of the baulked or fallen horses got going again to finish.

It was the fourth time in the history of the race that only one horse had completed a clear round, following Glenside in 1911, Shaun Spadah in 1921 and Tipperary Tim in 1928.

When John and his wife, Ann, returned to Chipping Warden, a stone's throw from Edgcote, they found the house covered in bunting by their neighbours with a notice proclaiming 'Buck-ingham Palace'. The next day he was invited on to *The Bob Monkhouse Show* at the London Palladium and, wearing a dinner jacket borrowed from amateur rider Roger Charlton (who in 1990 was to train Quest For Fame to win the Derby), he joined in the fun, although confessing the stage fright to be worse than the pre-National nerves. He later opened a few fetes and knocked down some charity piles of pennies, but he had been back at work at Edgcote the morning after the National. One outcome was that his number of rides markedly increased the following year.

He rode Foinavon several more times, though injury excluded him from the 1968 National when Foinavon was brought down at the water. Amazingly, he was on him when another mini 'Foinavon' happened. It was in a three-horse race at Uttoxeter; he was tracking the other pair three from home when one ran out and took the other horse with him, leaving Foinavon to jump and gallop home alone again. 'The crowd simply went mad,' John recalled. Of the Grand National win, he said, 'It could have happened to any horse in the race, it just happened to be Foinavon. Although he was lucky, I still think he was a good horse who would not have been disgraced; he was one-paced but always stayed on and I'm sure he would have been in the first dozen.'

John Buckingham continued racing for a few years but eventually, at the age of thirty-two, with his rides dwindling and a young family to support, he was offered and accepted a job of jockey's valet – a role he revelled in, for it kept him in the weighing room in the midst of the atmosphere he knew and loved so well. Before he retired, John rode a further three times in the National and remained convinced that he would have won on merit on Limeburner had that horse not fallen at the penultimate when lying close-up third in 1971. He died in December 2016 aged seventy-six.

Luckiest, unluckiest, and now the most gallant loser . . .

13

Crisp

Most gallant loser, 1973

When former jockey Richard Pitman talks about Crisp the enthusiasm in his voice bubbles as freshly as if the whole thing had happened yesterday, instead of heading for half a century.

The admiration and awe he feels for that magnificent Australian chaser is as strong now as it was then. Fifteen years after the ride he said, 'Crisp was incredible. When he first arrived in Fred Winter's yard from Australia, the first thing that hit you was his size; he was so strong, with a great shoulder, and to ride he was exactly as he looked: he would wear you out, he carried his head low and you just had to sit and suffer.'

Within days of his arrival to a British winter as a seven-year-old in November 1970, having won all there was to win in his sunny native clime, Crisp started growing an extra coat. Soon it was two inches long and wafted in the breeze like the ripples of a cornfield; but he proved virtually impossible to clip – a normal dose of tranquilliser did not so much as shut one eye and in the end a drug used by a zoo on elephants and rhinos did the trick.

Brian Delaney, who was Fred Winter's head lad, also recalled Crisp's arrival at Uplands, Lambourn, and admitted that they felt a little sceptical: 'We had heard this horse was coming who was the tops in Australia, but at the time our stable was the top in the world, with such as Pendil, Bula, Killiney, so there wasn't great anticipation, not like when Jay Trump came in our very first

season and we were all agog.' Brian remembered the shaggy coat
and the time it took Crisp to acclimatise. He, too, was impressed
by the size and strength of the dark brown horse – 'a wonderful
stamp of English three-mile chaser, the sort that aren't around
much'. Tall, angular, with long, slightly loppy ears, kind eyes and
a gentle nature, Crisp had character written all over his face.

Crisp's first run in England was a handicap at Wincanton;
he was allotted automatic top weight of 12 stone 7 pounds because he had not had the requisite three runs in the country to
enable the handicapper to assess him. No one knew quite what
to expect. A good round would have been satisfactory. What followed staggered onlookers. Crisp, ridden by Paul Kelleway, took
up the running after a mile and then drew clear to win the race
easily. Fred Winter himself had disbelief written all over his face
as his horse trotted up.

Before the National, Crisp had won the two-mile Champion
Chase (prefixed since 1980 by 'the Queen Mother') at the Cheltenham Festival and broken several track records, including at
Newbury, by pulverising the opposition into the ground, usually
ridden by Paul Kelleway or Richard Pitman. Richard recalled,
'He gave a sensation that money simply cannot buy; his jumping
was electrifying and it was all so *easy* for him. He was magical.'

Owner Sir Chester Manifold had sent Crisp over to England – he
finished third in the Colonial Cup, South Carolina, on the way –
to have a stab at the Cheltenham Gold Cup; he was entered for
the race in his second season. But, as he had run so sensationally
over two miles, there was a fear that he might not last the trip.

His rider tried to settle him but that didn't work. He pulled
for a bit, then gave up, like many another front runner who feels
frustrated when restrained, finishing a disappointing fifth. Unfortunately, the result encouraged the view that the horse did not
stay, so it was back to the Champion Chase the following year,
when he finished third. His former Australian rider, the ex-British

Tommy McGinley, was convinced it was wrong to hold him up.

Anyway, Crisp was entered for the Grand National and, being such a high-class horse and taking account of his English form, was allotted top weight of 12 stone. Fred Winter and Richard Pitman discussed tactics at length: if he was held up, there was a danger his spectacular jumping would land him on another horse's back, so it was decided he would do best if allowed to jump off and then slow down the pace from the front. That was the theory. In practice, Crisp had other ideas, resulting in the most breathtaking National run in living memory.

Thirty-eight runners milled round at the start; the joint favourites at 9-1 were the improving Red Rum on 10 stone 5 pounds and Crisp. How right the bookmakers were to be proved.

Richard Pitman lined Crisp up on the inside – always Fred Winter's favoured position, where the drop fences are bigger but the danger of interference less – and they were off.

Crisp devoured the big fences as if they were bales of hay strung across the course. Every time he saw one he gripped harder on the bit and attacked it boldly, always fast, always totally accurate, and he was away from it again in a flash, as well as saving many lengths by going on the inside so that he gained ground all the time without even trying. Big, with a wide-open ditch, the third fence is the downfall of many; to Crisp it was no more than an upturned dandy brush, and to his exhilarated rider he exuded confidence: 'I just thought: he'll never fall. It was so easy to him it was laughable; there wasn't a fence on the course that would even make him blink.' All Richard could do was try to sit against him, conserving what energy he could, all the time conscious of his stamina limits: had he simply let him go, the horse would have burnt himself out before the halfway point. Becher's Brook came and went as if it didn't exist. The Canal Turn was executed in the style of a top three-day eventer taking a corner fence; Crisp went so close to the inside of the 90-degree turn that he brushed the marker post.

The crowds were mesmerised; what a performance! Incredibly the horse drew even further away so that, when they headed out into the country for the second time, he was an amazing thirty lengths clear. As Crisp and his partner went down that long line of fences which culminate in Becher's Brook there were signs everywhere of those who had not been so lucky: big holes in the fences, disconsolate jockeys on their feet, one holding a bridle – not another horse in sight. Richard, out on his own, had time to reflect: poor sod, he hasn't even got a horse under him and mine is jumping as if the fences don't exist. He found the silence the strangest thing of all. Normally there is the crashing of fences as horses plough their way through, the swearing of jockeys, the thud of hooves.

At Becher's the second time, another doddle for Crisp, Richard distinctly heard the Irish voice of racecourse commentator Michael O'Hehir say, ' . . . and Red Rum is breaking away from the pack some twenty lengths behind.' David Nicholson, another jockey who had fallen on the first circuit, called out, 'Kick on, you'll win.'

The brilliant horse jumped the Canal Turn perfectly again and at last the stands came back into view. But they were still a long, long way from home: six fences and that gruelling run-in of nearly 500 yards.

The mental obstacles were well out of the way now: to get over the third and remain alive; to clear Becher's and have the bogey fence out of the way; to complete a circuit and start being a jockey; to jump the Canal Turn again and know that completion of the course should follow; and, if well in front at that stage, to collect thoughts and make the best way home . . .

It was at the second last fence that Crisp began to falter. The pounding, relentless gallop was beginning to tell, and Richard felt the horse's strength 'fall out of him'. It got worse: those loppy ears sagged lower; his legs, instead of stretching out forward, began swinging sideways; his whole body swayed as if he were drunk.

And now their pursuer was within earshot: Richard could hear the snorts of the 'high-blowing' Red Rum and the rhythmic drumming of his hoof-beats on the firm ground. The threat was still nearly twenty lengths back but drawing ever nearer. Richard described the feeling graphically: 'It was like being tied to a railway line with an express train coming and being unable to get out of the way.'

They jumped the last all right, but Richard will never forgive himself for what happened next: 'Crisp was out on his feet but I made the basic riding error of picking up my stick in my right hand, with the intention of waking him up. He just fell away from it towards the left and away from the angle of the racecourse. I had to put down the whip, gather him up again, and get him back on course for the elbow, where there was the running rail to guide him. I am stuck with that mistake for the rest of my life and I know that someone like John Francome would not have made it. I lost the National for all those people who so deserved to win it: the owner; Fred Winter, the trainer; the horse's lad, Chippy Chape.'

At that moment, Crisp was still in front. To the thousands in the crowd and the millions watching on television it was the most agonising few moments they had ever seen in the Grand National: if willpower alone could have got Crisp first past the post, he would have been home and dry. They had witnessed the most devastating, compelling performance under top weight.

All was not yet lost. As Crisp felt his lighter-weighted rival draw up to his quarters, he tightened instinctively and tried to give more when he had in truth given his all. Red Rum went by, just two strides before the post, in record time.

Form book publishers Raceform Ltd paid a vivid tribute to the loser:

Crisp, flicking over these enormous fences like hurdles, pulled his way into a twenty-length lead after jumping the water. Sailing down to Becher's he actually increased his lead and, turning for the long haul home after Valentine's, looked to have an unassailable advantage. He started to tire at the second from home but was still at least ten lengths clear at the last. Then, suddenly, Crisp the flying rocket became painful flesh and blood with air-starved lungs and limbs like stone. Rolling about, out on his feet, he started to hang towards the dolls guarding the Chair and it was all Pitman could do to wrench him back on to the racecourse. Though by now he appeared to be standing still and looked certain to be caught, it was only in the last few agonising yards of the interminable run-in that the dogged Red Rum finally cut down perhaps the greatest hero of them all.

To many, the spectacular Australian chaser was the most gallant loser ever. Little did they know how exceptional the horse who had beaten him was to prove . . . The emotion provoked by Crisp's defeat was overwhelming.

From Fred Winter, one of the best respected men in racing, there was not a word of recrimination. From the owner, there was a cash present 'for disappointment'. For Richard Pitman there was the sorrow at losing for all those people who deserved to have won.

Sitting at home in his bungalow at Uplands, watching the television, Brian Delaney recalled the agony: 'We were *screaming* for him to last home; my mother-in-law's poodle went crazy and jumped on to a glass ashtray, smashing it to smithereens. We have had some horses jump round Liverpool, but nothing like that before or since. Crisp made those fences look like hurdles; I hate seeing it all again.'

The night of that epic race, amazingly recovered from his exhaustion, Crisp ate up every oat. And although he did not run in the National again, he gained revenge on Red Rum in a match at

Haydock the next year in yet another bold display, his superior class telling at level weights.

Fred Winter had ridden and trained a total of four Grand National winners, but he unhesitatingly put a loser as the best Grand National horse he had been connected with – and considered Crisp probably the best of all National horses in living memory. 'His performance was unforgettable,' he said some fifteen years later. He added with a tinge of real regret, 'the only sad thing is that Red Rum is the one who will be remembered and Crisp is not. People don't realise what his run amounted to. He has to be the best.'

Crisp ended his days with Mr John Trotter and his wife, Joy, hunting with the Zetland in Northumberland, where the wide-open spaces suited him admirably. In 1985 he died of a heart attack doing what he loved best, out galloping and jumping with the Zetland. He was twenty-one years old.

Within a couple of years Richard Pitman, too, had retired, and quickly established himself as a polished paddock commentator for BBC television, as well as writing for several newspapers and magazines, becoming involved in the bloodstock business, and being in demand as an after-dinner speaker.

Inevitably, this story is followed by the only horse, so far, to have won the National three times.

14

Red Rum

Most wins, 1973, 1974 and 1977

Red Rum became a better-known celebrity superstar than most human beings. He epitomised courage, professionalism, triumph over adversity and, yes, he liked to show off in front of the cameras. He was a living legend, winner of the Grand National a record three times and placed second in his other two attempts; he landed first over the last fence for five years in succession.

Hard-raced under both rules from an early age, Red Rum's future looked decidedly ordinary – and in jeopardy altogether when found to be lame in a foot – but he was blessed with that overriding essential, the will to win; he was a survivor no matter what the odds. He was the horse for whom the overused word charisma could have been invented.

Born and bred in Ireland, he was sold as a yearling for 400 guineas. In his early days no one could have predicted him as a future National winner. By the miler Quorum out of a winning mare called Mared, who was said to be virtually unrideable, his breeding did not indicate that he would win over the maximum distance.

Few could have foretold his greatness the day he first ran at Liverpool, in a five-furlong selling race for two-year-olds (the minimum distance and lowliest type of race) in which he dead-heated with his former stable companion, Curlicue.

'Just imagine the derision I would have been greeted with if I'd offered a two-year-old sprinter as a future Grand National winner,' recalled auctioneer John Botterill in later years. 'I'd have been laughed out of the ring!'

So began Red Rum's love affair with Liverpool and with life.

Fledgling trainer, second-hand car dealer and part-time taxi driver Ginger McCain liked the look of the horse that day but did not stay for the post-race sale because 300 guineas was twice as much as he could then afford. His first win as a trainer had come courtesy of a previously broken-down fourteen-year-old in a selling chase at – where else – Liverpool.

Red Rum was to have five trainers and some hard races; twenty-four different jockeys, including Lester Piggott and Josh Gifford; was to win three flat races, three over hurdles and twenty-one steeplechases, and was placed thirty-five times. He was beaten a short head in the Hennessy Gold Cup and won the Scottish National in the same year as one of his Grand Nationals (another record); he never fell at a fence, once slipping up on the flat and once having his jockey knocked off at the first fence. His overall Liverpool record was won four and second three times from his seven runs.

The character was there from the start. 'The horse always had a high opinion of himself and it got bigger and bigger,' Ginger McCain recalled in the 1980s.

It was a few years after that selling race that Ginger McCain picked up a cab fare from Mr Noel Le Mare; he was a wealthy businessman who shared Ginger's ambition of winning the Grand National, the fare became a regular one, and friendship blossomed. A slim, dapper octogenarian, Noel Le Mare was always immaculately dressed, with starched cotton shirt and silk socks, often wearing a bowler hat and neat glasses. His one concession to advancing years was a morning lie-in; a glass of sherry before lunch and, come 6 p.m., he would enjoy a whisky and cigarettes sitting in a chair by the fire. He kept an immaculate Daimler and chauffeur and eventually, at his family's insistence, spent his final years on the Isle of Man. A grandson, Michael Burns, ran the Red

Rum fan club and was chairman of the company that looked after Red Rum in retirement.

Mr Le Mare told Ginger he could go up to 7,000 guineas for a horse at the Doncaster Sales; the Grand National was the aim. Ginger bought Red Rum for 6,000 guineas – but next day the horse pulled up from exercise lame. He paddled in the sea and, miracle of miracles, emerged sound. The seawater saved Red Rum who in earlier years had suffered from the foot complaint pedalostitis.

Thoughts of a fan club were in no way entertained during Red Rum's early days at Southport. He was housed in the stable nearest to McCain's house; the stables had been converted by Ginger from old brewery-horse stalls and garages; the garden gradually gave way as more stables were built, until only a central tree remained as a feature of the yard. It was set in a shop-lined back street typical of any town: washeteria, post-office-cum stores, coal merchant and, just before the level crossing where trains sped by at regular intervals, the modern showrooms of D. McCain, car salesman. Only a few streets away was the seaside pier and a huge, garish funfair on one side of a roundabout; on the other side stretched two miles of coastal road carving through bleak sand dunes uninhabited save for the wildlife and McCain's horses at exercise on the sandy beach, until it reached a Pontin's holiday camp.

The seawater, sea air, sand and rarity of formal grass gallops stimulated Red Rum's vigour for life and he bloomed.

The transformation Ginger wrought in the cocky rich bay was swift. After the horse's fifth win in barely six weeks, on ground ranging from good to hard, *Timeform* commented that he was 'still cherry ripe and reflects credit on the trainer'. Before long he was being spoken of as a National prospect, and in that spring of 1973 he was allotted 10 stone 5 pounds for the race that saw him claw back Crisp in one of the most memorable Nationals of all time.

In 1974 it was Red Rum's turn to carry top weight of 12 stone, and he was again ridden by Brian Fletcher. Dual Gold Cup winner L'Escargot carried one pound less and was second favourite; the favourite was Scout, who finished eleventh ridden by Tommy Stack. Red Rum was third favourite – but he made the race look incredibly easy. He had cruised to the front at the second Becher's and even after the last fence he increased his speed until eased down before the post by his rider with the race well won.

Grand National winners traditionally return home to a hero's welcome, but the greeting which the Southport suburb of Birkdale gave Red Rum after his second victory was such that, with crowds thronged so many deep, the police gave up trying to let traffic through and closed the road. Even the chimney stacks along the lines of houses were occupied by cheering fans. The only scenes reminiscent of that occasion in Ginger's memory were those of VE Day, when Ginger was a lad of thirteen.

L'Escargot finished second that year, but the tables were turned in 1975. That was the only time Red Rum had to contend with soft ground; he hated it so much that halfway round Brian Fletcher even thought of pulling him up. Yet Red Rum ploughed on to such effect that again he landed just in front over the last fence.

It was different against Rag Trade in 1976, when Red Rum was ridden by Tommy Stack. Carrying top weight for the third successive year, and overtaken by Rag Trade (receiving 12 pounds) just after the last, he was regaining ground all the way up that long run-in.

The third-placed Eyecatcher was ridden by the deposed Brian Fletcher. Apart from his two wins on Red Rum he had also won the National in 1968 on Red Alligator, joining the only other jockeys on three wins each: Ernie Piggott (Lester's grandfather) with Jerry M and Poethlyn twice (once at the First World War substitute course at Gatwick); Jack Anthony (1911 Glenside, 1915 Ally

Sloper and 1920 Troytown – also second twice and third once from twelve rides); Arthur Nightingall (1890 Ilex, 1894 Why Not and 1901 Grudon – second, third four times and fourth once from fifteen rides); Tom Olliver (1842 Gay Lad, 1843 Vanguard and 1853 Peter Simple – also second three times and third once from nineteen rides); Tommy Pickernell (1860 Anatis, 1871 The Lamb and 1875 Pathfinder – also two seconds and a fourth from seventeen rides); and Tommy Beasley, whose three wins we have seen in Chapter 4. George Stevens' five wins, described in Chapter 2, see him still the rider of most Grand Nationals one and a half centuries since his last victory.

By 1977 Red Rum was twelve years old but felt better than ever. His whole programme was geared to one single race, the Grand National. Yet again he had top weight but it was down to 11 stone 8 pounds. Could he possibly win again? Would his luck in running hold up or would, finally, some faller bring him down? McCain was given stick from some uninformed quarters for even contemplating another attempt.

'But he was fit and still relatively young,' said Ginger, 'and Mr Le Mare, at eighty-eight years old, had given up golf. Red Rum was his only remaining pleasure and we were not abusing the horse.'

For some reason McCain never doubted that his horse would win that day. Possessed of superior intelligence, Red Rum simply never met his fences wrong; he could shift his shoulders from four strides out to put himself right, and would change direction in mid-air if he spotted a faller on the other side; indeed, he was his own race-reader. What was more, he was king and knew it, bearing himself with majesty.

Down at the start there was a delay. Red Rum was *bursting.* He was so *sure* of himself. He swaggered round his kingdom and Tommy Stack had never felt anything quite like it in a horse before. It was a mystical moment that brought incredible confidence.

In the event, there might just as well not have been any other horse in the race. From Becher's second time round Rummy drew further and further ahead, making the fences look like matchsticks, and won as he liked by twenty-five lengths, to tumultuous applause. Here was the little flat-race selling plater turned greatest Grand National horse of all time. Grown men wept openly.

This time the whole of Southport joined in the official celebrations. There were two bands in the parade through the seaside resort's streets, which were lined with cheering admirers. There were people with no interest in horses, those who had never so much as had a Grand National flutter, but here they could admire and praise this horse of so many great qualities: guts, hard work, professionalism, enthusiasm, the ability to come back for more and more – above all, that will to win against all odds, to survive.

The next year, 1978, at thirteen, Red Rum was in good form and all set to run again, until the last minute: a week before the National he pulled up from work slightly lame behind; the tried and tested seawater treatment quickly brought him sound again, but then on the eve of the race he was again slightly sore behind. Ginger's heart sank; he was certain he would have won not only then but also the next year, too, at fourteen.

Instead, Red Rum immediately began his new role as a highly sought-after celebrity, and he paraded before the 1978 race, kicking and squealing and full of joie de vivre. But as vet Ted Greenway had reasoned with Ginger the day before, 'If the foot goes in the race, the crowd will hang you.'

The horse seemed so well, turning himself inside out to the extent that an unkind few claimed his apparent injury had been a bookmakers' ploy! But the country and the world of racing at large loved the horse as their own and perhaps breathed secret sighs of relief in the knowledge that Becher's and the rest could no longer hold any hidden perils for 'their' horse.

In his early retirement, as Rummy made numerous appearances, it became apparent that other people were cashing in on the act – Red Rum tea towels and other souvenirs appeared. To prevent this, the Red Rum Ltd company was formed.

That summer of 1978 a huge sum was offered by a Japanese restaurant owner for that company, with promises to keep Ginger with a say in the horse's movements, but an antagonistic crowd put paid to that, and Mr Le Mare stipulated, 'Red Rum is not for sale to anyone at any time or any price; he stays with Ginger for life.'

Red Rum's new life could hardly have been more hectic, varied and interesting, and he revelled in it. In one typical week that first summer he went to Ireland by boat, to Exeter the next morning, up to Scotland the following day, down to Wolverhampton, then home – all the time opening fetes (he once ate a vicar's button-hole), parading at shows, opening betting shops and new stores, coming on stage, and being used at business conferences as an example of all that is good in British industry.

So how did Red Rum, whose exuberance and bucks and kicks were the trademark of his love affair with life, cope with slippery stages, narrow doors, bright lights, hotel foyers, lifts, shop floors and clapping and cheering in confined spaces?

'It is the survival thing,' said Ginger. 'He will turn himself inside out on grass or sand but he won't act the fool when he's unsure of his surroundings and thinks it may be slippery. He's very intelligent.'

His twenty-first birthday was celebrated lavishly with a huge marquee at the home of Noel Le Mare's grandson; only Noel was missing, having died at the age of ninety-two. Red Rum's achievements certainly altered Ginger's life but he retained his affability, amused grin and modest manner – and ability to be contentious and outspoken at times. Red Rum had opened doors for him and given him the assurance that, given the material, he could do the job.

Twenty-seven years after Red Rum's third win, and having moved from Southport to beautiful parkland at Bankhouse,

Cholmondley, in 1990 looking for a change of luck, Ginger proved he was no back number by again training the winner of the Grand National in 2004. The horse was Amberleigh House, a twelve-year-old, owned by Halewood International and ridden by Graham Lee. Unusually, eight years later Graham Lee switched successfully to being a jockey on the flat.

Bankhouse became a 'go-to' destination for owners and the stable thrives. Ginger retired from training in 2006, handing over to his son, Donald, who had learnt the craft in some top stables, both riding and as assistant trainer besides growing up embroiled in it all. He in turn won the 2011 National with Ballabriggs; Ginger McCain died in September of that year, two days before his eighty-first birthday.

When the great Red Rum died on 18 October 1995 at the age of thirty it made headline news. Appropriately, he was buried by the Aintree winning post, where his epitaph reads: 'Respect this place, this hallowed ground, a legend here, his rest has found, his feet would fly, our spirits soar, he earned our love for evermore.'

During Red Rum's race to his third victory, another little piece of National history was being made . . .

15

Charlotte Brew

First woman to ride, 1977

When the Sex Discrimination Act came into effect in January 1976, it meant that women were finally allowed to take on men as equals. Many, already competent point-to-point riders, were swift to take up the challenge. By finishing fourth in the Aintree Foxhunters over the big fences on Barony Fort that year, Charlotte Brew discovered her mount had automatically qualified for the 1977 Grand National. (That rule has since changed due to tighter race conditions being brought in.)

Charlotte could not remember a time when she had not wanted to ride in the great race. Now she could. Although Barony Fort had been last of the four finishers in the Foxhunters he had been beaten only sixteen lengths overall, and he had actually jumped his way into the lead three out before running wide on the last bend. Of the other five runners, three fell at the first and the other two at the third, the Chair; one of those remounted only to fall again. Jumping is the name of the game. (Another rule change since then: jockeys are no longer allowed to remount a faller in any race.)

Once Charlotte's parents, Richard and Judith Brew from Coggeshall in Essex, had agreed to the previously inconceivable – that their daughter should ride in the Grand National – they backed her wholeheartedly, and proved a great source of strength. Charlotte, for her part, spent months training herself as well as her horse, learning all she could about the big race, and studying the course.

Charlotte was twenty-one and had had three seasons' point-to-pointing on him, winning and placing several times. The form book recorded that Barony Fort 'jumps brilliantly', 'stays extra well', and 'Charlotte Brew has done really well with him'.

Once news of her historic intended ride broke, the public supported her, but many of those within the racing industry did not. When some jockeys threatened to 'lynch' her if she crossed them in the big race, the quietly spoken maestro Fred Winter commented, 'If professional jockeys can't keep out of her way, then *they* don't deserve to be in the race.'

The lengths to which Charlotte went to prepare for the Grand National would have silenced many critics if they had realised just how much effort she put in. She even engaged a 'personal trainer' long before that became commonplace. A downside of all her gym work was that the extra muscle made her put on weight. At 5 feet 10 inches tall, and set to carry the minimum weight of 10 stone, just imagine what cannon fodder that would have made if she'd gone out overweight. In the end she rode on a paperweight saddle with about two ounces to spare.

She was constantly under fire from the press, to the point she stopped reading their reports; years later, she came across a number of articles that had been hidden by her mother. Critics claimed that the fairer sex were simply too weak to ride in the National; others that she was too inexperienced (to which she replied: how many male jockeys have much experience of Aintree?); others that she and Barony Fort were too moderate and were 'courting disaster'. Certain well-known trainers were 'really unpleasant' and some criticism was 'vicious'. Even some fellow female jockeys were against it. The Grand National fences were rapidly becoming the least daunting obstacles she had to face.

Happily, not all the publicity was bad. There were those who admired her pluck and courage. The inhabitants of her home village of Coggeshall adored her; and she received two pre-race telegrams she will always cherish, one from champion National

Hunt trainer Ryan Price, the other from Bruce Hobbs, who won the race when only seventeen, both admiring her and wishing her luck. She had never met either of them.

Barony Fort and his human entourage set off in their old trailer from Essex to Aintree on the Wednesday before the race – and were greeted by stable manager Ossie Dale, who had helped Charlotte so much the previous year to prepare for the Foxhunters, with a bottle of champagne.

The night before the race, jockey and long-time pal Ian Watkinson persuaded her to go dancing . . . and some of the press even berated her for that.

She rode out once more on Saturday morning – far away from others – then returned to the hotel for breakfast, one cup of black coffee in her case. Afterwards, she had yet another walk of the course, this time with Richard Pitman and Ian Watkinson, and the reality and enormity of the whole thing began to dawn on her – there was no turning back now. The Chair looked enormous, and Ian clowned about in it, pretending to be mountaineering. 'Don't, you're tempting Providence,' Charlotte cried. It was at the Chair that Ian fell in the race.

The short walk from the weighing room (she had a tiny ladies' convenience for changing in) was a nightmare, with police warding off the mob around Charlotte. Once she had the familiar feel of Barony Fort beneath her, she felt better and, after the parade, they cantered nicely down to the start. She was struck by the tremendous noise of the crowd. Soon the forty-two horses moved into line: they would be off any second now . . .

Suddenly a protest group marched out in front of them, waving banners, probably a 'welfare' issue. Jockeys turned their horses in anticlimax, as police removed the demonstrators. They were called into a line again, then – 'Hold it!' rang out the cry. A policeman's helmet was lying on the grass in their path. For Charlotte, the last remnants of tension disappeared with that sight, and within moments they were off.

Because of all the haranguing she had received, Charlotte settled at the back on the wide outside. Her horse was soon loving it all, and jumped superbly. Although she had no hope of winning, she was determined to get round.

They avoided a seven-horse pile-up at the first fence, and thereafter managed to steer clear of the loose horses, but she was soon slipping further and further behind. She needed to have jumped off smartly at the start for such a one-paced horse as Barony to get into the race properly.

Throughout the race, a separate television camera was focused on Charlotte, to record the historic ride for posterity. As she approached Becher's for the second time – 'It was like jumping off the end of the world' – there were three horses ahead of her, but two refused and the other fell. To his eternal credit, Barony Fort kept going and the crowds cheered the pair as they conquered each fence.

Barony Fort negotiated the Canal Turn expertly for the second time, but as they approached the fourth fence from home, which was the final big open ditch, he was losing more and more impetus. To Charlotte's despair, she could not get him over it. To her, it was failure. In fact, they had reached the twenty-seventh fence, further than any other non-finisher. 'The last three fences all had big holes in them, but not that ditch. I felt a terrible sense of anticlimax as we returned to the stables; I'd set my heart on getting round, and we so nearly did – but Mother and Ossie came rushing out to greet me and they were over the moon that we'd got that far.'

Meanwhile, even greater history had been made, as Red Rum galloped to his unique third win.

Women pioneers of the twentieth century

From 1977 until the end of the twentieth century, fourteen more Grand National runners were ridden by women. Jenny Hembrow fell at the first fence with Sandwilan in 1979 – imagine the outcry that would have caused by opponents had it been the first ever attempt – and she officially pulled up at the nineteenth the following year on the same horse, at 100-1 both times.

Of her first attempt, she was caught out like so many before her in galloping too fast on the long run to the first fence where she was one of four to come down. Sandwilan stood off too far, over-jumped and turned over.

It was different in 1980, when Sandwilan, now twelve years old, gave her the thrill of a lifetime. This time she put him right in the race and by the eighth fence the pair were lying in third, the horse was loving it and jumping superbly. She was no longer so close up at the nineteenth, a big ditch, where she was denied by both a horse who refused and ran along the fence and a loose horse bumping her from behind, pushing Sandwilan into the ditch.

Jenny was the mother of a young daughter; the next woman to compete, Linda Sheedy, was the mother of twins. She, too, got as far as the nineteenth, where Deoipea, also 100-1, refused in 1981.

There were two notable landmarks for women jockeys in 1982: the first Grand National to feature two female riders, and the first female jockey to get round. This was Geraldine Rees on Cheers, while the other was Charlotte Brew having a second crack, this time on Martinstown at 100-1 – half the odds that Barony Fort had been – but they were unseated at the third.

Geraldine Rees, riding the 66-1 shot Cheers, also had to contend with enormous prejudice and some extraordinarily antagonistic statements. What both women found most galling was those decriers who claimed they were in it for the publicity. There were those who contended that Geraldine was 'just a housewife who thought it would be fun to hop on a horse and pop round Aintree'. Nothing could have been further from the truth, for she was stable jockey to her trainer-father, Captain James Wilson, and had been the leading female NH rider. Cheers was a 'spare' ride

and was one of those neat, agile horses who gave a tremendous
feel, as if he had springs in his heels, and, apart from pecking
slightly as he landed over the crucial first fence, he was foot-
perfect. He gave her confidence, as did 'Big Ron' Barry, calling
out to her in Irish all the way down the first three fences, along
the lines of 'stick with me'.

Jumping Becher's 'felt like flying' and she was 'in the van' ex-
periencing the exhilaration of riding a good jumper in the world's
greatest steeplechase. It was from Becher's second time that
Geraldine encountered an Aintree phenomenon – the cheering
crowds. 'It was like going down a funnel and was deafening –
but it was also euphoric and the crowd carried us on, willing us
home.'

Cheers jumped the last fence fine but fatigue set in up that long
run-in; nevertheless, he became the first female-ridden runner to
complete – and enabled punters who had backed him to do so to
collect their winnings.

Geraldine tried again the next year, riding 500-1 shot Midday
Welcome, but they fell at the first. American Joy Carrier was also
in the line-up on King Spruce at by far the shortest odds of that
century, 28-1, but the previous year's Irish National victor was
hampered and his rider unseated at the first Becher's.

More good names tried without completing: trainer's daugh-
ter Valerie Alder (whose father, John, finished ninth in 1965 on
Tant Pis); Jacqui Oliver, who had turned professional and rode
the winner, Aonoch, of the Aintree Hurdle immediately before
the National. Three girls tried in 1988: trainer's daughter Gee
Armytage, whose brother Marcus won in 1990 on Mr Frisk;
Venetia Williams (now a Grand National-winning trainer with
Mon Mome); and trainer's daughter Penny Ffitch-Heyes. In 1989
Tarnya Davis, a professional (who is married to National-winning
trainer Oliver Sherwood, of Many Clouds fame), pulled up at the
twenty-first on Numerate.

In 1994 there was a great ride from Rosemary Henderson who completed in fifth place on Fiddler's Pike at 100-1. Rosemary was fifty-one years old and received special dispensation from the Jockey Club to ride her own horse. The pair knew each other well. The big, white-faced horse had proved a thorough stayer in point-to-points, in which field Rosemary, a late starter to the sport, had had many successes. She and Fiddler's Pike were a familiar sight around the Cornish point-to-points – they won five and placed in a further six, and they were successful in hunter chases at Warwick and Towcester, as well as second in the Champion Hunter Chase at Cheltenham. In 1993, with Fiddler's Pike now twelve, the pair contested top handicap chases like the Midlands National and the Whitbread Gold Cup, and in December that year they finished second in the Welsh Grand National; in spite of all this they were 100-1 for the 1994 Grand National three months later.

Her aim was to get round. The pair did more than that. In a race in which there were many fallers, Fiddler's Pike kept lobbing away on the outside, avoiding trouble, jumping well and ably assisted by his rider.

At one point, one of the commentators rather disparagingly said, 'And Fiddler's Pike is doing his own thing.'

There was a different tone on the second circuit. 'And one that is very handy on the outside is Fiddler's Pike, having a great run.' He pecked on landing at the twenty-first but at the next fence, Becher's Brook, he was again 'very handy' and with two to go, 'Fiddler's Pike is one of the very few brave horses to keep going'. At the second last a loose horse ran across him, but still he plugged on for a hugely deserved fifth place; the only other finisher was a long, long way behind him.

Rosemary Henderson and her husband, veterinary surgeon Bill, moved to New Zealand to run a flying vet service. Bill played a huge part in Fiddler's Pike's longevity (he raced at a lower level for another three years) and Rosemary was on board her old favourite for all fifty-two of his races, including point-to-points and, most memorably, the Grand National.

Remarkably, it was to be another eleven years until another woman rider contested the Grand National. This rider also finished fifth and, after a plunge from punters, started at odds of just 8-1. Different century, more acceptance of women riders, better opportunities . . .

There has yet to be a fairy-tale win for a woman rider, but the victory of Bob Champion and Aldaniti was little short of a modern miracle . . .

16

Aldaniti and Bob Champion

Greatest fairy-tale win, 1981

When Bob Champion went out for the 1981 Grand National, defeat was unthinkable. Victory was as certain to him before that race as death had seemed in his fight against cancer less than two years earlier.

All the ingredients of a fairy tale were there: the broken-down horse, recovered not once but *three* times from leg trouble; the back-from-near-death jockey; the incredible loyalty and patience of the supporting cast; and a girlfriend waiting in the wings.

Of the seventh generation of a hunting family, Bob Champion loved riding to hounds by the time he was nine or ten years old. But something stirred him even more. Seeing Pathé News film of the Grand National, he thought: I'd like to ride in that one day.

His first race was an unofficial one, but he won it just the same. His father, Bob Senior, was huntsman to the Cleveland and at the end of the hunt's annual point-to-point Bob and two or three other whippers-in set themselves a two-mile course over the track. 'I've got to be fair and admit that I was on the best horse and was also considerably lighter than my opponents,' Bob recalled with a grin, 'but I just got up in a stirring finish and thought: this is fun.'

The real thing was not at first so jolly. Bob took such a purler when disputing the lead at the last fence at Larkhill, after which the horse rolled on him, that he began to think he was not cut out for racing after all. But, as was to be the case so poignantly in later life, he soon came back – and, what's more, he won on his first ride as a professional.

Bob built up a solid career as a freelance, taking a retainer from Josh Gifford at Findon on the South Downs. He was regularly finishing in the first half-dozen in the jockeys' table, riding forty to fifty winners, and enjoying life to the full, when he received the jolt that was to alter his whole future and bring his life to the very brink: the seemingly fit, healthy young man had developed testicular cancer. 'You just think you are going to die when you are first told,' he recalled. 'You never heard about the people who recover.'

Because of this, after his recovery, Bob agreed to help publicise the cancer survival rate, helping to make a star-studded film *Champions*, promoting it all over the world, and setting up a trust fund in which his winning ride, Aldaniti, himself would play an integral part. One thing the film did not portray with total accuracy was the ghastliness (in those days) of the treatment – though, goodness knows, the portrayal was harrowing enough – because they did not want to put people off. But, Bob said, that was in the early days of chemotherapy, and its side-effects had been vastly reduced by the late 1980s. 'Yes, I felt like death during the treatment, but even at the lowest ebb I felt I would get better; I just didn't want to die, basically,' said the master of understatement.

When that traumatic, painful period, which he had borne so bravely, was over, he had to regain fitness; the thought of riding Aldaniti, himself sidelined through injury, in the Grand National was the invisible spur. 'And that was even harder,' says Bob, whose muscles had wasted, his whole body washed out and limp. Aldaniti was slowly but surely getting better from breakdown, re-toning lost muscles, hardening the damaged leg, so Bob just had to make it. His turning point was a spell in America with trainer friend Burly Cocks, and the magic tonic of riding a winner on his comeback ride, and on the flat too!

It had been a full three years earlier when Bob had predicted that Nick and Valda Embiricos's Aldaniti would win the National. 'I really meant it, ask anyone,' he says. 'I had won the Eider Chase on Highland Wedding [winner of the 1969 Grand National]. I won Rag Trade's first novice chase [winner of the 1976 Grand National]. I "did" Rubstic at Toby Balding's as a two-year-old, when he was the slowest thing on four legs! [Rubstic won the 1979 Grand National.] I even fell off Corbiere [winner of the 1983 National]. They all shared common likenesses: they had low head carriage, were very well balanced, and gave the same type of feel. They all won the National, and when Aldaniti came along and felt just the same I was always certain he would win too.'

Bob had not, of course, been on any of those earlier winners and his own National record was mixed. Riding Country Wedding his first time, he decided to follow a proven Aintree horse, picked the previous year's winner Gay Trip, tucked in behind him and when Gay Trip fell at the first, he was brought down. He got further the next year on the same horse, falling at Valentine's – 'but at least I'd jumped Becher's!' With Hurricane Rock, Money Market and Manicou Bay he finished in the first half-dozen or so, but then it was back to a first-fence fall with Spitting Image. Purdo fell at the first Becher's when in the lead. Then it was all up to Aldaniti in 1981. Could it be done? Could this pair of former crocks, who had had just one pre-National race together and gloriously won it, really make a fairy tale come true? There are so many imponderables and bad-luck stories in a race like the National that, to the huge crowds and watching millions, it seemed to be asking too much of fate, but if their collective wish could bring about the result they would make sure it did.

It was much simpler for Bob Champion. 'The race was just a formality, I simply couldn't see myself being beat,' he stated, dismissing the loose horse factor and admitting that his first-fence bogey was the only thing he was genuinely afraid of (Aldaniti himself was to fall at the first fence the following year). 'But that's where Fred Winter won it for me. He said you've got to "break the horse's jaw" after crossing the Melling Road approaching the first fence, to get it back on its hocks. It's a long, long way to the first* and such a cavalry charge that most horses are on their forehand.'

Even with the good advice given to Bob, the pair nearly capsized at the first. Aldaniti over-jumped and 'paddled along with his nose on the ground, but we got away with it'. Bob will never forget the moment. At the second, he dropped his hind legs and the thick stakes obviously hurt him. The next was the big ditch – and from then on, he jumped to the manner born.

For the early part of the race Aldaniti tracked popular amateur John Thorne on the favourite Spartan Missile, both of them going down the outside, which trainer Josh Gifford favoured for his horse. The ground was good, Aldaniti made light of 10 stone 13 pounds, and as early as the twelfth fence had jumped his way to the front.

It was plenty early enough to be leading but the horse was obviously loving it and so were the crowds. He gave them an extra treat by jumping the huge Chair in front of the stands superbly. 'He gave me a dream ride,' says Bob. But there was one more anxious moment to come. 'We were on the wrong stride going into the last and I didn't know what to do; but he sorted it out himself, drifting left and he fiddled it.'

Now there remained that long run-in. Bob knew the horse nearest to him, Royal Mail, was a spent force – 'that's who I thought I was beating' – but unbeknown to him, it was John Thorne and Spartan Missile who were eating up the ground in hot pursuit,

* In 2013, the start of the race was brought 90 yards closer to the first fence, in an attempt to stop horses getting up too much speed before it.

having been badly hampered at the Canal Turn. 'I knew if I got to the running rail after the elbow first, I would win,' says Bob – and it was by four memorable lengths that he did so, arm raised in triumphant salute, that always-engaging smile spread across his face for the world's cameras to capture.

The crowd applauded to the skies. It was the perfect result; and there were many who felt that John Thorne's turn could surely come in next year's National. But, shortly before then, the true amateur was killed in a fall at his local point-to-point in Warwickshire.

Now all eyes were on Bob Champion and Aldaniti, trainer Josh Gifford, owners Nick and Valda Embiricos, lad Peter Double, stud girl Beryl Millam, doctors and nurses from the Royal Marsden Hospital for cancer sufferers, the vets, the families: it was a happy ending for the press to lap up and the whole world loved it. And it heralded a new role in life for Bob Champion.

From then on, he would find himself telling and retelling his life story. He was the inspiration for cancer sufferers, who saw that they could get better and lead a normal life again. But Bob found that as his role of ambassador for cancer research increased, his life was no longer his own – he had become public property. His marriage, which set such a happy seal on the story, was to last only three years.

Bob Champion has a shy manner, and he found more loneliness than glamour as he travelled the world, shaking countless hands and giving interviews.

He set up as a trainer in an attractive hamlet near Bury St Edmunds, but an average of three nights a week were taken up attending charity functions, balls, race-nights and so on, and many days he would be parading Aldaniti at some county show, or attending a cricket match – not his favourite game, but it was all for the cause. Such engagements hindered his training and, inevitably, his income; he needed better horses to make his mark; in many ways the freshness had gone.

'You get used to it,' he said resignedly six years after his momentous win, by which time a lacklustre element had crept into his once-ebullient frame, now heavier than it used to be. 'The reaction was far more than I expected, especially in the length of time it has gone on,' he admitted. 'Every charity wants you and you are always expected to go. It was all forced on me a bit, but I'm glad really.' Speaking in 1987, he calculated that he had had just twenty-six days off since 1977.

'I know I've been round the world promoting the film *Champions* and so on, but that was twenty-five-hours-a-day stuff, no glamour but bloody hard work.' Bob's promotional itinerary ran something like this: depart London; five-hour delay Bahrain; 10 a.m., first interview in Sydney, Australia, interviews all day; film premiere in the evening; 6 a.m., plane to Melbourne; 7 a.m., breakfast television; more interviews through the day; another late-night premiere, another early morning flight for the next stop . . .

It was an endless whirl, taking in Adelaide and Perth, on to Christchurch and Auckland in New Zealand, Hong Kong, Tokyo, South Africa . . . And it was enough to bring the toughest spirit down. Despite travelling first-class and staying in the top hotels, sleep became a thing of the past. 'I slept more on planes than in bed, and once, in order to do any sightseeing at all, I was taken round a city, Perth, at 3 a.m., just so that I could see something for myself.'

Very much on his own, Bob never knew from one day to the next whom he would be meeting, but always it was the same round of handshakes and the same set of questions. In Tokyo, instead of having one press conference and photo call, he was required to speak to each reporter and pose for every cameraman separately: 'It was in a riding centre and I was meant to pop a horse over a pole; I must have jumped it three hundred times and it took five hours . . . Yes, it does get boring; I can see why actors go funny. It is such a false life.' But then his face lit up again as he said, 'Home is still a haven.'

He retired from training in 1999.

Shortly after the National victory, Professor Peckham, finding that so many uninvited donations were being sent to the Royal Marsden Hospital, suggested a trust fund should be formed. Thus came into being in 1983 the Bob Champion Cancer Trust, with Bob as patron and Clive Nicholls, QC, chairman of nine trustees and two executives. In 1988 it had raised over £1,500,000, including the ambitious, far-seeing 250-mile charity walk with Aldaniti from London to Aintree. The walk ended minutes before the 1987 Grand National, with Bob himself in the saddle for the last mile; horse and rider cantered past the packed, cheering stands. Bob and Aldaniti remained an inspiration wherever they went.

The walk caught the public's imagination. The 250 people who rode one mile each came from all walks of life, ranging from famous film stars, celebrities and royalty to Pony Club members. For every yard of the 250 miles, stud girl Beryl Millam was at Aldaniti's side. 'Aldaniti and I were both very fit by the end of it,' she said a few years later. She had looked after him devotedly since he was a five-year-old and nursed him through his various injuries. 'Everybody used to like to ride or groom him, he is so kind. He just wants to please. He rises to the occasion and is the most wonderful horse ever to look through a bridle.'

The idea of the walk was for each rider to raise £1,000 in sponsorship, with the aim of netting £250,000. That it raised three times as much – some £750,000 – is testimony to the Bob Champion story. It was fitting that Bob should ride the last mile. And it was particularly moving that Jonjo O'Neill should ride the first mile while fighting his own successful battle against the illness.

Today, in 2019, the fund has raised in excess of £15 million. 'All thanks,' says Lucy Wilkinson, executive director of the

Bob Champion Cancer Trust, 'to the fairy-tale story of Bob and Aldaniti's triumph over adversity.'

Its principal work is for the Bob Champion Cancer Research Laboratory, at the Institute of Cancer Research in Sutton, Surrey, which forms part of the largest male-dedicated research facility in Europe, and for the research team at the Bob Champion Research and Education Building at the University of East Anglia in Norwich, Norfolk.

The research has been so successful in finding treatment for testicular cancer that survival rates have gone from 5 per cent to 95 per cent; as a result, most of the laboratory's work now concentrates on prostate cancer.

Today, Bob lives in Newmarket and is an amusing after-dinner speaker.

Aldaniti died in March 1997, at the age of twenty-seven. Fifteen years earlier, when Aldaniti was among ten fallers at the first fence, the race was won by the oldest jockey ever to claim a National victory . . .

17

Dick Saunders

Oldest winning rider, 1982

To have one ride in the Grand National; to win the race at twice the age of many jockeys; and then to retire . . . Dick Saunders, Northamptonshire farmer and lifelong countryman, did all this and more. At forty-eight years old, he was by far the oldest winning jockey (Tommy Pickernell was forty-one when he won on Pathfinder in 1875); he was the only serving member of the Jockey Club ever to have won; and he was the only current Master of Foxhounds to have done so. Two other amateurs have won on their only ride: Mr E.C. Hobson on Austerlitz in 1877, and Lord Manners in 1882 on Seaman.

But there was nothing either old or flukish about Dick Saunders' win on Grittar in 1982. One of nature's gentlemen, with an abiding interest in racing and all things rural, he was a consummate horseman with a practised eye across country, who had already, from seven attempts, filled the first five places in the Liverpool Foxhunters over part of the Grand National course. This meant he had more experience of the course, if not the National, than many professionals. His win in the Foxhunters had been on Grittar himself, in 1981, and so the scene was set . . .

Saunders was an efficient man with a direction of purpose so strong that, once he decided something was worth doing, he would make sure he did it well. That was the clue behind his success in farming and racing, his involvement in the Jockey

Club and with the Injured Jockeys Fund, and as a Master of the
Pytchley Hunt for ten seasons.

The horse scene began for Dick, as for many a farmer's son,
with Pony Club, hunting and a natural progression to point-to-
pointing. He used to win the Pytchley Hunt members' race quite
regularly until, as a young man, he was given 10 acres of his be-
loved Northamptonshire by his father, use of farm equipment,
and left to get on with it.

Get on with it he did, fulfilling his ambition to farm 1,000 acres
within ten years (he ended farming 3,000), but it meant hanging
up his boots during that period, without any thoughts of ever
returning to riding, bar in the odd members' race.

Any idea he may have entertained of winning the Grand National was more dream than ambition, for, like many an amateur,
he would not be able to make the minimum weight – and horses
with a good chance and bigger weights were mostly claimed by
top professional jockeys.

But in Grittar he had the ideal partner, similarly from an 'amateur' background, that of Leicestershire farmer Frank Gilman
in the Cottesmore hunting country. Gilman not only owned him
and trained the horse under permit, but had bred him too, his
dam, Tarama, having won two novice hurdles for him. Grittar
was by a sprinter, Grisaille, who sired little else besides a few
hurdlers.

A neat, compact bay with an attractive white star, and a good
buck in him, Grittar stood only just over 16 hh., but was beautifully made and balanced, capable of adjusting his stride as the
occasion demanded – an attribute which time and again has
proved its worth at Aintree. He started his racing life early, running unplaced twice as a two-year-old, ridden by Pat Eddery, and
began to show some form after switching to hurdling.

Frank Gilman's stable jockey was Terry Casey (who went on to
train the 1996 winner Rough Quest), and his head lad was Derek

Lane (who went on to take the same role with Terry Casey). It was Terry who rode Grittar to his first two victories in large, competitive, novice hurdle fields, and placed six times in sixteen outings.

In 1979, Grittar began point-to-pointing. As Dick Saunders had ridden Mr Gilman's point-to-pointers and hunter-chasers for about fifteen years, he was the natural choice for jockey, getting off to a highly promising start in a quiet run at Newton Bromswold, which was one of the best-tended point-to-point courses. For Grittar's next run, Dick was sidelined through injury, so the ride went to his young daughter, Caroline (now Caroline Bailey, a trainer), who was then twenty. During two seasons they won several point-to-points and hunter-chases and placed many times. By the end of that period, however, Grittar was beginning to get a bit 'knowing', often finishing second when perhaps with stronger handling he might have won.

The female touch had worked wonders mentally on Grittar after some hard hurdle races, but it was agreed that the time had come for Dick to regain the ride, which, in 1981, he did with devastating results. After an initial fifth, the pair were unbeaten in four races, including the two prestigious Foxhunter events at Cheltenham and Liverpool.

But after his last run at lowly Southwell on firm ground (the all-weather track came in 1989), and unbeknown to the racing press, both Grittar's front legs blew up. Frank remembers showing him to Dick a few weeks later at grass. Dick's face dropped. Grittar's tendons were bowed. It would be long odds against getting him fit to race next year, let alone tackle the Grand National.

It was not surprising, therefore, that the two men did not immediately think of the Grand National after that successful 1981 hunter-chasing season; but when the horse got off to a good enough start under Rules next season, having made a complete and speedy recovery, the whole racing world was talking of him as a Grand National prospect. He was third first time out in a handicap chase at Leicester, second in a handicap chase at Ascot, won a hunter chase at Leicester, and finished sixth in the Cheltenham Gold Cup.

As his chances in the National were more and more widely discussed, so was the question of his jockey. Surely the best professional should be put up rather than an ageing amateur, the pundits urged. Dick raised the question with Frank just once, suggesting he book the best professional available, probably John Francome. Frank replied, 'If he runs, you ride him.' End of conversation.

Frank Gilman said, 'There was never any question of a professional riding, and you don't want to put a professional on an amateur-ridden horse – it wouldn't know what was happening. Dick is anyway one of the finest horsemen I have ever seen, with marvellous hands.'

Frank Gilman was a man of his word, even though John Francome did ride Grittar once before the race, to do a lower weight, which further fuelled speculation about the horse's Grand National jockey.

Dick Saunders rode Grittar into that highly satisfactory sixth place in the Cheltenham Gold Cup as his warm-up race, then, on the opening day of Aintree, drove up to walk the course. He went alone, in peace and quiet, to chart out his intended route, to plan and hope and, very privately, dream. His wife, Pam, did not walk round on that occasion, having been frightened enough by the fences during previous Foxhunter forays.

Dick's Foxhunter rides had stood him in good stead. He had learned the hard way that it was worth dozens of yards to go on the inside; and that, in so doing, he was less likely to come up against the unreliable jumpers or timid riders. He had hunted all his life, had raced now for many years, and in the early days of team chasing had been without peer in planning and riding the stiffest cross-country courses.

Three horses headed the betting market in the weeks leading

up to the race: Grittar; the previous year's winner, Aldaniti; and a good class horse trained by Stan Mellor, Royal Mail, third the year before. But the punters' choice on the day was Grittar, and at the off he started clear favourite.

Once Dick had weighed out for the race and handed over his saddle, the daunting task he faced suddenly dawned on him. Not exactly the first jockey in the history of the race to do so, he found himself thinking: what the hell am I doing here? The tension remained until the jockeys were called out, and Frank Gilman put his jockey at ease. 'Instructions?' said Dick, speaking in 1988. 'There were no instructions, he just told a few jokes and was nice and relaxed, and left the riding to me.'

Naturally, they had discussed tactics beforehand and agreed to keep Grittar 'in the van' to make the best use of his stamina; not that he had ever tackled the distance before, but they both felt, correctly, that he would stay for ever.

As they lined up, and the thirty-nine jockeys jostled for position, Dick managed to obtain the berth just two off the rails, with Bill Smith on Delmoss, a proven pair, hugging that number one position.

Within moments they were off, and both Delmoss and Grittar got a good break. Grittar was at full stretch over the first two fences, then, as the race settled down, and with Aldaniti a faller at the first, Dick found he could track Bill Smith. Grittar jumped accurately and economically and had soon settled into an easy stride; he was still behind Delmoss as they came back onto the racecourse towards the end of the first circuit, and approached the mighty Chair fence in about fifth place.

By the second fence second time round, Dick could see that Delmoss was tiring, so he drew out a bit to pass him; Grittar met the second Becher's on such a good stride that he jumped into the lead and landed running. Dick recalled, 'I decided at that point that the race was hardly being run fast enough, so I took it up to make it a staying race.'

From then on the pair were never headed, though they had to survive one anxious moment. It was not a jumping error; Dick takes up the story as they were approaching the Canal Turn for the second time: 'It didn't go quite to plan, as you want to jump the fence at an angle with your foot brushing through the inside flag, to get the shortest way round the right-angled bend; but Grittar met it on a long stride, and I didn't want to disappoint him, so over we flew, jumping too well and landing right out so far that we had to come round wide; but luckily, as we were in the lead, all the others followed us, and so we didn't lose any ground!'

Although Dick remained in the lead, he could always hear horses just behind him, waiting, he was sure, to pounce, while he willed them not to. He met the last just right, popped over it and set off up the interminable run-in. 'It felt as long as the whole of the rest of the race,' said Dick with some feeling. 'I was sure we were going to be swamped by horses, but luckily Grittar had got them at full stretch.'

As he pulled up in triumph, fifteen lengths clear of Hard Outlook in second, the first person to come down the course and congratulate him was Bob Champion – and that was the first time Dick knew that Aldaniti had fallen, along with nine others, in a first-fence pile-up. Royal Mail had fallen at Becher's. (Twelve departed at the first fence in 1951.)

The last combination to finish were Cheers and Geraldine Rees, who thus became the first female rider to complete the race.

Immediately after the race, Dick Saunders, the ever-youthful forty-eight-year-old, announced his retirement. He and Pam drove home to Northamptonshire that night, scarcely able to take it all in, but soon had to face that greatest of all levellers in racing: their daughter, Caroline, after watching the National on a huge screen at their local point-to-point, took a fall, which resulted in the death of her horse. In addition, they had to spend most of the evening taking entries for their own point-to-point the following weekend, a difficult task with the phone going non-stop with calls from well-wishers.

That same evening Dick received a telegram from the Queen Mother. Countless letters followed, from old friends, acquaintances, and people they didn't know at all; they ranged from cartoons of old men jumping fences to a four-page personal letter from Prince Charles.

Dick secretly hoped that, with his retirement, Grittar would be retired too, but he ran in the race twice more, completing the course both times, for John Francome and Paul Barton. Grittar never won another race, and eventually broke down and retired on the farm.

Why did Dick Saunders, after seven broken collarbones, a number of broken ribs, a punctured lung, broken shoulder and back injuries during his career, retire at that time? 'I could never cap that, there was nowhere else to go.'

After that, Dick's life became increasingly taken up with work for the Jockey Club – he was a steward and chairman of the licensing committee for two years to the end of 1987 and chairman of the Aintree stewards' panel. As such he was responsible for giving the pep talk to jockeys before the big race. On what proved to be his last time there, in 2001, he made the decision to let the race go ahead in the quagmire that the ground had become after continuous heavy rain.

He remained involved with the Injured Jockeys Fund, with hunting, racing and point-to-pointing, to say nothing of farming 3,000 acres. Did he have time for any other interests? 'Occasionally I manage to cook the breakfast,' he smiled.

Dick Saunders died in January 2002 at the age of sixty-eight, just twenty years after his historic National victory.

A year after Grittar's win, the winning trainer was, for the first time, a woman.

18

Jenny Pitman

First winning woman trainer, with Corbiere, 1983

Jenny Pitman nearly gave up horses to work in a shoe shop. She credits Fred Winter with jolting her into making a go of things as a professional trainer.

That was in 1975. As a girl in Leicestershire, Jenny, one of seven brothers and sisters, had grown up with ponies, ridden in a point-to-point at fifteen, and worked in racing stables. After marrying jockey Richard Pitman she produced two sons and started taking in a few liveries, building up into a successful point-to-point yard and then becoming a private trainer.

This worked out fine while she was married but it was not enough to make a living after her marriage broke up. She had been a relatively big fish in the short-seasoned point-to-point pond (from February to May in those days); she would be small fry in racing. And earning an income was no longer an extra but a necessity. Some well-meaning friends advised her to quit. She was wavering. Working in a shop might not be lucrative, but it would be steady and safe. One day Jenny was given a lift to the races by Fred Winter, to whom she confided she was considering packing up the horses. 'He turned round and gave me the biggest bollocking of my life,' she said a dozen years later. She responded with the guts and common sense that became her hallmark. But with the decision came plenty of worries and rock-bottom moments: 'I was skint, but I always fed the horses the best and I always gave my owners a fair deal; luckily they paid me promptly.'

She moved to Weathercock House, Lambourn. It was derelict. Outside there were nineteen dilapidated boxes. There were no roads or paths to them and no drains; the whole place was up to the knees in slurry. The house was no better; a survey was dispensed with – it would have been too depressing.

Ten years later the house was a picture, tastefully furnished and decorated, and ruled over by a cheery assortment of dogs. She had turned the outside into a model yard, or rather several yards, new additions in smart red brick having been built as more money was earned along the way, totalling sixty-five boxes in all.

Just eight horses occupied the run-down stables when Jenny moved in, and six of those were swathed in bandages. For most of them it might have been the last stop before the knacker's yard, but soon Jenny started winning races with them. Her first winner was Bonidon, in a moderate selling race at Southwell.

Soon after, she met a Shropshire owner considering putting two horses with her. Over lunch he changed it to six and Jenny nearly fell out of her chair. In time, that owner's string built up to fourteen. It was the sort of break she needed; when all fourteen were eventually taken away over a point of principle (something that has happened before and since) it was a desperate blow.

In the 1980–81 season, Bueche Giorod won six races, including the Massey Ferguson Gold Cup at Cheltenham. The racing world was beginning to sit up and take notice of Mrs Jenny Pitman.

There were lean spells, there were crises. Somehow, something always came along to pull her out of the mire. Horses such as Fettermist, one of the unsung heroes of National Hunt racing doing a job of work, could be relied upon to provide the odd win or two when most needed. 'If a carpet was pulled out from under my feet and I was slapped down and feeling desolate, there would be a horse like him to come along, as much loved in the yard as the Corbieres of this world.'

Corbiere joined Jenny's yard as a three-year-old and there he remained throughout his career. He had been given as a twenty-first birthday present to Bryan Burrough, a member of a Henley brewing family, and, from day one, Corbiere, or Corky as the stable knew him, was a 'character'. A chestnut gelding standing just over 16.1 hh., with that familiar broad white blaze down his face, he looked almost as broad as he was high, certainly more of a hunter than a racehorse. That was how it seemed on the gallops, too. 'When he was learning, his gallop was like a baby elephant's, even the Labrador could go faster,' Jenny recalled. 'But whatever the weather, come snow or driving rain on the downs, he never turned his head away but always faced it head-on.'

And that was the way Corbiere was to face his racecourse battles: head-on. He never did become a fast galloper, but he was a gem with a heart of gold, a will to win, guts that told him never to give up. It was not easy for a horse like him. While Burrough Hill Lad could cruise in third gear for most of a race before moving into top gear (and even had a fifth gear to call up if needed), Corbiere would be there galloping his heart out right from the start of the race until the end, just in order to keep up.

Conditions contrived to be the worst imaginable for his first race, a two-mile National Hunt 'bumpers' flat race at Nottingham. 'It was like a ploughed field,' recalled Jenny. 'The jockeys' colours were so plastered in mud it was impossible to tell who was who, and then coming out of the pack, stomping his way home, was Corbiere.'

When Corbiere was turned out to summer grass as a five-year-old, farmer Alan Davies, who was keeping an eye on the horses, predicted he would be a Grand National winner. There was an avenue between two fields bounded on both sides with fencing at least 4 feet 6 inches high; Corbiere kept jumping out of his field, crossing the avenue in one stride and jumping into the opposite field, where a filly was the subject of his attraction.

Jenny believes Corbiere would have been a star in whatever sphere he went into; from the start he would do anything to please – although he could show a bit of cupboard love, too. 'If you had a packet of sweets for him, he would rob you until they were all gone, then he wouldn't want to know you.'

He was a crackerjack when he was pulled out for exercise in the morning, bunching himself up and arching his back. After he had worked on the gallops, he would regularly buck the whole way home, and the lads on his back often reckoned they had seen all the way to the Severn Bridge. If there was an audience, he would rear and plunge and generally show off.

He built up a solid race career, mostly in long-distance events, always doing it the hard way, galloping resolutely, never giving up. By the start of the 1982–83 season, when he was rising eight years old, he had won six races and been consistently placed. That season he added the Welsh Grand National to the list, and became a firm favourite for the Grand National. When the weights were published and he was allotted 11 stone 4 pounds, support for him was greater than ever.

The ebullient Jenny told the world and his wife that he would win – 'a dangerous thing, which I don't do any more,' she said a few years later. 'Everyone knows that the Grand National is a lottery and a horse can be brought down at the first fence, but I did think he had a real chance.'

She arranged for her parents, who had given her much moral support, to attend, but as the day grew closer so the nerves became worse – not least because the young owner and his parents would not contemplate defeat! To them victory was a foregone conclusion and Mr Burrough Senior not only arranged a party at the Bold Hotel, Southport, where they were staying, but also brought up two coachloads of his brewery's workers complete with crates of champagne! 'If we lose, I think the safest place I can escape to is the car park,' Jenny confided to her friend and assistant trainer David Stait as the pressure mounted.

She need not have worried. Stable jockey Ben de Haan rode a peach of a race on the stable favourite, always well placed, jumping superbly, and at halfway he was lying third. Excitement and tension were heightening in the box where Jenny and her family were watching. Approaching Becher's for the second time, Corbiere took a fractional advantage. I'll give up smoking or anything, Lord, for a safe jump now, Jenny prayed fervently. Inside the box was pandemonium. Every time somebody said, 'He's going to win,' Jenny pleaded with them to shut up, fearing such predictions would bring bad luck. The Canal Turn was past, the last big ditch, they were back on the racecourse with two to jump.

Mandy, Jenny's sister and her secretary for six years, burst into tears. It set Jenny off, as her Corky jumped the last and touched down in front . . . Her family were hysterical now, all hell let loose, shouting until they were hoarse – and here was Grease-paint coming. He was catching up. 'It's going to be another Crisp and Red Rum,' groaned Jenny, 'it can't happen again.'

It didn't. That most courageous of horses hung on, finding that little bit more from his drained reserves when he felt his rival at his quarters. He won by three quarters of a length.

Victory didn't sink in for a minute. Then David Stait burst in, calling, 'You've done it!' It hit Jenny then, although she felt as if in a dream world while the two mounted policemen escorted her hero in, and she scrambled through the crowds to reach the winner's enclosure. She was then swept up in a whirlwind of interviews, television, radio, press reporters, being led from one assignment to another in the protection of two burly policemen. She was overwhelmed. All she wanted was a cup of tea, a ciga-rette, and a moment's peace.

'Hang on. I've got to go in there!' she said to them suddenly as they passed the queue for the ladies' toilets.

'You can't, the television crew is waiting.'

'I must.'

And with that the women patiently waiting parted to let her through, slapping her on the back as she went. She leaned against a basin for a moment, gathering her thoughts. It was a haven. She lit a cigarette, laughed and joked with the rest of the women, and emerged refreshed. It wasn't the first time she had found such a haven. In the late 1970s, with girl riders so new on the scene that they were yet to have their own changing rooms, make-do provisions were made: a caravan on the concourse, a screened-off section of the first-aid room and, at Aintree, an upstairs ladies' toilet. Jenny, gasping for a smoke and desperate to get away from the press for a few moments, found refuge then, too.

Jenny drove home that night, leaving about midnight, and soon her passengers were curled up sound asleep. She imagined what it must be like to be on drugs, for she was on a high as her adrenaline flowed and she sang the whole way.

When she reached home at about 3.20 a.m., she found, to her amazement, the house filled with flowers. 'Where anybody had been able to get them from on a Saturday night I don't know,' she said. She was far too alert to go to bed, and sat mesmerised, watching the video of the race through several times. After a shower she was in bed by 4.30, totally at peace and contented, but quite unable to sleep.

At 6.30 she looked out of the window and found a crowd already gathering to welcome Corbiere home. When he arrived, many motorists having hooted and waved out of their windows en route in tribute, people crowded so close that she was afraid Corbiere would kick out, but he seemed to know not to.

By the time Jenny went back into the house, it was high time for food; but, save for one crust and a piece of old Brie, the house had been eaten and drunk dry!

Jenny was staggered by everyone's kindness and especially

moved by the amount of mail she received. It came from all over the world, from people she had never met; it took four people two hours each for two days to open it all. 'It was wonderful to know thousands of people are supporting you; I had felt alone and fighting my own battle in the past. They did me a world of good, and it couldn't have been done without the team around me.'

For Jenny, the best thing of all was that her parents and sons, Mark and Paul, had been at Aintree for the race; and the next day her three brothers and three sisters arrived to join in the celebrations at Lambourn.

Corbiere ran in each of the next four Nationals, and save for an uncharacteristic fall at the fourth fence in 1986, he showed all his courage, finishing third under big weights in both 1984 and 1985, and completing safely in 1987. He was then deservedly retired, Bryan Burrough giving him to Jenny, and the horse then acted as a schoolmaster to the young lads and loved going hunting in the winter.

Only one year after becoming the first woman to train a Grand National winner (women having only been allowed training licences since 1966), Jenny Pitman pulled off a similar record in the Cheltenham Gold Cup. 'Yes, the horses have been good to me,' she said. 'Burrough Hill Lad was like a Ferrari, Corbiere a Ford Escort beside him, but he was a magic old horse . . .'

Ten years later, Jenny Pitman's runner Esha Ness was first past the post in 'the National that never was', voided because most of the runners failed to realise there had been a second false start. The starting tape was wound round the neck of jockey Richard Dunwoody, preventing him from taking part, and only eight other jockeys obeyed the false start call.

It was not a good year for the National.

*

Two years before that debacle, in 1991, Jenny had again won the Cheltenham Gold Cup, this time with Garrison Savannah, a victory made even sweeter because he was ridden by her son, Mark. The pair looked like recording a remarkable double when holding a clear lead over the last in the National, but were caught on the run-in by Seagram – so father, Richard (with Crisp), and son both suffered the same fate on that long, long run-in.

Four years later, in 1995, the winning Grand National trainer was again Mrs Jenny Pitman, with G. and L. Johnson's 40-1 shot, the ten-year-old Royal Athlete, ridden by Jason Titley.

Jenny Pitman married her long-time partner and assistant trainer, David Stait, in 1997, and she retired from training in 1999, handing the stables over to her son, Mark.

Jenny Pitman had three horses first past the post in the Grand National, if one includes the void race of 1993. Only one horse has ever finished twenty-third, and he went by the name of Canford Ginger.

19

Canford Ginger

Most finishers, 1984

Racing was fun for Tony Sykes when he was host of the Savernake Forest Hotel near Marlborough, Wiltshire. His Canford Ginger still holds the record for being the only horse to finish twenty-third in the Grand National, in Hallo Dandy's year of 1984. There were twenty-two finishers in 1963, 1987 and 1992, and in 2005 there were twenty-one.

Tony Sykes was a lover of congenial company, good food and fine wine, which he dispensed convivially at his delightful Victorian country hotel on the edge of the ancient Savernake Forest; after he sold it subsequent owners did not do so well, and the house has now been converted to flats.

One of those myriad of 'small owners' who make up the backbone of National Hunt racing, Tony Sykes had been hankering after having a horse in training for some time when he read an article about the then up-and-coming trainer David Elsworth. When they met, Tony immediately liked David and realised he would enjoy having a horse with him. 'Half the fun of owning is visiting the stables and feeling involved and being made to feel important, even if you only have a moderate horse,' said the jovial Tony. He had a useful hurdler in Remezzo, then David bought back Canford Ginger on his behalf.

David Elsworth had originally bought the bright chestnut as an unbroken four-year-old at Doncaster Sales for a firm of solicitors in Canford, Dorset, hence his name. After a while the horse was switched to Jim Old's yard, nearer his owners, but, when he came up for sale again, David, who always had regard for him, bought him back for about £1,500 – 'One of my better purchases,' he mused.

To begin with, it appeared that the horse simply did not stay, even over the minimum two-mile trip. Eventually he was tried over a longer distance as a last chance; if he failed again, it would be off to the sales ring.

In November 1982 he ran over the three miles two furlongs of Fontwell, where the course arrangement, three times round an attractive figure-of-eight, means that the gallop is unlikely to be exceptionally strong. Canford Ginger hacked up and duly remained in his current stable. He won two more chases and was beaten a short head in the four-mile amateur race, the National Hunt Chase, at the Cheltenham National Hunt Festival, at last showing the potential David Elsworth had believed he had.

Canford Ginger was always a superb jumper, and it was decided to take his chance in the 1983 National for experience, in preparation for a serious crack at the race a year later.

Tony Sykes and his family loved the atmosphere of Liverpool and all the build-up. In 1983 they stayed at the Black Swan, Bucklow Hill, where among other guests was Ben de Haan, who won the next day on Corbiere. They walked the course the night before, Tony's wife, Isabelle, then vowing not to watch the race itself.

Early on National morning the familiar figures were back on the course, where all the horses were being exercised, the trainers were exchanging good-natured banter, and bacon sandwiches and brandy-laced coffee were being passed round.

Canford Ginger was unluckily knocked out of the race, and lost his form in subsequent races, so that when he returned to Liverpool for the 1984 National, David Elsworth was feeling, in his words, 'very negative about his chances'. His one asset was his jumping, and so his connections backed him at about 10-1 to complete the course.

Colin Brown, his rider, takes up the story of the 100-1 outsider: 'I knew the connections stood to win about £1,000 if he completed the course; I'd known the horse since he was a three-year-old and he was a superb jumper. He was not far off them when he started to tire after Becher's second time and got a bit slow; but I didn't pull him up because I kept thinking of the money on him. If he'd been out for the count, I wouldn't have been cruel and continued, but he was still popping away and anyway there wasn't much birch left in the last two fences. By then I was trying to look after him and just get him round.'

That year, Tony and Isabelle, busy at their hotel, did not attend. Various guests at the hotel shared in the thrill which goes with having a runner in the National, watching the race on television with Canford Ginger's owners, after enjoying a special Scouse lunch prepared by the chef, and likely to have included lamb and kidneys along with vegetables, herbs and seasoning in a home-made stock.

Tony Sykes, delighted at winning his bet, did not immediately realise that his horse had set a new National record, but when David Elsworth mentioned the fact that evening it made as good an excuse as any to carry on with the celebrations!

As for strategy, the first part of David's instructions had been complied with to the letter: to run the horse at the back to help him get the trip. 'The only thing is, the back is where he stayed!'

Later that year, Canford Ginger was sold at Ascot Sales for 5,000 guineas to go point-to-pointing, which he did without success for a couple of years.

The twenty-three horses who completed, in the order in which they finished, were: Hallo Dandy, Greasepaint, Corbiere, Lucky Vane, Earthstopper, Two Swallows, Fethard Friend,

Broomy Bank, Jivago De Neuvry, Grittar, Hill Of Slane, Tacroy, Doubleuagain, Beech King, Eliogarty, Spartan Missile, Yer Man, Fauloon, Another Captain, Mid Day Gun, Poyntz Pass, Jacko and Canford Ginger.

Hallo Dandy

Hallo Dandy was the first horse Richard Shaw ever owned – and he had been bought with the specific intention of winning the Grand National.

Richard Shaw's sporting passion had always been golf until a good friend, Tim Sasse, talked him into buying a Grand National prospect as they imbibed at a dinner party one day in 1982. Chief executive of Lowndes Lambert, then an insurance broking subsidiary of Hill Samuel, Shaw was far more used to frequenting the likes of Sunningdale than Catterick or Cumbria. It was at Catterick that he first made the acquaintance of his purchase, Hallo Dandy, when Mr Shaw flew up to the Yorkshire track: 'I tried to pat him but he threw his head up and hit me in the face – that's how little I knew about horses.'

For a man who had undergone massive open-heart surgery, Richard Shaw stood the strains and stresses of Aintree remarkably well. Later in the year he had Hallo Dandy brought to the City of London and paraded with a police escort from Tower Bridge to his owner's office in Cheap Street, so he could be seen by staff and clients, many of whom had had a bet on him, and also to raise money for the British Heart Foundation.

Hallo Dandy was a gelding by Menelek, out of Last Of The Dandies. He was bought as an unbroken three-year-old at Ballsbridge Sales for £10,000 by Mr Jack Thompson, former chairman of David Brown tractors, who initially put him with Ginger McCain, for whom he won three races and was consistently placed, but he developed a spot of leg trouble and was fired;

when he came back into training he was sent to Gordon Richards at Greystoke, Cumbria.

After a couple of seasons, in which Hallo Dandy won another three races and again was consistently placed, Gordon Richards told his owner, 'I think your horse could win the National.'

'Terrific,' was Mr Thompson's immediate reply. But a few days later he said, 'My wife will divorce me if we run a horse in the National.'

It was agreed to sell the horse to someone who *would* like a runner in the race, on condition he stayed in the stable. Of the many callers to Gordon Richards, once news of the sale got out, it was Richard Shaw who secured the purchase of Hallo Dandy for £25,000.

The horse finished fourth behind Corbiere in the 1983 National on soft ground. Connections set their eyes on 1984 and had an ideal preparation. It went perfectly in the race, too, when he wore down the Irish trier Greasepaint and the weight-carrying Corbiere.

So it was victory for Richard Shaw, the second-season, one-horse owner who had hosted a hospitality tent for his colleagues, clients and family including his eighty-one-year-old mother.

It was a memorable day, too, for jockey Neale Doughty and his proud parents, retired Welsh steelworker Arthur and his wife Joyce. They had scrimped and saved so that their son could have the pony he longed for as a kid, and here he was, twenty-six years old, riding the winner of the Grand National.

Neale Doughty, who had taken over as Richards' stable jockey on the retirement of Ron Barry, having been his 'understudy' for a couple of years, had produced Hallo Dandy at precisely the right moment. At what point in the race had Gordon Richards first thought he might win? 'Well,' he said, 'you never know until you're past the post; but from a mile out he held a lovely position and I knew he should win if he proved good enough.'

The following year, Hallo Dandy joined the roll of past winners to become a first-fence faller. He completed the course in 1986, and then retired to the hunting field for eight seasons. However, in 1994, ten years after his National victory and aged twenty, he was found in an emaciated state in a field. Richard Shaw immediately took him back and gave him to the then embryonic British Thoroughbred Centre at Halton in Lancashire, where he became a success story and their flag-bearer. He lived until the ripe old age of thirty-three.

20

Mr Frisk

Course record, 1990

When a young Kim Bailey went to the Doncaster Sales in 1986, he refused even to look at the chestnut point-to-point winner Mr Frisk, of whom the form book wrote 'should improve in time'.

'He was by a horse called Bivouac and they're all nuts,' Kim said baldly. His then wife Tracey, herself a competent horse-woman, liked the horse and when he came into the ring kept nudging Kim until eventually he bid for, and bought him, for 15,500 guineas.

Within days, people were ringing him up to say, 'Whatever else, get rid of the horse.' 'Friskers' was nuts all right. So highly strung, he would start dripping with sweat at the very sight of a saddle, and to ride him was virtually impossible.

His breeder and former owner, Ralph Dalton, a farmer from Cleveland, assured Kim that the horse would go on fast ground and so he sold him to American Mrs Lois Duffey because her annual visits to England were in early autumn when the ground was usually firm.

But the training went from bad to worse, and when galloped with two moderate horses he finished 150 yards behind.

Mrs Duffey, in her late seventies, flew over from Maryland as planned and travelled to Devon and Exeter to watch Mr Frisk's first race, in September 1986. A rather bashful Kim told her apologetically that he was afraid he had wasted her money. He suggested to the jockey, Alan Jones, that he should jump him off in front for he knew, at least, that Mr Frisk was a good jumper. Then he settled back nervously to watch with Mrs Duffey, confident only that the horse wouldn't run very well.

What followed left him dumbfounded: the bright chestnut not only set off in front as planned but stayed there throughout the three miles to win, hard held, by fifteen lengths.

'I was genuinely shell-shocked,' Kim recalled.

Their problems were not yet overcome, although the sore back that Mr Frisk acquired in that race eventually turned out to be a blessing in disguise, but not at first.

Wanting to run him again quite soon at Carlisle while Mrs Duffey was still in the country but unable to put a saddle on him, Kim sent him swimming for exercise – or rather he tried to. Only one attempt was made, when 'Friskers' tried to 'walk on the bottom' and drowning looked imminent.

Instead, with the back still too sore to take a saddle, Tracey tried leading him off her former advanced eventer and team chase horse, Barnaby. Off they went down the drive and along the roads with Mr Frisk bucking and kicking all the way. But for once he was not sweating, and so the venture continued, Tracey always afraid her charge would get loose, especially when they started cantering on the stubble, and the situation not helped by Barnaby pulling like a train.

'My heart was in my mouth, but we went for weeks like that,' she said, while Kim watched them work, laughing at the unusual sight. At least the horse was not dripping buckets of sweat.

When Carlisle came round, Mr Frisk actually tried to lie down in the saddling box and it took two handlers to lead him round the paddock – but he won easily by seven lengths, having put in a particularly flamboyant leap at the first fence.

He was still a bad traveller and so they tried stabling Annabelle the goat with him, a ploy that can work with a highly strung horse. Mr Frisk was not too bothered one way or the other and when the goat began eating first his food and then Tracey's garden plants, the idea was abandoned.

The unorthodox training continued, although by this time Tracey would occasionally tie Barnaby to a tree, leap on Mr Frisk's back to give him a gallop, then lead him back; this way he gradually accepted being ridden again and eventually, with extra age and experience he was ridden out with the string on daily exercise.

But that first season, he felt the saddle literally only on race days, and from nine runs he won seven races. Already the couple were thinking of him as a future Grand National horse, but his owner, Mrs Duffey, would not contemplate the notion.

Lois Duffey, brought up in New York, became embroiled in hunting and racing. Her father, Walter Salmon, not only bred and raced three Preakness Stakes winners but also bred Discovery whose daughter Geisha produced Native Dancer, whose grandson was Northern Dancer, and he produced the likes of Sadler's Wells.

Northern Dancer was a Canadian horse who was far and away the best thoroughbred to come out of that country. Northern Dancer was so small, barely 14.3 hh., that he didn't fetch his $25,000 reserve as a yearling, but he quickly proved that lack of size was no barrier to success, winning seven of his nine starts as a two-year-old with a career total of fourteen wins from eighteen starts. As a stallion, by which time he had grown to 15.1¾ hh., Northern Dancer proved every bit as successful as on the racecourse. He sired the great Nijinsky and other Derby winners such as Secreto and The Minstrel, as well as Irish Derby winners El Gran Senor and Shareef Dancer. His influence as a stallion is still strongly felt in Classic races throughout the world. A number of his sons became great sires, especially Sadler's Wells. Tiger Roll has Sadler's Wells on both paternal and maternal sides of his pedigree.

Lois Duffey married steeplechase rider Harry Duffey, and in 1946 the couple took up farming in Maryland. In 1968, on a visit to Ireland, they were persuaded to go into steeplechasing as owners. A few years later they moved their 'entire operation' (one horse) to England. In time, Mrs Duffey kept three in England, initially with Tim Forster, and three in Maryland with Charlie Fenwick.

The press latched on to Mr Frisk prior to the 1989 Grand National, for which Mrs Duffey allowed her horse to be entered but stipulated that she would not actually let him run. The ground became heavy and he was duly withdrawn.

The following season produced a perfect preparation but there was still the question of obtaining Mrs Duffey's permission. Kim told the story: 'On the day entries closed Mrs Duffey was in Mexico, but I had her number and rang it; I only let the telephone ring once before putting it down, then I made the entry. We agreed we would pay her back the entry fee if she was still adamant.'

Next he had to pluck up the courage to admit what he had done, and wrote Mrs Duffey an obsequious letter, dated 22 January 1990:

Dear Lois, I tried to ring you without success as I would have liked to have asked you if I could enter Mr Frisk in the National. As I couldn't get hold of you, I took the liberty of entering him. I know you will most probably be absolutely livid with me for doing so but I really would like to run the horse as you already know. I feel that he has matured mentally and physically enough now to take the challenge and also, as they have already made numerous changes to the course since last year, the race has become much less dangerous than it used to be. Becher's Brook, as you know, has been filled in which really takes away from a lot of people's point of view the glamour of the race.

I know we are going to have to have our annual battle but if the ground was good I would more than anything else like to run him.

If you haven't already ripped up this letter by now, Tracey and I would love you to come and stay on 7 April.

The alterations he spoke of had come about following a vigorous press and public opinion campaign the previous year when two horses had been killed, one of them breaking its back when it slipped back into the ditch made infamous by Captain Becher all those years ago. Indeed, the modifications could be deemed to have come about after more than 150 years of campaigning.

It was not until after the National weights had come out (for which Mr Frisk had been allotted a reasonable 10 stone 6 pounds) that Kim heard back from Mrs Duffey.

The phone rang about 10 p.m. 'I've got your letter,' she told him, and continued to make small talk for what seemed an eternity, 'and I've spoken to Charlie [Fenwick]; I'm not getting any younger, and we'll never have such a chance again, and I know that if you weren't happy you wouldn't run him – so let's go for it.'

Although Tracey was expecting their second child in June, she continued to exercise Mr Frisk (now with a saddle) until two days before the National when she entrusted him to the sympathetic hands of stable girl Rachel Liron, who was also a major influence in calming him down.

As race day approached and the tension mounted, with Kim and Tracey aware that 'Friskers' had never been better in his life, Mrs Duffey said she would not be coming over. She felt the strain would be too great, especially as she was still recovering from a broken ankle. The Baileys were already in Liverpool when they heard the Aintree executive had persuaded her to come and booked her into the prestigious Adelphi Hotel.

Dinner, not surprisingly, was a stilted affair between the three of them, with Kim and Tracey both thrilled and terrified at the same time. They pledged not to talk about tomorrow's race but their strained conversation kept coming round to it.

The question of jockey had been sorted out some time in advance. While Dunwoody would always have been Kim's first choice (and had ridden the horse three times), Richard had something like six regular rides entered before he could consider Mr Frisk, and so Kim engaged Marcus Armytage, who had already ridden him six times notching three wins. But even that was an added strain, for no matter how good Marcus was, he was still an amateur and the odds against an amateur winning were great. The only other post-Second World War amateur to win was American Charlie Fenwick, ten years earlier on Ben Nevis, and in 1946 the Scots Guards former amateur champion Captain Bobby Petre on Lovely Cottage. Otherwise, the flamboyant Spaniard the Duc De Albuquerque added much colour in his various gallant but failed attempts during the 1950s, 60s and 70s. A handful won earlier in the century; and the remarkable Jack Anthony three times in 1911, 1915 and 1920, on Glenside, Ally Sloper and Troytown. In 1906, Ascetic's Silver was ridden to victory by Aubrey Hastings. In the nineteenth century, many winners were amateur ridden.

One of the traditions of Grand National morning is the pre-breakfast 'pipe-opener' given to contenders out in the centre of the course, watched not only by trainers and connections but members of the public willing to get up early enough. This tingling atmosphere was the last thing that was needed for a horse with the nervous disposition of Mr Frisk, who would have burnt up unnecessary energy instead of saving it for the race. So he stayed firmly in his box until all the other horses had finished and then he was just led out for a short while.

The Baileys had been dreaming of how they hoped the race would go for weeks past. Mrs Duffey joined them on the packed stands for owners and trainers. Mr Frisk and the other American-owned horse, Uncle Merlin, matched strides going a tremendous gallop on the fast ground, until Marcus settled his mount in just behind.

At Becher's second time round, Uncle Merlin just missed his footing and Hywel Davies unluckily found himself bumping along the ground.

Kim Bailey knew then they should win, but he suffered an agony, for there was still all that way to come home. He not only chain-smoked, but at one time had three cigarettes alight in his hand, some of them burning his fingers. Like Jenny Pitman before him, he found himself vowing to give up smoking if his horse won.

Up in Yorkshire, Mr Frisk's breeder, Ralph Dalton, was attending a local point-to-point. While spectators crowded round a television screen, he returned to his car to listen on the radio as the son of a mare he had bought for £150 galloped his way into the record books.

Mr Frisk skipped over the last fence but after it, Durham Edition came on to the scene, his stamina carefully conserved by Chris Grant. Would the National yet again see a long-time leader overhauled on that testing run-in?

Mr Frisk did not possess all that character and nervous energy – for so long the bane of the Baileys' life – for nothing; he stuck to his task tenaciously. Even more importantly, his young amateur rider kept his cool, did not panic, kept the horse together and, some yards from the post, began drawing away again. They had won! And it was a new course record, the first sub-nine-minute race in the National's history, having clipped an incredible fourteen seconds off Red Rum's time in 1973.

Tracey, in tears throughout the race, fearful that something would go wrong, jumped up and down so violently that jockey John Mackie's wife, Mary, grabbed hold of her to calm her down, fearing for the safety of her pregnancy.

Feeling numb, Tracey linked arms with Mrs Duffey. Together the unlikely pair – the seven-months-pregnant former model who had played such an unusual role in the winner's training and the near octogenarian recovering from a broken ankle and so wearing plimsolls, along with an old beret – forced their way through the crowds to the hallowed unsaddling enclosure.

Kim Bailey, the tall trainer who had saddled his first winner, Shifting Gold, at the age of twenty-four only seven days after taking out a trainer's licence, was there to greet his gallant chestnut and level-headed rider.

It was a dream come true.

Within weeks, Mr Frisk was to become the first horse to win the Whitbread (now the Bet365) Gold Cup at Sandown in the same season as the Grand National, giving a scintillating display of bold front running and jumping over three miles five furlongs, again beating Durham Edition. His style and character deserved to catch hold of the public imagination as much as Desert Orchid or Red Rum.

He was ridden in all the remainder of his races by Marcus Armytage, including an amateurs' handicap in which, at 4-1 ON, he carried 12 stone to beat the runner-up on 10 stone. On softer ground, and carrying a stone more than the previous year, Mr Frisk ran in the 1991 Grand National but pulled up.

In 2016 the Grand National course was shortened by two furlongs between the start and the first fence in an attempt to reduce the cavalry charge (and so, in theory at least, reduce the number of fallers), meaning that Mr Frisk's record over the original length cannot be beaten. Only Many Clouds (over the shortened course), along with Mr Frisk, has produced a sub-nine-minute time in the history of the Grand National.

Mr Frisk was a 'one-off' horse, and the same could be said of the jockey featured in the next chapter.

21

Richard Dunwoody

Most modern wins and places

Call it a day. Every working person has to at some stage, National Hunt jockeys earlier than most.

Call It A Day happens to be the name of the horse Richard Dunwoody rode into third place behind Bobbyjo in his last of fourteen Grand National rides, giving him an eighth placing to go with his two memorable wins on West Tip and Miinnehoma.

But Call It A Day had a joke up his sleeve. As a mass of Carberry siblings, parents and friends rushed on to the course to greet their hero Bobbyjo, Call It A Day stopped dead after passing the post and whipped round 180 degrees to the right, sending his hapless jockey straight over his ears on to the famous turf. Meanwhile, the prankster horse had galloped off in the wrong direction and Richard Dunwoody had to get hold of him in order to weigh in.

Richard was twenty-one when he rode in the race for the first time in 1985 on the horse that was to become his Grand National stalwart, West Tip. Trained by Michael Oliver in Worcestershire for owner Peter Luff, West Tip ran in the race six times, the first five of them ridden by Richard Dunwoody – but the horse nearly didn't make it to the track at all. Before then, he was hit by a lorry on his hindquarters while out on exercise and badly injured; he bore a large scar the rest of his life. The trainer's wife, Sarah Oliver (now chief executive of the Amateur Jockeys Association), and team spent many hours nursing him back to health – and by the time of the 1985 Grand National he started joint favourite with Michael Smurfit's Greasepaint, who had been placed in the previous three Nationals.

Richard Dunwoody was the youngest rider in the race, but the pair of debutantes took to it like old hands. They had eased their way to the front coming into Becher's for the second time, only to crumple on landing. 'When we came down at the second Becher's I vowed we would come back next year and win,' Richard said.

That, of course, is exactly what they did.

The 1986 National was a race full of Aintree talent, past and future. Race favourite Mr Snugfit had finished runner-up the previous year; Corbiere, winner three years earlier, had finished third for the last two; Last Suspect, the surprise winner the previous year for Arkle's owner, Anne, Duchess of Westminster, was in again; 1984 winner Hallo Dandy, fourth in 1983, was back; and tasting the National for the first time was future winner Little Polveir (1989).

Richard Dunwoody recalls the race: 'I was still very young but the horse made it very easy for me. He was right up there with them. Corbiere fell at the fourth and by the Canal Turn West Tip was in a good position, just on the inside of Classified, and Last Suspect was at the back.

'West Tip was travelling well at the thirteenth and I gave him a breather; he put in a big leap at the twentieth and turned neatly round the Canal Turn. There were about nine left in with a chance three out, and we were in second place [behind Young Driver] at the last with his ears pricked. I only had to give him a couple of smacks.'

West Tip lined up in the next four Nationals, finishing fourth to Maori Venture and then to Rhyme 'N' Reason the next two years and then, at twelve years old in 1989, he and Richard Dunwoody, sharing their fifth partnership in the race, produced a fine second behind Little Polveir. West Tip ran like a horse much younger than his twelve years, sharing the lead and then leading for much of the way from the Chair until heading for Becher's the second time, where he was overtaken by the eventual winner and several others.

His chance looked well gone two out, but while another twelve-year-old Little Polveir had gone beyond recall, West Tip, ever the dour stayer and by now a true Aintree specialist, stayed on past other horses to finish a gallant second.

West Tip finished tenth the following year ridden by Philip Hobbs, who went on to become one of England's leading National Hunt trainers. Finishing four places higher was Richard Dunwoody on the second-favourite Bigsun, allocated 10 stone but on whom he had had to put up 2 pounds overweight; that sixth placing was as close to the front as the horse ever reached in the race won by Mr Frisk. Richard teamed up with Bigsun again the following year and was once more well-fancied. That year they were in closer touch with the leaders, until a serious mistake at the second Becher's saw Bigsun slide along on his belly. His horseman jockey stayed on but he pulled up after the next fence.

The well-fancied Dunwoody mount Brown Windsor was knocked out of the contest by a loose horse at the first Becher's in 1992. Fate was to deal a far scarier occurrence the next year: Richard went to the start of fifteen Nationals but one of those was the voided 1993 race – and it was round Richard's neck that the miscreant starting tape was wound, preventing him from galloping off. The name of his horse that day? Prophetically, it was Wont Be Gone Long . . .

After a lean few years, it might have seemed that Richard Dunwoody's Grand National name was destined only to be associated with West Tip. Not a bit of it. Before the 1994 race he had moved to Martin Pipe's innovative and all-conquering Somerset stable.

The trainer watches his string at work from the top of the gallops. As usual, it means he is also on hand to catch a loose horse, should there be one, and ride it back to its dumped lad or lass.

But oh, no, not this one. He bucks everyone off. Martin Pipe puts on a brave face (no hard hats in those days), gets on and rides Miinnehoma back down to long-established work rider Mary Horswell.

'Mr Pipe, Mr Pipe,' she calls as her boss approaches, 'what are you doing, you shouldn't be riding him. You still love me then?'

They laugh. There is not a rider in the yard, no matter how experienced, who has not been bucked off this particular stable star, sired by Kambalda.

'But he was a very kind horse,' Martin is quick to point out, 'his bucks were only in play.'

The story goes that while in Ireland, Miinnehoma was impossible to break until he was taken into the sea, where he couldn't buck.

Miinnehoma came to Martin Pipe as the result of an out-of-the-blue phone call from comedian Freddie Starr. 'I want to win the Grand National,' he said. At that time, the four-year-old had yet to jump a stick, let alone an Aintree fence.

'I thought, "that's interesting",' recalls Martin, 'but we'll do our best.'

It was a race Martin longed to win, and it wasn't for lack of trying that he hadn't. (In 2001 he was to run ten horses, a quarter of the field.) Born in 1945, he had grown up dreaming of the race; in his youth he had worked in a betting shop, taking bets; Merryman II in 1960 is the first National winner he remembers.

'The National is the greatest race in the world,' he says simply.

Martin Pipe began with humble horses in converted pigsties on a derelict farm, but he was a trainer ahead of his time in many respects. He paid particular attention to the horses' health, physical and mental; to ensure they did not become bored, most went out for exercise twice a day. He introduced interval training and saw to it that his horses could run and jump alone at the head of the field so that their supreme fitness could produce results. Not surprisingly, he built up a mighty reputation.

'All a trainer can do is have his horses fit and healthy, enjoying their life and training at home and placing them to the best of their ability. You can't make them run any faster but you can make sure you don't overface them.'

Martin Pipe had been training for fifteen years before he became champion trainer, but he held that title for another fifteen years before retiring in 2006, in the process enabling Peter Scudamore, Richard Dunwoody and Sir Anthony McCoy to be champion jockeys.

It did not take long for Martin Pipe to realise that he might, indeed, have a National horse, as Miinnehoma was quick to show his prowess and his stamina. He had been first, second and third in his three bumpers for original trainer Owen Brennan.

In his first season with Martin he won his first four hurdle races, all over at least two miles six furlongs, culminating in a Listed three-mile hurdle, but then he finished fourth in an Aintree hurdle and was off the course for almost two years.

He returned by winning his first two novice chases and then the RSA Chase at the Cheltenham Festival by half a length over Bradbury Star (a horse I was lucky enough to own following his retirement after a distinguished career which included eight wins at Cheltenham). The next season, 1992–93, saw Miinnehoma place in his first three chases and the National became the focus, but in his next run Miinnehoma pulled up, after which he was off the course for more than a year with a stress fracture to his pelvis.

He came back from that with a win and Martin Pipe began urging everyone to back him to win the National; that Miinnehoma did just that speaks volumes for the care in the yard and determination from the horse.

Richard Dunwoody's chief concern when he teamed up with Miinnehoma for the Grand National was that the heavy ground was potentially a drawback. But Miinnehoma took to the unique fences well, and in fact Richard struggled to keep him from hitting the front too soon, fearing he was likely to idle if leading.

'He was a small horse to ride but clever and good with his feet; he took to it. I was happy passing the stands the first time and we kept clear of several fallers. Jamie [Osborne] on Garrison Savannah and I chatted about how well we were going, then a loose horse wiped out Jamie and I was very lucky to avoid that – Miinnehoma did a sidestep, he was clever.'

It was a National with a high attrition rate, in which twenty-three of the thirty-six runners lost their riders, either through falling, being unseated or brought down. Miinnehoma nearly joined the list of fallers when, at the second Becher's, he came down on one knee, but again he was clever enough to regain his balance. Adrian Maguire, Richard Dunwoody's up-and-coming rival in the jockeys' championship, came into view on the race favourite Moorcroft Boy.

'Are you going to beat me again?' Richard called over.

Young Hustler was running loose and gave him the lead he needed but he zig-zagged badly approaching the last, where Moorcroft Boy jumped to the front, looking the probable winner.

'Miinnehoma was idling and I thought Adrian had us beat [but Moorcroft Boy broke a blood vessel and faded into third], and then the gigantic head of Just So – known as Just Slow – was at my boot. I couldn't believe how well he was travelling. But I gave Miinnehoma a couple of slaps and he went on.'

The winning margin was one and a quarter lengths over the Henry Cole bred, owned and trained Just So and jockey Simon Burrough. Naturally, Martin Pipe and his stable team were ecstatic.

But, highly unusually, there was one rather important person missing: the owner. Freddie Starr was not present, said to be because of other commitments, or, according to another report, possibly superstition. It was Martin Pipe's head lad Chester Barnes and the horse's stable lad, the ginger-haired Jason Barron, who led the winning horse and rider into the hallowed winner's enclosure, where George Malde, another of Martin Pipe's owners, joined the winning group.

Then it was bring on the party. When the Pipes returned to Pond House at Nicholashayne in Somerset, they could hardly get down the drive for all the press cameras and well-wishers.

'It was such an exciting day, to win the greatest race in the world,' Martin says. 'Eventually we managed to get Freddie Starr down by telling him we'd send a helicopter to pick him up for nothing. We partied all night. The owner enjoyed all the publicity, too, and having his photograph taken with the horse.'

The following season, Miinnehoma won his first race and placed third in the Cheltenham Gold Cup, but did not run too well back at Aintree. He spent his retirement in the paddocks at Pond House along with other retirees of all abilities and Martin Pipe 'loved every one of them'. It is rare for a thoroughbred to live for three decades, but Miinnehoma made it to thirty.

At the time of his win on Miinnehoma, Richard Dunwoody was, by his own admission, a driven man. For most jockeys, winning the National was the ultimate dream. But for Richard it was another one on the clock, one more towards beating his nemesis Adrian Maguire in the jockeys' championship. It was the year that ran to the wire, ending with Dunwoody 197, Maguire 194; the latter haul would normally have won a championship outright, but Adrian, who had to retire early through a neck injury, never won it.

His was a huge talent, and every time he beat Richard Dunwoody, Richard was gutted. It was doing him no good – and it certainly wasn't doing his marriage any good.

'Poor Carol, having to live with me, I don't know how she

put up with me, I was a nightmare.' Their separation happened shortly after the couple had been part of a *Hello!* magazine photo-shoot celebrating Miinnehoma's win.

Richard rode in the National five more times with mixed luck. He was reunited with Miinnehoma the following year, but the horse made a mistake at the first and never went well thereafter. He was tailed off by the twelfth and pulled up before the twenty-first.

The winner in 1996 was another up-and-coming rider, Mick Fitzgerald, beating his idol Dunwoody on board Rough Quest. Richard Dunwoody rode the Mark Pitman-trained Superior Finish for a never-nearer third.

He rode Smith's Band for Jenny Pitman the following year, the postponed 'bomb scare' race, and was contesting the lead when his mount fell at the twentieth and broke his neck, a gut-wrenching experience for him and the stable.

Samlee for Philip Hobbs saw him a plodding-on third – but placed yet again – behind Earth Summit in 1998. His mount in what turned out to be his last National in 1999 was the appropriately named Call It A Day, trained by David 'The Duke' Nicholson near Stow-on-the-Wold. Much as he would have liked to win for the Duke, who had been good to him when he was starting out as a rider, he placed third yet again, behind Bobbyjo.

To win two Grand Nationals and place in eight of fourteen rides; to win the Cheltenham Gold Cup and Queen Mother Champion Chase; to ride the public's great favourite Desert Orchid to seven of his wins including two King Georges; and to be champion jockey three times – success on such a scale would be enough to last a lifetime for most jockeys. The lucky ones move on, once their riding careers are over, to become trainers, agents, pundits, presenters, tipsters, jockey coaches, valets, or work for the British Horseracing Authority as stewards' secretaries, starters, clerks of scales, clerks of courses and so on.* They miss the adrenaline, of course, but most make do with riding out for trainers, schooling horses, reminiscing in the pub, or encouraging their children to take up the sport. For Richard Dunwoody, however, this was not enough.

Forced to quit race-riding at the age of thirty-five after suffering a neck injury in 1999, he took up TV presenting. He was used to travelling long distances to get to races, but now he began to see more of the world and found he'd been bitten by the travelling bug. He embarked on a round-the-world trip taking in Hong Kong, Australia, New Zealand, Argentina, Brazil, Peru and Canada, before meeting a mate in New York, but it was the trek to Machu Picchu in Peru that got him really hooked: 'That was responsible for what followed.'

He met up with David Hempleman-Adams, whose Duke of Edinburgh Awards achievements at school led to a life of adventuring, and whose charity work earned him a knighthood in 2017. Together they made a 150-mile trek across Baffin Island in 2003. A team race to the magnetic North Pole followed when, in spite of twice dislocating his shoulder (jockeys are used to putting up with injuries and pain), Richard Dunwoody and his teammate, former army commando Tony Martin, finished second. It was, he admits, 'very challenging' pulling a sled for 320 miles, not helped by the injury – which had happened, originally, not through racing but by falling off a dressage horse!

Next up, in 2008, was a 700-mile challenge following in the footsteps of Ernest Shackleton's 1913–14 expedition to the South Pole. Dunwoody was part of a team led by Doug Stoup, making their way on skis, dragging a provision sledge that weighed 120 kg when they started. The money raised was donated to

* JETS (Jockeys Employment and Training Scheme) does a great job in finding the right second career for retired jockeys, whether in racing or other professions.

Motor Neurone Disease, Spinal Research and Peter O'Sullevan charities.

How did he feel when they achieved their goal?

'Knackered . . . But it was an amazing experience and probably the hardest thing I have ever done.'

In 2017 it was a 2,000-mile walk, the length of Japan's three largest islands, in 101 days. The money raised by that trip went to Sarcoma UK.

In a break between expeditions, in 2011, Richard Dunwoody took a nine-month photography course in Paris and now takes stunning photographs worldwide, none more so than in spring 2013. This trip saw him and his camera in Guatemala, India, Pakistan and Egypt illustrating the challenges facing the Brooke Hospital for Animals. The resulting photographs featured in an acclaimed exhibition in early 2014 at St Martin in the Fields, London.

He says, 'I am still called up to do the odd shoot now and again.'

He has also been involved with the renowned Mongol Derby and taken many photographs there. In 2009, he was invited to start the race and ride in the first leg of 40 kilometres.

Now fifty-five, he lives with his partner, Olivia, in Madrid with their three-year-old daughter, Milly (Amelia), because 'we love Spain, Madrid is a good hub and Milly has a great school'.

He shows no sign of slowing up. In addition to his photography, he occasionally leads riding safaris in Namibia – but the long walking treks are a thing of the past and his last marathon run in 2018 (after a gap of more than a decade), 'a different, almost surreal experience', was, he says, his swansong. Such ventures are now committed to the memory bank – along with his two Grand National wins on West Tip and Miinnehoma and eight places in the great race – and not forgetting the equine that really started it all for him as a six-year-old newly moved to Gloucestershire from

County Antrim: Tony the Pony. Doubtless there will be a pony for Milly one day.

There are already ponies for the children of Mick Fitzgerald, who beat his hero Richard Dunwoody in 1996 and found himself in the National winner's enclosure – but in bizarre circumstances.

22

Rough Quest

Surviving a Stewards' Enquiry, 1996

Imagine the elation of riding the Grand National winner and then only moments later learning that you must face a Stewards' Enquiry. Young jockey Mick Fitzgerald, who had got no further than the first fence on his only previous ride, thought, 'I've just won the world's greatest horse race and I might be about to lose it.'

Only twice in the previous 180 years of the race had this happened, both more than one hundred years before: in 1878 the unfortunate jockey was Tom Beasley, and in 1891 Captain Roddy Owen. In both cases the objection was overruled.

These days, of course, the presence of camera patrols means that every yard of the race can be scrutinised, and from every angle.

As Mick Fitzgerald had cantered down to the start on Rough Quest he had many reasons to be grateful to be on board. He had a dismal record over the Aintree fences, including falling at the first in his only previous National ride. He had finished second on Rough Quest in the Cheltenham Gold Cup only two weeks before (to Imperial Call), so the horse was not expected to turn out again so soon afterwards for the National marathon. And then with Rough Quest having displayed his well-being and eagerness at home, Mick expected his hero, the experienced Richard Dunwoody, to be called up because he was without a ride in the race and had ridden Rough Quest a few times before.

To Mick's eternal gratitude, owner Andrew Wates and trainer Terry Casey remained loyal to the man who had ridden Rough Quest in seven of his last ten races.

Now, as the big strong bay, standing a good 16.3 hh., headed off towards the start it was, in Mick's words, 'like sitting in your favourite armchair; he felt perfect'.

Some horses take to Aintree's awesome fences and thrive on the challenge; others say 'no thanks' and a jockey will know his fate early on; occasionally a previous winner will return and say 'not a second time, thank you' – in fact, a few winners have tried again only to fall at the first fence (Aldaniti was one, Hallo Dandy and Gay Trip two more, and going way back, Poethlyn, winner in 1918 and 1919, promptly fell at the first fence the next year). Others will thrive year on year: Manifesto finished in the first four six times, including two wins from a record eight runs; Red Rum was first or second five times from five runs; West Tip and the nineteenth-century mare Frigate both won and placed four times. Those with a win and two places include Royal Tan, L'Escargot, Mr What and Corbiere, while Edward Courage's home-bred pair Tiberetta (1957–59) and her son Spanish Steps both placed three times.[*] In more recent times, State Of Play finished in the first four three times.

Now Mick Fitzgerald was to enjoy the supreme thrill of a horse who takes to Aintree. He recalls, 'Rough Quest landed so surefooted over the first, and was so nimble over the third' – a big ditch and the first real test – 'Becher's just felt like any other fence to him, and he bounced over the Chair' – the biggest single fence on the course.

---

[*] Spanish Steps came fourth in 1973 behind Red Rum, Crisp and L'Escargot, all four beating the previous course record. In 1974 Spanish Steps came fourth again, and in 1975 finished third.

Mick was purposefully riding him on the middle to outer, giving him daylight and a chance to see the fences clearly. He was going so well that when they came to the first fence second time around, Mick persuaded his mount to 'fiddle' it in order to keep him back a bit. One thing he could not do was hit the front too soon for Rough Quest was one of those horses who, in that position, thought they had done enough. Horses, like humans, have their individual quirks and idiosyncrasies, and that was Rough Quest's.

From then on, having successfully dropped back a bit and relaxed as Mick planned, Rough Quest 'made ground without me having to do anything', Mick says. 'When I jumped the third last I suddenly thought, "I've only got two more to jump and I will have got round in the Grand National."'

By the second last he began to use the leader Encore Un Peu, ridden by David Bridgwater, as a buffer. Facing the daunting run-in, he still bided his time until about halfway up. At that point he considered squeezing up the inner but Bridgwater, just like Tommy Beasley more than a century and a half before, was not letting him in. Instead, Mick Fitzgerald found he had time to pull out and pass his rival on the right. Rough Quest then promptly leaned towards the running rails on his left, causing a modicum of inconvenience to Encore Un Peu, before running out the winner by one and a quarter lengths, with Mick not resorting to his whip.

He gave no over-the-top reaction as he passed the post, but leaned forward and patted his partner on his neck, and then reached his arm out to the losing jockey.

'I was elated to have just won the National but then I saw Terry [Casey, the trainer] walking towards me, and he said I might lose it.' There was to be a Stewards' Enquiry into possible interference.

Two police horses escorted him in, as is the tradition, and there were cheers from the crowd but they weren't resonating; to Mick the scene was muted. All he could think was, 'Shit, I'm going to be the first jockey to lose the National.'

The horse's owner, Andrew Wates, was at that time an experienced local steward. He had watched the race from the roof of the County Stand with his wife Sarah, and their good friends Patrick and Rita Vaughan with whom they had travelled to Aintree. Andrew had seen the incident side-on.

'I knew there would be an enquiry, but it was only when I saw the head-on replay that I felt concerned.'

He advised his jockey to 'keep it simple' to the stewards, to say he felt he was comfortably clear before moving over.

Along with David Bridgwater, Mick was taken into the stewards' room for what was to be the longest fifteen minutes of his life. Mick's scrambled brain thought only of the horrendous nightmare unfolding. He certainly didn't reflect on the path that had brought him to this point.

Born and raised in Camolin, County Wexford, Mick enjoyed the Irish pony racing circuit and then at sixteen began riding out for local flat trainer Richard Lister, before moving on to the Curragh stable of John Hayden. When he left school at eighteen he had begun putting on weight; like many Irishmen before him he moved to England and switched to jump racing, firstly with John Jenkins and then Richard Tucker, and he rode his first winner at the end of 1988.

But it was a slow work in progress, and Mick even thought about moving to New Zealand – he actually had a job lined up and tickets booked – but then he teamed up with Jackie Retter's West Country stable and also trainer Ray Callow and that changed his career. After he won an Easter Monday race at Hereford on his Sunset Sam, Ray Callow told the aspiring jockey he could ride all his horses the following season. One of those was a horse called Duncan Idaho. Some of his early rides, from 1987 still as a 7-pound claimer on the bay gelding by Busted, were at odds of

100-1, but in time Mick won four races on him, including one
that was televised – and his burgeoning prowess caught the eye
of Nicky Henderson.

Mick Fitzgerald's move to Seven Barrows, Lambourn in 1993
was the start of a long, fruitful and friendly association, starting
by winning the conditional jockeys' championship, through well
more than a thousand winners, right up until his enforced retirement due to injury.

That last was still in the future as he sat waiting for the Aintree
stewards' verdict.

Outside, Rough Quest and his handlers waited patiently in
the winner's enclosure. Bred by Michael Healy from Fethard,
County Tipperary, Rough Quest carried the British-bred tag
being by Crash Course (by Busted). The bay with a little white
star between his eyes and an almost mealy muzzle was sourced
for Andrew Wates by Arthur Moore in Ireland after placing
fourth in two bumpers. For his new connections he fell in his
only hurdle before a summer at grass to fill out and mature, and
then he promptly won first time out the next autumn in a novice
chase at 25-1, and quickly followed up with another.

From the start, Rough Quest was headstrong at home, even 'a
bit of a lunatic'.

'He "carted" me a couple of times,' Andrew Wates, himself a
top amateur, recalls.

In a race, Rough Quest had to be held behind until the last
minute, but he had a 'fantastic' cruising speed and was a 'wonderful' mover. At this time Andrew's private trainer was Tim
Etherington, until in 1994 he moved to North Yorkshire to train
on his own account.

Andrew Wates had originally trained under permit but when he
became too busy at work he took on a professional trainer, while
remaining hands-on himself, riding out once or twice a week,
seeing to the entries, and doing evening stables once a week.

With the move of Tim Etherington, he advertised for a new

trainer and one of many to apply was Terry Casey. Andrew had no hesitation in taking him on; Terry had some good horses at the time and was well regarded. The arrangement was that Terry would train Andrew's seven or eight horses and roughly the same number of other owners' horses that Terry brought with him. It was a win-win arrangement.

Andrew recalls a time at home when he was on Even Flow and Terry on Rough Quest; the plan was to do a couple of steady canters on his oval gallop. The two horses took each other on and galloped flat out.

Afterwards, Terry's verdict was, 'They really enjoyed themselves.'

It hadn't all been plain sailing en route to Aintree, as Rough Quest suffered a number of setbacks, but in the spring of 1995 he won three-mile handicap chases at the Cheltenham and Punchestown Festivals, ridden by Mick Fitzgerald in both. At last, his undoubted class was rising above injury problems that had plagued his early career.

He followed up with seconds in the Hennessy Gold Cup at Newbury and the Betterware Handicap at Ascot in the autumn of 1995, and a win in the Racing Post Handicap at Kempton, ridden by Richard Dunwoody, in February 1996 – good enough form to have him entered not only for the 1996 Grand National, but also the Cheltenham Gold Cup before it.

David Bridgwater reflected on the race. Encore Un Peu had been 'absolutely cantering' as he crossed the Melling Road for the last time, and jumped the final four lengths to the good. He'd thought he was going to win, until he looked behind, saw that Mick Fitzgerald on Rough Quest was coasting, and 'the world dropped out of my pants'.

And of the incident that was now under scrutiny he said later, 'Although it stopped my momentum, I wouldn't have beaten him. His horse was much better than mine.'

Despite being born into racing, 'Bridgie' harboured ambitions of being a professional footballer as a youngster, but racing won out. He initially joined Lester Piggott in Newmarket but then switched to jumping with David Nicholson in the Cotswolds, close to where he now trains. Neither were easy spells but both taught him a lot – about racing and about life.

Winners flowed once he joined Nigel Twiston-Davies, and when he later moved to Martin Pipe, he finished second in the jockeys' title with 132 winners; he was well on his way to this total as he sat beside Mick Fitzgerald at Aintree, yet it was at the end of that season that he left the Somerset yard.

For Andrew Wates the wait was 'a very funny feeling' when he went from the euphoria of winning to trying to keep very different emotions at bay.

As he waited anxiously with Terry Casey in the winner's enclosure, Andrew Wates knew better than most how the stewards would be deliberating. A former amateur rider, he was a local steward and had been a member of the Jockey Club since 1977 (he went on to become chairman of the United Racecourses and Racecourse Holdings Trust, or Jockey Club Racecourses as it is now known).

Andrew Wates also knew what it was like to win over the Grand National fences, having won the Foxhunters, 'the amateurs' National', on Lismateige in 1970. And he had experienced the downside, too, on his only ride in the Grand National two years earlier: his mount, Champion Prince, was brought down by Bassnet at the water jump in front of the stands and was killed.

'He had been going so well and was giving me a really nice ride, but Bassnet rolled over in front of him. It's a remarkable race, one of triumph and tragedy.'

Andrew Wates' mother Phyllis (Lady Wates) loved racing and was co-owner of Rough Quest, but would not go to Aintree after the loss of their previous horse. Now she was sitting in front of the TV in her Surrey home, also awaiting the outcome.

Irishman Terry Casey paced anxiously. He hailed from County Donegal where, to the concern of his parents, he'd run away from school at the age of fifteen hoping to join a stable on the Curragh. But the Gardai (police) hauled him back home where he was told in no uncertain terms that he was not to go into racing. But it was like a drug for the dark-haired lad, and he learnt much of the racing craft from the inimitable Aubrey Brabazon on the Curragh, for whom he had about forty rides on the flat. Once he switched to jumping, he rode forty-six winners for, among others, George Dunwoody, father of Richard. It was Terry Casey who'd taught the future three-time champion jockey much about riding.

When Terry became head lad to Frank Gilman, he kept up his riding licence and twice won on Grittar over hurdles. He next took out a licence to train on the Curragh before returning to England to train for John Upson, in whose name the licence was held, at Adstone, near Towcester in south Northamptonshire. From there, in the mid-1980s, Terry Casey built a reputation for producing super-fit horses and for rising to the big occasion. His success with Nick The Brief helped put Casey and his individual training style firmly on the map; Nick The Brief won or placed in twenty of his twenty-six chases.

Terry Casey had a spell of about six years training on his own from the lovely period stables of Derek Ancil in Thorpe Mandeville, near Banbury. Richard Dunwoody was his number one jockey, but realistically he was only available early and late season. In between, the rides fell to fellow Irishman Martin Lynch, who remembers Terry as someone who enjoyed the occasional cigar, and having a good laugh with his landlord and golfing partner, Derek Ancil. (When Martin Lynch joined them for a game, he discovered on moving on to the fourth tee that Derek and Terry had never made it that far – they'd disappeared off to the club room.)

Terry was subsequently coaxed to Surrey by Andrew Wates – and from there the path to Aintree glory – or was it about to be snatched away from him?

The stewards had by this time finished questioning the two jockeys, both of whom had given their version of events, and they asked Mick Fitzgerald and David Bridgwater to wait outside. Time hung. Every second seemed interminable. And not just for the jockeys.

Rough Quest had started 7-1 favourite for the race, which meant that many of the 70,000 or so racegoers at Aintree were clutching their betting tickets anxiously while around 500 million television viewers worldwide were sitting on the edge of their seats as they awaited the verdict. They did not have much longer to wait.

The stewards called the two jockeys back in and told them, 'The placings remain unaltered.'

'Everything drained out of me,' Mick recalls.

'Bridgie' turned to him and said, 'I wouldn't have felt I'd won a National if they'd given it to me.' He admitted Rough Quest was a much better horse who deserved to win.

'It was a huge relief when the outcome of the enquiry was announced,' remembers Andrew Wates. 'It was a fantastic time.'

Martin Pipe and his team had stood in the runner-up's berth with Encore Un Peu wondering if they might be trading places with the winner.

Martin recalls today, 'He ran a great race to finish runner-up in the 1996 Grand National. He was crossed on the run-in by Rough Quest but the winner kept the race after a Stewards' Enquiry.' He goes on to note that Encore Un Peu 'was only getting 7 pounds from Rough Quest . . . He carried 10 stone and raced from 9 pounds out of the handicap and was only beaten one and a quarter lengths. The top weight that year, Young Hustler, only carried eleven seven.'

Over in County Donegal on the west coast of Ireland, Terry Casey's brother, Frank, was committed to looking after a party of golfers at his Rosapenna Hotel and Golf Resort. When they were done, he snuck away to a television and saw the drama unfolding. That evening some of the golfers were idly discussing the 'other' sporting event that day when they noticed their host opening a bottle of champagne. Soon they discovered the reason and joined in the celebrations.

The first person to nab Mick as he emerged from the stewards' room was the BBC's Des Lynam, a tall, imposing figure in Mick's eyes. Thrusting a microphone under Mick's chin, he asked him how he was feeling. Still shell-shocked and certainly not taking on board that he was speaking to hundreds of millions of people, Mick came out with the immortal words, 'After that, Des, even sex is an anticlimax!'

Now that Mick is himself a TV horse-race presenter, he appreciates just what a gold nugget he innocently delivered to Des Lynam in the emotion of the moment.

'I can remember seeing the light flicker in his eyes,' he recalls. To the viewers, Des remained inscrutable, but Mick understands now how light bulbs flashed in the experienced man's head at that moment. It became such a well-known quote that the title of Mick's autobiography was *Better Than Sex.*

'And I still don't regret what I said,' he says, more than twenty years later.

In the *Irish Times* Michael O'Farrell wrote: 'I have not seen a better riding performance in a National, though his partner, Mick Fitzgerald, said modestly that Rough Quest had "done everything for him" and that all he had to do at one stage was to "take a pull". But the horse has never been the easiest of rides.'

Mick, of course, was much more than that one race. He went on to win the Cheltenham Gold Cup on See More Business in 1999 as well as the King George on the same horse, the Champion Chase on Call Equiname in the same year, the Hennessy on Trabolgan for his boss Nicky Henderson in 2005, and three Tote Gold Trophies.

He joined the elite band of jump jockeys to have ridden more than a thousand winners, but he also suffered many injuries; one of these nearly forced him to give up in 2007, but the Henderson yard was in such good form that he kept going.

In 2008 he lined up for the Grand National again, this time riding the François Doumen-trained L'Ami for owner J.P. Mc-Manus; A.P. McCoy had ridden him into tenth place the previous year but was now on the better-fancied Butler's Cabin.

Mick was looking forward to the ride; he had finished fourth on him in the RSA Chase as a youngster, and in the Gold Cup, too.

'I liked the horse and thought he was the right type and was really looking forward to it. He jumped the first really well and met the second on a lovely stride but he put in a short one instead of taking off.

'I thought, "Oh f*** this is going to hurt!" He flipped and when I came round I was paralysed. I was looking at my body and it wasn't mine, then it started to jump involuntarily. I told the paramedics not to move me, and they got me on to a spinal board and off the track.'

It was to be Mick's last ride. He had hoped and dreamed of returning to race-riding, but his last consultation with Professor Jeremy Fairbanks made his mind up for him.

'When a man with the experience and expertise of Mr Fairbanks is shaking his head, you don't argue,' he told Marcus Armytage of the *Daily Telegraph*. 'When I broke my neck the first time, I was happy to ride on his advice and I'm happy to accept what he says this time. With all the metal in there now, he said I'd be riding with a noose round my neck; it wouldn't be paralysis next time, I'd be dead.'

He admitted that what he would miss most was life at Nicky Henderson's, where he had been since 1993. 'It'll be hard to find a substitute for that.'

Mick lives in Lambourn with his wife, Chloe, and three children, Zac, Oscar and Lola. He is still a regular visitor to Seven Barrows, where he coaches Nicky Henderson's aspiring jockeys, and is also a well-respected key expert on the ITV live racing coverage every Saturday and on other big days in the racing calendar.

A number of years after his great training achievement Terry Casey began feeling a pain in his neck; it turned out he had inoperable throat cancer. He died in July 2001, aged just fifty-six. Many of his mementoes went to his brother at Rosapenna Hotel and Golf across the bay from where the brothers grew up; some of the hotel interior walls are festooned with photographs of Rough Quest and his talented trainer, with pride of place occupied by a portrait of Terry Casey and Andrew Wates cantering Rough Quest and another horse at home.

Mick Fitzgerald says, 'Terry Casey was a big race trainer, but the horse always came first; he was a good operator and a nice man who did a good job.'

David Bridgwater said, 'Looking back at what happened to poor Terry Casey, I'd have gladly given him the race anyway. Life's too short. At the end of the day it's only a horse race.'

Martin Lynch said, 'Terry was very, very good to me; he never deviated or changed, he was always himself: a total individual. It was unbelievable when he got ill.'

Rough Quest finished second in the 1996 King George to One Man but was then off the course for twelve months. The following year he was third in the King George behind See More

Business but fell in the 1998 Gold Cup before pulling up on soft ground two out in Earth Summit's Grand National.

In the spring of 1999, he ran in three hunter chases ridden by Mark Bradburne, winning one, and in a chase at the Cheltenham Festival for his old friend Mick Fitzgerald. He was pulled up and after one more race (when he fell in the Aintree Foxhunters) he headed off into well-earned retirement.

It was then a life of deserved luxury at the Wates' home in beautiful surroundings near Dorking in Surrey. There, he was looked after by David Arbuthnot, who took over after Terry Casey's death, and still trains for Andrew Wates.

'Nothing is too much for him,' says Andrew.

Of the owner, Andrew Wates, Mick Fitzgerald says, 'He is a lovely, lovely man and an absolute gent. I visited the horse several times in retirement and he was so well looked after, he had a great life.

'It meant so much to the Wates family to win a race like that.'

Rough Quest died in 2016, aged thirty, and is buried under the oak tree where he liked to stand in his field.

Richard Dunwoody and Mick Fitzgerald were stars of their eras, but waiting in the wings were two more whose paths were inextricably entwined.

23

Sir Anthony McCoy and Richard Johnson, OBE

The great racing rivals

Christmas Day, 2018. Lodge Down pre-training and point-to-point stables, Lambourn Woodlands. Run by Ciaran O'Brien. Owned by Sir Anthony McCoy. Twenty stables to be mucked out this morning, the same as every other morning. But today there is a difference. The staff have been given Christmas Day off. The man with the fork and the muck barrow is AP himself.

Sir Anthony McCoy – known at large as AP – was knighted after retiring in 2015 from a racing career in which he was champion jockey in all twenty seasons that he rode as a professional; he was also champion conditional in his first and only other season. He rode an incredible 4,358 winners, and beat Sir Gordon Richards' fifty-five-year-old flat racing record of 269 winners in a season by 20. They are the only two jockeys ever to have been knighted.

AP says that having Richard Johnson forever breathing down his neck made him strive even harder year on year to go that extra mile to notch yet more winners. Their careers were closely inter-twined and after AP retired there was no one more deserving of the champion jockey title than Richard Johnson, and he was to win it for the next four seasons.

Between them they have ridden almost eight thousand winners.

Their Grand National paths took similar routes also; for a period, they held the joint record of having ridden in it twenty times, but in 2019, Richard Johnson made his score twenty-one. Tom Olliver and Tommy Pickernell in the nineteenth century rode in it nineteen and eighteen times respectively; in the twentieth/twenty-first century Paul Carberry rode in it nineteen times and currently Barry Geraghty is on eighteen and counting. He was due to ride a leading fancy Anibale Fly in 2019, but broke his leg in two places the day before.

Richard Johnson also holds another outstanding record: he rode in the National for twenty years consecutively, beating Michael Scudamore's long-held record of sixteen. Actually, Richard holds a third record, but this is one on which he prefers not to dwell: he has ridden in the National more times than any other jockey without winning. His luck was out yet again in 2019 when he was brought down on Rock The Kasbah.

Sir Anthony McCoy

AP grew up near Moneyglass, County Antrim, where he learned to ride. He was the third child of six; along with his parents Paeder and Claire, his brother, Colm, and sisters Anne-Marie, Roisin, Jane and Kelly have been his stoutest supporters throughout his career.

He began riding out at the age of twelve for local trainer and early mentor Billy Rock, a huge influence on his life, before an apprenticeship and first win aged seventeen with flat trainer J.P. Bolger in County Wexford. Rising weight followed a broken leg, resulting in a switch to jumping and a career in England, first with another great mentor and spotter of rising young talent, Toby Balding, followed by the inimitable Martin Pipe, and finally as number one jockey for J.P. McManus.

Of the Grand National, AP says the race totally changed from his first ride on Chatham in 1995 to his last on Shutthefrontdoor in 2015, and added that older jockeys would notice it even more.

'It's the mindset of the politically correct, that's the way it is. You have five or six hundred million people watching it, and of them you have a thousand who complain [about perceived animal welfare issues]. They will complain about anything, that's their niche in life – and they're given too much air time; they're free to voice an opinion, but we shouldn't have to listen to it.'

He asks rhetorically, 'Why do so many people watch it? Because it's different, with different variables: excitement, the lottery element to it – even with the changes, there are still a few big-priced winners; so long as the lottery element is still there it will probably be OK.'

He adds, like others, that with the fences easier the biggest danger is speed, with horses simply going too fast, and that can cause falls. 'I hate to bring it up, but many of the changes have been since Synchronised's death.' AP has no hesitation in nominating Synchronised as the favourite horse of his career.

It was on Synchronised's dam, Mayasta (by Bob Back), that AP rode his first winner for J.P. McManus at the 1996 Punchestown Festival, wearing the green and gold with white cap that were to become so familiar. That evening he accepted an invitation to a party – and there he met his future wife, Chanelle. Mayasta's trainer, Frank Berry, was to become the quietly spoken, super-knowledgeable manager of JP's racing empire, while JP's wife, Noreen, was the breeder of Synchronised. So it's no wonder AP felt a special bond with Synchronised.

If you had to nominate AP's top half-dozen rides for sheer brilliance, his riding of Synchronised to win the 2012 Cheltenham Gold Cup would be among them. The horse made several mistakes but a masterly, tenacious ride from AP saw him overhaul, first, past winner Long Run and then runner-up The Giant Bolster on the run-in from an improbable position when his chance had looked well gone. Somehow the horse moved up through the gears and stayed on the best.

'If that was a thrilling finish to watch, just imagine how it felt to ride,' he said in his autobiography *Winner*.

Synchronised, sired by Sadler's Wells, was so well after it that he lined up for the National four weeks later, carrying top weight of 11 stone 10 pounds and going off at 10-1 behind 8-1 co-favourites Seabass and Shakalakaboomboom.

AP had no doubts about him running.

'Had I done so, I would have told JP,' he says. 'Jonjo genuinely believed he'd never been better than after Cheltenham.'

So well, in fact, that he spooked at something and decanted AP at the start. As described by AP in *Winner*:

> There was a line drawn on the ground about 50 yards before the start, a line that we weren't supposed to cross before the starter raised the tape to let us go, and as we were cantering down just to have a look at the first fence he spooked at that. Then he ducked at the starting tape that went above our heads. That's the type of horse he was: noticing everything. I came out over his head.

It took a few minutes to catch him while the other thirty-nine runners circled at the start, anxious to be off. Horse and jockey were reunited, and Synchronised took the fences well enough, but was caught out by the drop at Becher's, fence six, and fell. As AP gingerly stood up, he saw his white-blazed partner gallop off safely with some other loose horses. Feeling relieved about the horse but sore himself with two broken ribs, he took a lift in one of the official vehicles that follow the riders around, and headed back towards the stands. Having seen that his horse was fine made what happened next all the harder to take. He heard it over the two-way radio in the vehicle, someone saying Synchronised would have to be put down. Surely he had misheard – had the word been euthanised, not Synchronised, and was it about one of the other horses? When they reached the weighing room, the looks on Jonjo O'Neill and JP's faces told him the worst. What had happened was, unusually for a loose horse, Synchronised had fallen again, at the eleventh fence, and broken both the tibia and fibula in a hind leg. There had been no alternative but to put him down.

AP wept, and wept, and wept. All the way home; all that night; and for several days. You can still hear that choke in his voice seven years later. It was by a long way the worst equine day of his racing life (human fatalities were, naturally, much worse).

AP's greatest achievement by far, in his opinion, is not winning the Grand National, or the Cheltenham big four, or to have been champion twenty times, but to have beaten Sir Gordon Richards' record by riding 289 winners in a season.

'Jockeys who are not particularly good can win the National, but none of them will beat that record.'

He remembers his first National ride clearly. It was 1995 and he was twenty. Chatham had been a good horse in the past but his best days were gone. But for the conditional jockey to secure a ride in the National was a childhood dream come true.

'He wasn't a brilliant jumper but, to be honest, I'd have ridden anything. It was great to be a part of such a big race; you've grown up as a kid dreaming of it and it was like a fairy tale to be riding.

'It's a big day, the one day of the year for many jockeys that they are propelled into the spotlight.'

Chatham fell at the twelfth, but it meant AP had savoured the thrill of soaring over Becher's Brook.

The day he finally won the National, on Don't Push It in 2010, 'is right up there' as one of his best racing days, not least because his long quest to win it had become newsworthy in itself. The story goes that Jonjo O'Neill tossed a coin when AP, asked to choose his ride, couldn't decide between Don't Push It and Can't Buy Time, but ask Jonjo now and he says with that twinkle in his eye, 'Well, perhaps it was a double-sided coin!'

In early years Don't Push It was such a poor feeder that he

seldom ran, until Jonjo put a sheep with him. It sparked his competitive spirit, because the horse didn't want to be beaten to the feed by a sheep.

As a youngster, after an initial third in a bumper, Don't Push It won five of his next six races, a mix of bumpers, novice hurdles and novice chases – and in the other he was beaten three quarters of a length by a future Gold Cup winner called Denman.

On 10 April 2010, the full complement of forty horses set out on good ground, with Don't Push It and Big Fella Thanks 10-1 joint favourites.

It wasn't until halfway through the race that Don't Push It's name was mentioned by the race commentators, even though he was well up with the pace throughout. Black Apalachi was one of the leaders and ran a cracking race for Denis O'Regan and trainer, the late Dessie Hughes.

Don't Push It moved into fourth place on the heels of the leaders at the second Valentine's, but made a mistake at the next. Recovering quickly, he stalked Hello Bud, Big Fella Thanks and Black Apalachi, and the four of them drew clear of the rest, resulting in the great sight of four in line abreast at the last fence. From there it was Don't Push It just holding the renewed effort of the brave Black Apalachi. After the elbow, AP peeped over his right shoulder, saw he was clear and galloped to a five-length victory.

He told the press afterwards, 'I'm delighted for JP as he's the best supporter this game has ever had and ever will have, and I'm very privileged to ride a Grand National winner in his colours.'

He says now, 'There was a lot of satisfaction, but also a lot of relief.'

It also showed 'the power and scale of the National', because it led to other things, such as winning the BBC Sports Personality of the Year award.

His last Grand National ride was on Shutthefrontdoor in 2015.

'It was a great last ride and for a long time I thought we'd win.

'Ah well,' he adds a little wistfully, 'you can't have everything. But it would have been a fairy-tale ending.'

The horse ran a cracking race but couldn't quite stay the distance, as up front Many Clouds held off Saint Are. Shutthe-frontdoor finished a not-disgraced fifth.

Four years after retiring, AP still hungers for the thrill that can be no more.

'People keep telling me something will come along, but that something else will never be the same, because there's nothing like performing on a big stage.'

Is retirement tough? One detects a tremor again as he speaks. 'You just have to get on with it and accept it. I miss the routine, the structure, the discipline, even the danger – and the winning.

'There is nothing like going out in front of seventy thousand people at the Cheltenham Festival. It's a big stage; I watch it now and think I could still do it, but you just have to accept it [retirement].'

He keeps busy; he rides out from his point-to-point yard every morning that he's home; he does advertising shoots for former sponsors like William Hill and Albert Bartlett; he's contracted for sixteen days a year with ITV Racing, and he acts as an advisor to his former boss and sound friend, J.P. McManus.

Retirement, he admits, is a reality check. 'I'm lucky to have a great life and the children, Eve and Archie, they keep you alive and in reality.'

There was no prouder family than AP's at various milestones in his life: his 3,000th winner at Plumpton in February 2009, and his 4,000th at Towcester in November 2013, celebrated later that night in the Sporting Chance at Manton, near Marlborough. Both his children were present for his final day of riding, at Sandown in April 2015, and again in June 2016 when he was knighted at Buckingham Palace.

Richard Johnson

Richard Johnson has an exemplary record as a jockey – claiming the champion jockey title in 2015–16, 2016–17, 2017–18 and 2018–19 after finishing runner-up no fewer than sixteen times to A.P. McCoy during his great rival's twenty years at the top. He has ridden a century of winners in a season twenty-two times consecutively and topped two hundred in 2018–19. He is one of only three jockeys to win the big four at Cheltenham (along with AP and Barry Geraghty), and to date only AP has ridden more winners – but when it comes to his actual rides in the Grand National, his record is unenviable, and one about which he is understandably reluctant to talk.

'It would be lovely to win it,' he says, 'but I've had horrendous luck, the worst record.'

He is in good company: previous champion jockeys never to have won the Grand National include John Francome and Peter Scudamore, while Jonjo O'Neill, one of the sport's best and bravest, never even got round in eight attempts! And it took A.P. McCoy fifteen rides in the Grand National before he won on Don't Push It. Luck certainly plays a part – that lottery tag that makes the National unique, and it can work the other way round, as the late Brian Fletcher would have agreed: from nine rides he won it three times, was second twice, and even in the year he was 'jocked off' Red Rum, he came third on Eyecatcher.

Like Michael Scudamore before him, previous holder of most consecutive rides in the National (sixteen), Richard Johnson hails from a Herefordshire farming family; today, his father Keith and brother Nick carry on that tradition. As a small boy, Richard remembers his father digging out the first baby potatoes, and then, come harvest, of twenty tons being driven away.

But it was a pony called Tasty that set his mouth watering for racing; a love of speed, of jumping, and a desire to become a jockey. It was part of his DNA, with his father having ridden as an amateur, and his mother, Sue, holding a training licence. He started in the local point-to-points and as an amateur under Rules, riding his first winner on the track at his local course Hereford on Rusty Bridge in April 1994. Richard, aged sixteen, and the seven-year-old, trained by his mother and owned by his father, went off at 25-1 for the three-mile-one-furlong hunter chase, winning by a head.

Rusty Bridge was a true stalwart for the yard, and a great horse for amateurs to learn on, for he ran a total of eighty-seven times, winning three point-to-points and five hunter chases, and placing second or third thirty-two times under Rules. Richard rode him eighteen times, winning on him twice more and placing eleven times – there could have been no better schoolmaster.

Richard moved on to David 'The Duke' Nicholson's yard at Stow-on-the-Wold as a conditional jockey and his learning continued on an upward curve, ending the 1995–96 season as champion conditional, the year after Tony McCoy, the man who was to become his nemesis over the next two decades. When David Nicholson retired, Richard stayed on at the yard under Alan King, and then worked for Henry Daly before moving to Philip Hobbs, 'a very good man to ride and work for', for seventeen years and counting.

Richard's first ride in the Grand National was 1997, the year it was postponed for two days after the course was evacuated because of a bomb scare. Imagine the anticlimax: dressed in the silks for your first ride in the great race, only to have to leave the course wearing them. Two days later, Richard was enjoying a good ride on Celtic Abbey only for it to end at the Chair. 'I fell off,' says Richard simply. A.P. McCoy missed the National that year for the only time in his career, through injury.

In 1998 Richard Johnson's ride Banjo was not unfancied at 14-1 but he fell at the first fence, along with four others including AP on Challenger Du Luc, in the race won by Earth Summit.

In 1999, AP's mount, the seven-year-old Eudipe, fell fatally at the second Becher's, while Richard's mount, Baronet, fell at the fourth. Would a change of century bring either man better luck?

In 2000, A.P. McCoy was on Dark Stranger, the favourite, but they parted company at the third; Richard Johnson's mount Star Traveller, trained by Henry Daly, certainly had the credentials, having been out of the first three only once in his previous eleven staying chases, and he was sent off 10-1 second favourite. It all looked possible, too, leading or disputing the lead for much of the way and giving Richard a dream ride. But he hit the twenty-fifth hard and went lame, resulting in Richard quickly pulling him up. The race was won by Papillon and Ruby Walsh.

The following year, 2001, was memorable for the ground being seriously heavy; Richard Johnson's mount, Edmond, had won the Welsh Grand National on heavy ground and was accordingly favourite. The pair were having a super spin, but going into the Chair they were squeezed for room, 'got it wrong' and fell. Only two horses managed clear rounds: the winner Red Marauder, masterfully ridden by Richard Guest, and Smarty. When Tony McCoy saw only two remained in the race, he remounted* Blowing Wind; Ruby Walsh followed suit on Papillon, and they finished third and fourth.

Hopes were high in 2002 when Richard Johnson had the ride on What's Up Boys, whose last run had been in the Cheltenham Gold Cup and whose season had begun by winning the Hennessy Gold Cup at Newbury. The Grand National nearly started with five joint favourites at 10-1, but in the end A.P. McCoy on last year's remounted third, Blowing Wind, was sent off 8-1 favourite. Once-a-year punters often had their flutter on AP, but even more so for any grey horse and one of those was What's Up Boys, an eight-year-old trained by Richard Johnson's principal trainer, Philip Hobbs.

* A practice no longer allowed.

Nine horses fell at the first fence but What's Up Boys, hampered at the seventh (the first Foinavon), otherwise put in a clear round, and as the race drew towards its climax the first grey to win since Nicolaus Silver in 1961 looked almost certain.

Richard brought his mount through to contest the lead with long-time leader Bindaree at the second last, and the pair jumped the final fence together. Then Richard and his grey partner, carrying 11 stone 6 pounds, seemingly cruised past him and took a three-length advantage. At last, Richard looked like winning the Grand National. On reaching the elbow, Jim Culloty switched Bindaree to the rail. As they neared the finish, with Richard believing the race was about to be his, Bindaree, carrying only 10 stone 4 pounds, found new legs. As What's Up Boys hung right just before the line, it was Bindaree and three-time Gold Cup (on Best Mate) winning jockey Jim Culloty from County Kerry that hit the front. It is unusual for the leader in a staying chase to get up to win after surrendering the lead at or after the last fence (Dawn Run memorably achieved that in the galvanising hands of Jonjo O'Neill in the 1986 Gold Cup).

Richard Johnson recalls his defeat with characteristic understatement, 'It was not a great feeling,' adding that What's Up Boys ran really well. Remarkably, it was the first time Richard Johnson had completed the course.

Next behind Richard was A.P. McCoy, some twenty-seven lengths back, carrying a full stone less than his rival.

Victory in 2003 went to Ireland via Monty's Pass for Cork trainer Jimmy Mangan and rider Barry Geraghty. Richard's mount, Behrajan, for trainer Henry Daly, pecked at the first fence and made a number of other errors but came in tenth – so he had got round again. AP was on the seven-year-old 8-1 shot Iris Bleu, but the horse made several bad jumping errors and after blundering at the Chair he was pulled up.

Richard was back with What's Up Boys for 2004; the horse knew the course and had been second two years previously, but this time Richard was among the nine whose dreams ended at the sixth fence, Becher's Brook, first time round. (AP had already fallen at the fourth with Jurancon II.) It was Amberleigh House who got the better of a three-horse battle for glory – and an incredible fourth win for trainer Ginger McCain three decades on from the mighty Red Rum.

The form book summary for Richard's 2005 ride on Jakari for Henry Daly says it all: '. . . mistake first, behind sixth, pulled up when tailed off before 20th'. Not a performance to remember. Often, a jockey will say he knows his fate within the first few fences: a horse either takes to the unique Aintree track or it doesn't. The French-bred Jakari clearly didn't; though he managed to win five chases in his career, he found his métier in point-to-points as an eleven-year-old when he won three and placed in his other three.

As for AP, in 2005 he was certain he was winning. His mount, Clan Royal, was running a great race and went into the second Becher's just behind the leaders when, from his right, a loose horse veered left across him and in one swift blow wiped him out of the race. AP was gutted. He told trainer Jonjo O'Neill that it was a disaster.

'No,' Jonjo replied calmly, 'disaster is when you're lying in hospital waiting for the doctor to come and tell you whether you are going to live or die.' He had been in that position and knew.

That put it into perspective for AP, who told the new ITV Racing team in a feature about Jonjo in January 2017, 'that made me change from then on'.

The newly built and re-sited winner's enclosure was in use for the 2006 meeting, but Richard Johnson still came nowhere close to entering it. He was on the shortest-priced of Martin Pipe's five runners, Therealbandit, at 50-1! A mistake at the water may have put paid to his chances, and they pulled up after the twenty-sixth fence. Up front, joint favourites Hedgehunter (Ruby Walsh), the 2005 winner, and the previously unlucky Clan Royal

(A.P. McCoy) finished second and third behind Irish-trained Numbersixvalverde.

So the first eight of Richard's Grand National rides can be summarised: UR, F, F, PU, F, 2, 0, BD, PU, PU.* Like his friend and rival A.P. McCoy, he was beginning to wonder if he would ever make it into that hallowed winner's enclosure.

Which brings us to 2007, but ask Richard about his ride that year, Monkerhostin, and he says baldly, 'He had no chance.' Yet he was sent off at 8-1 co-favourite of three! But to say he was not a horse to take to Aintree is putting it mildly – by Foinavon, the seventh and smallest fence on the course, he said no more and refused. AP got round in tenth place on L'Ami.

The next two years brought falls for Richard. In 2008 Turko was only a six-year-old (seven is now the minimum age) but he got as far as the twenty-fifth, Valentine's Brook, where he fell. The following year, Parson's Legacy fell at Becher's second time round.

In 2008 AP was in the leading bunch with Butler's Cabin when they fell at the second Becher's, leaving victory to Comply Or Die. In 2009, he was reunited with Butler's Cabin and got round to finish seventh.

So, we're a decade into the new century – and as we have seen, a great result for Tony McCoy, Jonjo O'Neill and J.P. McManus with their horse Don't Push It. Richard Johnson finished ninth on Tricky Trickster, replacing Barry Geraghty, who in turn replaced the injured Ruby Walsh on the joint favourite, Big Fella Thanks, and finished fourth.

In 2011 Quinz did not jump all that well, broke a blood vessel and Richard Johnson pulled him up after the Chair. AP was reunited with Don't Push It, but try as he might, he had no answer for the impressive Ballabriggs who recorded a second victory for Trevor Hemmings; he was trained by Ginger McCain's son,

* UR = Unseated, F = Fell, PU = Pulled Up, BD = Brought Down.

Donald, and ridden by Jason Maguire. In second was Aintree specialist amateur Sam Waley-Cohen on Oscar Time, with Don't Push It third.

For AP, 2012 brought the devastating loss of Synchronised, already described. Richard Johnson, meanwhile, finished twelfth on Planet Of Sound, who gave him an eye-catching ride before fading at the end. History was being recorded up front when Neptune Collonges won by the narrowest margin (see Chapter 3) and became the first grey to win since 1961, and when Katie Walsh, in third, became the first female jockey to place in the race.

Balthazar King, a neat little horse by King's Theatre, who became a people's favourite, was not unfancied in 2013 when he made most of the running up until the first Foinavon fence; he then took the lead again after the water but was headed two fences later, hit the twentieth when weakening and faded into fifteenth place. Colbert Station and AP parted company at the fifteenth, the Chair.

The next two renewals gave Richard Johnson both his best and worst Nationals. In 2014 he nursed Balthazar King round towards the outer and, largely missed by the race commentators, just kept creeping nearer and nearer. By four out he was on the heels of the leaders and at the last only Pineau De Re was ahead of him; Richard felt his moment had come at last.

'I hoped he was going to win,' he recalls. But his gallant partner could not claw back the winner.

Behind him in third came AP on Double Seven, trained for J.P. McManus by Martin Brassil, who trained the 2006 winner Numbersixvalverde. So it was the second time the rivals had finished second and third in the race.

Naturally, Richard Johnson's hopes were really high for 2015. As so often before, for his last ride in the National punters' favourite AP went off favourite on Shutthefrontdoor, while Balthazar King was third favourite.

Little Balthazar King looked to be going fine but at the eighth fence, the Canal Turn, he took one of those horrible, crashing, heart-stopping falls that are awful to witness. As he sprawled along the ground a horse behind – Ballycasey, ridden by Ruby Walsh – had no way to avoid him, landed on top of his prostrate body and was brought down. While his horse galloped on loose, Ruby Walsh got to his feet, but both Balthazar King and Richard Johnson lay injured on the ground. The green screens were quickly erected around them, and with so many attendants seeing to both casualties, Ruby volunteered to join an official as one of two men to run to the front of the fence with a black and white chequered flag to wave the runners round it as they galloped towards the obstacle on the final circuit.

'Yes, it was my worst National,' Richard recalls ruefully. He was severely bruised and sore for a few days, but for his mount it was touch and go. He had had at least one rib broken and a punctured lung, and he spent six weeks in intensive care at the University of Liverpool Equine Centre. The public took the warrior to their hearts as he fought for his life, sending many cards and titbits.

Eleven months later, fully recovered and raring to go, he contested a cross-country race at Cheltenham, where before his Aintree fall he had won four similar events and another two in France, but he fell again and was immediately retired.

Today, he spends his retirement trail hunting in Wiltshire for Izzy Beckett, wife of Classic-winning flat trainer Ralph. The only tell-tale sign of his 2015 fall is a dip in his side due to muscle wastage from the broken rib.

In 2016, with AP now retired, Richard Johnson got as far as the fourth last fence on 33-1 chance Kruzhlinin, but was well tailed off and pulled up. He was without a ride for 2017 and 2018 (nothing good enough was on offer), and in 2019 he was brought down on Rock The Kasbah.

'You can't do it without the horse,' he says – but he hasn't given up hope of filling that one gap in his hugely impressive CV. Another remaining ambition: to beat A.P. McCoy's 'unbeatable' career tally of 4,358. With Richard on just over 3,620 at the end of the 2018–19 season – he notched his 3,500th winner in September 2018 – and aged forty-two, it is still within the realms of possibility. He has the understanding and support of his wife, Fiona, and children in his quest.

In December 2018, Richard was awarded an OBE in the Queen's New Year's Honours list for services to horse racing. It was an immensely popular reward within racing and a surprise to the jockey when he opened the letter informing him.

'It's a massive honour,' he said. 'Racing has been my whole life . . . I've been very fortunate to have a fantastic career and I'm lucky to be honoured for something I love doing.'

Philip Hobbs praised him as the complete role model: 'He's so reliable and there's no side to him at all.'

The same is true of A.P. McCoy. The two friends and lifelong rivals have been, and continue to be, excellent ambassadors and a huge credit to the great sport of steeplechasing, never more so than in the Grand National.

The National itself was the winner in 1997 when the human players responded to an unforeseen threat in defiant manner.

24

Lord Gyllene

The bomb scare National, 1997

Owners chatted in nervous, excited huddles as their horses paraded in the build-up to the 1997 Grand National. In one group, Staffordshire-born Stan Clarke was looking forward to his first runner; in another, unrelated Irishman Frank Clarke was anticipating his. In all, forty horses were parading and the jockeys were about to be called out to join their connections, to receive their instructions, mount and set off for the most keenly anticipated race in the jumping calendar worldwide. Suddenly, a posse of policemen walked towards them. Owner Frank Clarke's first thought was 'What have we done wrong?'

Then a Dublin barrister, now Chief Justice of Ireland, Frank Clarke had dreamt of having a runner ever since his first visit to the race while in his last year of studying for the Bar – 1973, the year of Crisp and Red Rum.

'There was no chance after that of my enthusiasm for the race dissipating.'

Twenty-four years later, he finally had a runner, Back Bar, jointly owned with Stephen Lanigan-O'Keeffe and fellow barrister Patrick McCarthy, and trained by Arthur Moore. And now they were being told they must all leave the course: there had been a viable coded IRA bomb threat.

As thousands of people wended their way towards the car parks, the atmosphere was one of perplexity mixed with confidence that any delay would be short and then the big race would be off. Then came another announcement: the car parks were declared out of bounds; everyone was to evacuate the course immediately. There was to be no pausing to collect bags, keys, coats, or anything they may have put elsewhere. In their hundreds, racegoers abandoned the Canal Turn area and the stands, heading for gates onto the public highway, most of them walking as if in a trance.

Meanwhile the BBC team, headed by Des Lynam, kept up a running commentary, interviewing well-known personalities.

Up until the preliminaries of the big race itself everything had been going to plan. Then Jim McGrath noted a lorry with flashing lights. 'Security is always tight here,' he told viewers. And it was true, with a police helicopter, 500 police officers and private security staff forming part of the core team.

As announcements could be heard in the background warning people to get as far away as possible from the stands, Jim McGrath kept up his commentary: 'This has caused chaos and a delay to the Grand National.'

Mounted police were ushering people away and, with largely good-humoured co-operation from the crowds, they cleared the stands. BBC cameras captured the desolate scene.

Des Lynam reappeared on screen again, interviewing some of the jockeys.

Jamie Osborne said, 'We were about to put our hats on,' adding, 'it turns the fiasco of three years ago* into insignificance'.

Richard Dunwoody agreed, adding, 'So long as everyone is safe, that's the main thing.'

At this stage it was widely assumed that a hoax would be declared and everything would soon return to normal.

Jamie Osborne said, 'It's going to take a long time to get back, so long as there's daylight.'

Julian Wilson reminded viewers that it had happened at the

---

* The void Grand National, actually four years previously.

Irish Derby on the Curragh once, but the race went ahead. 'We can only hope.'

Richard Pitman noticed that many people had been climbing over fences to get out, causing damage that would need to be repaired before the race could be run.

Peter Scudamore said, 'I feel sorry for the horses; it's all very, very sad. People don't know where anything is, especially families split up.'

Toby Balding, twice the winning trainer, had three runners for races after the National. 'Horses are not as easy to move as crowds.'

The inimitable Jenny Pitman came on and described the scenes in the stable yard.

'We have had to leave our horses – it's a disgusting act, don't tell me these people love animals, horses. Let them run, we cannot be held to ransom, we cannot give in to them.'

At this point, Chief Executive of Aintree Charles Barnett said complete evacuation was required.

'Everyone, including you [directed at Des Lynam], must leave and get out on to the highway. There will be no racing today, it's rather a sad day. The police are taking this very seriously indeed.'

In due course it was announced that the race would be re-scheduled for 5 p.m. on Monday, two days later. All bets would stand, but those on non-runners, of which there were two, would be returned.

The Tannoy system was inaudible because the speakers were all facing the wrong way; eventually a police helicopter equipped with loudspeakers began issuing instructions. The crowds, who had left the stands in stoic good humour and orderliness, were beginning to get frustrated, angry and cold as it began raining – and many were desperate for toilet facilities.

Once the message to evacuate had sunk in, Frank Clarke and the rest of his coachload of Irish visitors were at an advantage: while thousands of spectators, officials, jockeys, trainers and owners were denied access to their cars or coaches in the various car parks (some seven thousand vehicles were to be individually inspected), they could go straight to their coach. This was because Walter Greacen of Leopardstown Tours always parked the coach for his Irish clients outside the course ready for a quick getaway to the airport – not that he would ever have envisaged the advantage it was about to give them now.

So, while jockeys still in their silks – no coats, no kitbags, and certainly no vehicles – along with similarly deprived members of the public, searched for somewhere to stay overnight, Frank Clarke and the rest of Walter Greacen's clients were already sitting in front of their Irish televisions for the *Nine O'Clock News* and watching the scenes unfold in Liverpool.

At the other end of the scale, family and friends of Stan Clarke were not just stuck, in spite of having three helicopters there, they were also split up; in particular, his daughter Jane Gerard-Pearse had become separated from her five-month-old baby, Emily.

The family were all excited to have a runner but their main hope was that he would run well and that he would come home safe. They had enjoyed a sumptuous lunch in a private box then some of them had gone down to the parade ring; the baby girl had been left asleep in the care of a friend.

In the evacuation that followed, Jane was not allowed back into the stand to collect her baby – and then she got separated from her husband, Mike, too. Their special day had turned into a nightmare. Luckily, once she had phoned home, Jane learned that her baby and some of the others had managed to get out in one of the helicopters; the remaining craft had been despatched to Liverpool Airport, and eventually the couple, separately, made their way home.

As soon as they were allowed to leave, most of the horses travelled back to their stables, while others were moved to Haydock

Park racecourse stables. About a dozen remained in the stables at Aintree overnight, under the overall care of stable manager Derek Thompson.

Stories of how the people of Liverpool opened their doors and took in stranded racegoers have become legendary. Many compared the atmosphere to the days of the London Blitz during the Second World War.

The Salvation Army began dispensing tea from a van, and many stranded racegoers were taken to Fazakerley High School and to Everton Park Sports Centre, where basic food such as baked beans was on offer, and blankets were provided for people to sleep on the floor, on benches, on chairs pushed together – wherever they could find a spot. Hotels, mostly already full, squeezed in as many more as they could. One couple even slept in the sauna cubicle at the Feathers Hotel. Some householders took in complete strangers and made them welcome. No one had any night clothes; the lucky ones were those who had coats with them.

A Methodist church was opened and its urn put on to boil water for tea. A family typical of many began by offering a couple of rooms but ended with people on every carpet and sofa; at one point the queue for their loo stretched down the stairs, through the garden and out to the road.

Before the total evacuation was announced and everyone had to be shepherded onto the public roads, thousands stood milling around near the course. A band of thirty-three Gurkhas in full uniform, including weapons, and bearing musical instruments, had been due to play before the big race. Now, they began playing and the crowds fell in behind them, like children following the Pied Piper, as they made their way along the Melling Road.

Finding accommodation for the Gurkhas was difficult as they were considered a security risk because of their weapons. Eventually, cold and bemused, they were taken to Chester Barracks for the night.

For many of the jockeys it was a night out at the Adelphi Hotel, scene of so many post-race antics in the past. In the words of Richard Dunwoody, the sight of jockeys on its famous dance floor still dressed in silks and breeches was 'a surreal, heart-warming, uplifting sight on a day of such unhappy dislocation'.

He remembers, 'I think I stayed with my girlfriend Emma Heanley in a hotel in the centre of Liverpool. We didn't have the mad night that some did, and I remember going to a Cheshire point-to-point on the Sunday.'

On Sunday, drivers were allowed to return for their cars, and the new race time for the next day was confirmed. It was to be free entry and a standalone event, the only race on the card. This happens every year in America for the Maryland Hunt Cup, a social event with picnics and parties and just the one outstanding race.

A crowd of ten thousand was expected for the re-run, but in a show of defiance and goodwill some twenty thousand people attended on the Monday evening. It was not the first time the race had been postponed. Back in 1858 the National was postponed for three days because of snow; it was won by legendary flat race jockey Fred Archer's father, William, on Little Charley.

In 1997, thirty-six horses stood their ground, the winners between them of 265 races (including one Gold Cup winner, Master Oats). Altogether, some nine jockeys put up overweight, having had their usual dietary routine interrupted. One of these was the previous year's winning rider Mick Fitzgerald; he was riding the favourite, Go Ballistic, who started at 7-1; the grey Suny Bay was 8-1; two were on 12-1 and four on 14-1, including Stan Clarke's Lord Gyllene, trained by Steve Brookshaw in Shropshire, and ridden by Tony Dobbin. Frank Clarke's Back Bar was out at 100-1.

So, at 5 p.m. on Monday, 7 April 1997, the runners circled at the start and formed a line. Peter O'Sullevan, commentating on the race for his fiftieth and last time, said, '. . . and it shouldn't be long now'. But the runners had to take a turn and line up again. 'That's it,' Peter O'Sullevan called, and the tapes went up on the delayed running of the Grand National.

It turned out to be one of the most impressive Nationals for decades. There were fancied horses taking part, but from the first fence it was Lord Gyllene's National, closely accompanied by Suny Bay.

Full Of Oats fell at the first for debut rider Jim Culloty (his turn would come five years later on Bindaree) but all the runners negotiated the first Becher's safely. The next, Foinavon's, saw Frank Clark's Back Bar brought down.

Very often an early front runner will fade, or not make that stamina-sapping, gruelling long run-in, but from a long way out the race was all Lord Gyllene's – although not without its heart-stopping moment: at the water, in front of the stands, a loose horse came very near to carrying him out. He had a superb rider in Tony Dobbin, a true horseman with a good head, who managed to straighten his gallant partner. He had done his homework in advance and had decided to make the running. The horse was obviously loving the Aintree experience. The pair were as one, jumping from fence to fence, and the big bay horse with the white star and snip had his ears pricked throughout; they saved lengths by cutting the corner at the Canal Turn.

Loose horses continued to run near him down the line of six fences to Becher's Brook, but there was no interference and he was beginning to leave Suny Bay behind. At Valentine's, Mick Fitzgerald, well back in the field, performed acrobatics to stay in the saddle on the favourite Go Ballistic, and four out Suny Bay's rider Jamie Osborne also made a brilliant recovery. But it was all about Lord Gyllene. Far from tiring, Peter O'Sullevan noted, 'He's jumping brilliantly, as if he had only just started the race . . .

'. . . And at the elbow Lord Gyllene is sprinting away – it's a fantastic performance of jumping, a terrific performance.'

By the winning post, Lord Gyllene had put twenty-five lengths between him and Suny Bay. The nine-year-old was the third New Zealand-bred winner, following Moifaa in 1904 and Seagram in 1991. Lord Gyllene only ran twice more, without success, following a break of nearly two years after his win. Seven of his thirteen UK chases were at Uttoxeter, the racecourse that was owned by Stan Clarke. Lord Gyllene died in 2016, aged twenty-eight. The 1997 Grand National became known as the Monday National, but it should have been called Lord Gyllene's.

A Staffordshire man through and through, and a long-time patron of Steve Brookshaw, Stan Clarke had humble beginnings but an aptitude for business and fair play. After being apprenticed as a plumber he went into business on his own. This eventually led to him building up a property empire and he also acquired several racecourses; whatever he bought, he improved. In the beginning of his horse-racing interest he trained a few point-to-pointers himself, and then went into breeding. In 1997, the year of his Grand National success, he bought Dunstall Hall, Staffordshire, along with 1,250 acres and set about restoring it. Dunstall Hall, near Burton-on-Trent, was where his mother had been in service as a child and where as a child himself he used to do a bit of poaching. The previous owner, Sir Robert Douglas, had given Stan his first major plumbing job.

Stan Clarke was a philanthropist and (like owner J.P. McManus) most of his gifts were given on condition that they were kept secret. He would share profits of a large deal among his staff. He was also an active fund-raiser for charities, and for Lichfield Cathedral. He was knighted in 2001, and served as High Sheriff of Staffordshire in 2003–04, but he died in 2004, aged seventy-one. He was a loss to much more than just the horse-racing world.

Northern Irishman Tony Dobbin, 'Dobbs', retired in 2008 having ridden more than twelve hundred winners, and is assistant trainer to his wife Rose in glorious rolling countryside not far from Alnwick in Northumberland.

Steve Brookshaw, part of a well-known Shropshire racing family, had held a full training licence for only two years before his success with Lord Gyllene. He was formerly a top point-to-point and amateur rider for some three decades; he rode in point-to-points from the age of fourteen (before it was raised two years for young men and reduced two years from eighteen for young women after the Sex Discrimination Act, thus creating an equal playing field). His father, Peter, won the Aintree Foxhunters and his uncle, Tim Brookshaw, was a professional jockey who was paralysed in a fall.

Apart from Lord Gyllene in the National, Steve Brookshaw also trained the winners of the Foxhunters and the Topham (twice) over the National fences.

Lord Gyllene was plagued by leg problems and only ran in thirteen races in his life, of which he won five and placed in five. He spent his retirement with his owner's family and died in December 2016 at the age of twenty-eight.

By contrast, Frank Clarke's horse, Back Bar, ran a total of sixty-four times during his long career. He may have been brought down in the 1997 National but he gave his connections a memorable weekend. A print of the legendary evacuation hangs in pride of place in Frank Clarke's Dublin chambers. Among the crowd in a pencil side drawing is a man with a coat and a boy beside him – the Hon Mr Justice Frank Clarke, Chief Justice of Ireland, believes it depicts him and his then ten-year-old son, Ben, now himself a member of the Bar.

'I led him sufficiently astray and now, aged thirty-two, he has been to the Grand National twenty-one times.'

Frank Clarke is currently an Irish steward at courses like Leopardstown, the Curragh and Fairyhouse. He is a man who loves his racing – and most of all the Grand National; 2019 was his forty-first visit in forty-five years. He may go into ownership again once he retires from being a judge, and will doubtless look for a National-type horse.

For the record, Back Bar's list of riders during his long career looks like a *Who's Who* of Irish jockeys, including Tony Martin who, as an amateur, rode him in the four-mile National Hunt Chase at Cheltenham; Tom Taaffe, Paul Carberry, Francis Woods, who rode the Strong Gale gelding to three wins in the 1995–96 season; A.P. McCoy, who was brought down on him in the Heineken Gold Cup at the Punchestown Festival; Richard Dunwoody, Barry Cash, Conor O'Dwyer and, after Back Bar was sold and moved to Ginger McCain, Timmy Murphy; and he ran a second time in the Grand National in 1999, this time at 200-1, ridden by another Irishman, Dean Gallagher, to finish fourteenth to Irish combination Bobbyjo. Back Bar's last few years were spent point-to-pointing right up until he was fifteen years old.

Probably the coolest and calmest person on Grand National day, outwardly at least, was Peter O'Sullevan – for a full fifty years.

25

Peter O'Sullevan and Peter Bromley

Legendary commentators

'And they're away – oh, and once again the tape has snagged, and it's a recall . . . It was caught round Richard Dunwoody's neck, the tape. And they've been recalled – but the majority don't realise that it is a recall! They're going down to jump the first, they're going to!'

Thus did Peter O'Sullevan convey the second false start to the void 1993 Grand National on a cold and windy day. Nine riders obeyed starter Ken Brown's recall flag; Richard Dunwoody was anyway incapacitated and could not have got away with the others. But thirty jockeys apparently did not see the assistant starter waving his recall flag.

Richard Dunwoody wasn't frightened by what happened to him – other horses stood on the tape so that it was soon flowing out behind Richard as he heard Jamie Osborne, who was on his outside and nearer a loudspeaker, call out, 'It's a false start.' But most of them had gone beyond recall.

'We tried to stop the others when they came round to the Chair with flags but most took no notice,' Richard Dunwoody recalls. 'The story goes that one Irish jockey said, "I think they want us to pull up," and the other replied, "I'm going too well," so on they both went.'

Peter Scudamore was one who did stop, along with a couple of others, and as they headed away on the second circuit so did a number more, but most continued to 'race'. Of those, three fell and one refused at the twentieth, another fell at the twenty-first, and one refused and another unseated at the twenty-fourth, leaving seven to complete. First past the post was Esha Ness ridden by John White and second was Cahervillahow with Charlie Swan in the saddle. Behind these two were Adrian Maguire on Romany King and Norman Williamson on The Committee.

Peter O'Sullevan continued to commentate but reminded viewers every so often that 'it's got to be a void race'. As the depleted field crossed the Melling Road for the last time with two fences left, a saddened O'Sullevan, who loved the Grand National, called it 'the greatest disaster in the history of the Grand National'.

Richard Dunwoody remembers some incongruous moments from the 'incredible' aftermath: Richard Pitman's normally neat trilby being squashed on his head like a pork pie; the enormous trench coat his horse's owner, Robert Waley-Cohen, put round Dunwoody's shoulders as they waited to see if the race would be re-started – 'the coat was about ten sizes too big for me' – and the general mayhem.

Incidentally, the runners in the 1857 National suffered no fewer than seven false starts; the race was eventually won by Emigrant and Captain Charles Boyce in pouring rain and heavy ground.

Twenty years before he retired, Peter O'Sullevan called home Red Rum to an unprecedented third Grand National victory: 'The crowd are willing him home now. The twelve-year-old Red Rum, being preceded only by loose horses, being chased by Churchtown Boy . . . they're coming to the elbow, there's a furlong now between Red Rum and his third Grand National triumph. And he's coming up to the line, to win it like a fresh horse in great style. It's hats off and a tremendous reception, you've never heard one like it at Liverpool. Red Rum wins the National.'

*

Peter O'Sullevan was rightly known as the Voice of Racing. It didn't happen by chance. He spent hours in preparation for any and all of the races that he was to call, learning the colours and the names of the horses that were to bear them, producing charts to have in front of him as an aide-memoire should he need it during a race. Back when he started, they were not allowed to give the betting odds on television, either before or after the race.

The 1997 National, which was to go down in history as the Monday – Lord Gyllene's – National, had begun with the unveiling of a bronze bust of Peter O'Sullevan, to mark the occasion of his fiftieth and final commentary that afternoon. He stood to one side, wearing his trademark fur hat, as Princess Anne drew back the cloth covering the likeness, sculpted by Angela Connor.

Viewers were shown pictures of Peter O'Sullevan's detailed notes and colours beside each entry in his racecard. He explained that two horses in the race, Turning Tricks and Gold Cup winner Master Oats, had virtually identical colours. He also revealed that there were ninety-eight steps up to his commentary box. His large, heavy binoculars had come off a German submarine, and they were placed in such a way that he didn't have to hold them up. He admitted that, once the race was over, he could then enjoy it retrospectively.

Asked what was the hardest part of commentating on the Grand National, he told viewers it was going down to the Chair and on to the water because that was 'not a long hop'.

'Next year,' he added, looking forward to his retirement, 'I will still have all of the adrenaline but none of the anxiety.'

Lord Daresbury (Peter Greenall), Chairman of Aintree, pointed out that in calling his fiftieth Grand National, Peter O'Sullevan would have covered one third of all the Grand Nationals in history.

Born in Northern Ireland, spending his early years in County Kerry before a permanent move to England, where he was educated, Peter O'Sullevan was blessed with one huge advantage in his commentating role: a naturally good voice. Its distinguished, mellifluous sound was instantly recognisable.

Sir Peter began his racing correspondence life for the Press Association in 1944, and two years later began broadcasting for the BBC. When the Grand National was first televised in 1960, in black and white, it was Sir Peter who called home Merryman II ridden by Gerry Scott. He also wrote for the *Daily Express* as chief horse-racing writer and tipster from 1950–86.

One of Sir Peter's finest accomplishments was when he called home his own horse, Attivo, to win the 1974 Daily Express Triumph Hurdle, the four-year-old hurdlers' crown at the Cheltenham Festival, with all the aplomb and calmness as if it had just been any other horse in the race: true professionalism.

Although Peter O'Sullevan is best remembered for his commentaries, he was also a perceptive and erudite writer; apart from his newspaper columns he wrote a number of books, including his acclaimed autobiography titled, appropriately, *Calling the Horses*. He also had good manners, high intelligence, a brilliant memory, a huge love of life – in particular horse racing and betting, never more so than on his own horses – and he was an extremely affable bon viveur with a great sense of humour.

Jimmy Fitzgerald, who trained for him in later years, recalls in *Coming to the Last*, a tribute book edited by Sean Magee, an occasion in London at which Sir Gordon Richards was guest of honour. A film was shown of Sir Gordon winning the 1953 Derby on Pinza; not only was this black and white but it was also silent. So up stands Peter O'Sullevan and, from memory and knowledge of the thirty horses, gave an impromptu, and perfect, commentary. It made hairs stand up on the backs of innumerable necks and the place erupted in applause at the end.

Jimmy Fitzgerald wrote, 'As an owner he's been wonderful. As a commentator he'll be irreplaceable.'

When he started out as an owner in the post-war years, Peter O'Sullevan had possessed a series of non-eye-catching horses, so moderate that any wins they did gain were likely to be in selling races.* However, as betting was part and parcel of his mien, no doubt they managed to earn him a bob or two.

All that was to change when two of Peter O'Sullevan's horses burst on to the racing scene with such success that they are remembered still: the colts Be Friendly and Attivo. Be Friendly, bought for 2,800 guineas at the Newmarket Sales, turned into one of the best sprinters, winning ten races at the top level in the late 1960s. Only a few years later, Attivo too won ten races; five on the flat, including the 1974 Chester Vase and Northumberland Plate, and five over hurdles, most memorably the 1974 Triumph Hurdle.

A full brother of Be Friendly was another chestnut Stay Friendly; he managed to win a seller on the flat, but failed when he tried hurdling and was given to Mike Pelly in Frant, East Sussex. He twice finished third in the Eridge Hunt race at Heathfield on him.

Valerie Frost, the racing secretary at the *Daily Express*, regularly rode out at Mike Pelly's in-laws', the Peates', stables, now subsumed into Tunbridge Wells. She described Sir Peter in *Coming to the Last* as a perfectionist who worked, 'and I mean worked', seven days a week, and as someone who hated coming into the Fleet Street office. Instead, he would dictate copy from a phone box; and he thought nothing of driving one thousand miles a week. But during that golden time he would throw excellent Fleet Street parties to celebrate a win, with personalised wine for all his guests.

---

* Sellers are generally the lowest class of horse race, and the winner is immediately put up for auction afterwards (the owner may bid for his own horse). These races are contested by horses who may have lost their way or become jaded, or who are simply slow; sometimes they are targeted by betting owners and trainers.

She recalled that during 'the salad days of the Be Friendly/ Attivo era' she would wear outfits of black and gold to go with his racing colours. She ended her piece in *Coming to the Last*: 'Since the day I started working with the *Express* I have never been less than totally proud of working for him. Apart from "the voice", the figure and the clothes, he has an elusive charisma that makes him stand out in the crowd.'

On one occasion the phone rang in my kitchen and the instantly recognisable, inimitable voice of Sir Peter came on; scrambling for the nearest piece of paper to the corded telephone – probably a shopping list – I made notes as he generously spoke of his life for one of my books. It was the fact that he had rung me, following my initial letter (these days emails), rather than the other way round, that made it extra special.

Sir Peter O'Sullevan (he was knighted in 1997), a gentleman to the last, with a sharp brain and fully involved with his animal welfare charities, died in July 2017, aged ninety-seven.

In retirement, he had become almost as well known for his charitable work as he had been as a broadcaster. Animal charities had long been a favourite cause; he had been a supporter of the Brooke (believed to be the largest equine charity, founded in 1934, with its slogan 'action for working horses and donkeys') for a number of years. With the extra time that retirement brought, in 1998 he established the Voice of Racing: The Sir Peter O'Sullevan Charitable Trust; it supports six charities: Blue Cross, Brooke, Compassion in World Farming, World Horse Welfare, Racing Welfare and the British Thoroughbred Retraining Centre. In February 2019 the Trust announced it had now exceeded £9 million in donations to good causes. Apart from its six nominated charities, it also helps other, mainly equine, causes.

Nigel Payne is manager and administrator of the Trust; he was formerly Press Officer at Aintree, and also co-owned Earth Summit, the 1998 Grand National winner, and co-wrote *Everyone*

Must Leave, the story of the bomb scare National the previous year. He said the Trust had received sixty applications, all of which were carefully considered, before making their decisions. The Trust also agreed to continue its support for the hugely popular Lambourn Open Day held on Good Friday, the Retraining of Racehorses racecourse parades and the World Horse Welfare annual conference.

He added, 'Our aim is to decide whether Peter would have wanted to support the particular cause and then to ensure his name is used in perpetuity.'

One such enduring legacy will be the Injured Jockeys Fund Peter O'Sullevan House in Newmarket. The Injured Jockeys Fund came about as the result of the injuries leading to paralysis to jockeys Tim Brookshaw and four months later to Paddy Farrell in the 1964 Grand National.* It was the brainchild of John Oaksey, himself a leading amateur and horse-racing writer who rode in the National eleven times. The Fund has helped over a thousand jockeys and their families and has paid out more than £18 million in charitable assistance. One of its most popular fund-raisers is its annual sale of Christmas cards.

The Fund has a team of eight Almoners who liaise directly with beneficiaries on a support basis and also a team of thirty volunteer visitors who keep in touch with old and isolated beneficiaries offering friendship and company.

The IJF also works closely with racing authorities and other organisations on many initiatives such as funding on-course physios and medical services and research into improved riding protection equipment for jockeys.

It was fitting that John Oaksey opened the first IJF Rehabilitation and Fitness Centre, Oaksey House, in Lambourn in 2009,

---

* There have been casualties and fatalities since the National's early days. In 1862 in a small field of thirteen runners, jockey James Wynne was killed when his mount, O'Connell, fell at the Chair. Fifteen years earlier, Wynne's father, Denis, had won the race on Mathew.

where a life-size statue of him was also unveiled. In 2015 the IJF opened its second such facility, Jack Berry House in Malton for northern-based jockeys, named after the retired trainer who did so much to bring it about. And in the autumn of 2019 a third, the Peter O'Sullevan House, is due to open its doors in Newmarket, sharing the British Racing School premises where the IJF already has its offices.

In the words of Nigel Payne, 'This will be Peter's flagship.'

Peter Bromley

Peter Bromley became as well known to radio listeners for his racing commentaries as Peter O'Sullevan did to those on course, and also enjoyed a long innings: forty-one years from 1960 to 2001. He covered every Grand National in that time, his last one being in the atrocious conditions that saw Red Marauder plough through the mud to victory. In some pundits' books, the race should have been called off but, apart from the sodden turf providing a soft landing for fallers, it was also the year that the Cheltenham Festival had been lost to foot and mouth disease and officials, owners, trainers and jockeys were keen to get the show on the road.

Peter Bromley's early life was about much more than horse racing, although he gained a passion for it close to home. He grew up in Winchcombe, near Cheltenham, and one day he watched a race from beside a steeplechase fence and 'couldn't believe horses could jump fences at such speed. I went home, pulled up my leathers, practised and practised and from then on I was hooked.'

Other sports entered his life when, after National Service, he became a cavalry officer, and was such a good shot that he won the Bisley Cup for shooting in 1951, and in 1952 was short-listed to represent the country at Modern Pentathlon in the Helsinki

Olympic Games. He was posted to Catterick, where he often rode with the Bedale Hunt; and when he was posted south, he rode out for a local trainer and took part in a few point-to-points. He then served in Tripoli, but decided to resign his commission and come home. The night before, in high spirits, he was concussed after a fall in a bike race and so couldn't travel – the plane on which he was due to fly next day crashed . . .

Another accident off a horse at home nearly put paid to his future career and dashed his hopes of riding as an amateur at Cheltenham; he fractured his skull, was unconscious for two days and was sidelined for more than a year with clotting complications. It also left him partially deaf. It was during this time that he listened to Raymond Glendenning's race commentaries on BBC Radio and the seeds for his future were sown – along with a growing love of betting, at which he became semi-professional.

It was not until the 1950s that there was any racecourse commentary; this was pioneered by Goodwood. Before that, all races were run in silence. The Jockey Club did not agree with the idea of commentary, afraid that it could influence the judge and highlight malpractices publicly, and horse owners and trainers held that racegoers should be left to read the races for themselves. The reality was, without full sight of the course, and with no prior knowledge of how many runners there would be (there were no four-day or overnight declarations in those days), punters were at a disadvantage and it was in the stables' interest to keep them that way because prize money was low and they relied on betting to keep them afloat.

Although there was no on-course commentary there had been BBC radio commentary, on the Grand National at least, for some time. In 1952, the redoubtable Mirabel Topham, Queen Bee of Aintree, fell out with the BBC and decided her staff could do their own live commentary of the race. Try listening to the staccato voices, the stumbling efforts to identify horses – and calling the winner, Teal, a faller at the first fence.

Obstructed visibility is a commentator's nightmare, but Peter Bromley believed strongly that the public were entitled to good viewing, too. The most important thing, he told me back in the 1980s, was to have 'exceptional eyesight and the ability to *use* the eyes in conjunction with big, powerful binoculars'.

When he first had to wear glasses, he was afraid it would spell the end of his career; but the only problem came when they steamed up, at which point he would calmly wipe them while still commentating.

It can sometimes be fatal to take the eyes off the runners for even a split second, in bad light for instance, and then 'the most important thing is to eliminate panic, or the mind rats on you. I call it "relaxed tension": you have got to have the adrenaline and yet you also have to keep cool; your mind is checking, checking all the time.'

Peter Bromley's first racecourse commentaries were for southern tracks like Fontwell and Plumpton, the now-gone Folkestone, and the long-gone Wye for a fee of £20, and no travelling or other expenses. It was then suggested he join the television team as understudy to Peter O'Sullevan who, the powers-that-be thought, would retire before too long. Peter Bromley evidently possessed more clairvoyance than they did, deciding instead to stay with radio – and taking over from Raymond Glendenning for a long and accomplished radio career, remaining with the BBC throughout.

Television didn't lose him entirely, as he presented excellent features not only on Arkle, but also on the two Russian horses and riders who took part in the 1961 race won by Nicolaus Silver (neither Russian completed, one unseating and the other refusing, and both had to carry 12 stone, not having earned a handicap in Britain).

Thanks partly to Peter Bromley's urgings, the BBC racing radio broadcasts increased from fifty a year in the 1960s to more than two hundred and fifty two decades later. A bigger influence was

Contrasting luck: many champion jockeys have never won the National including Richard Johnson seen here with Edmund jumping perfectly – only to fall later on, resulting in his jockey seeking shelter under the fence. It took AP McCoy many attempts but here he celebrates as Don't Push It breaks his duck in 2010.

Left Trainer Jonjo O'Neill, AP McCoy, and owner JP McManus at the presentation.

Top A mounted policeman guides people out after a bombscare in 1997.

Above Lord Gyllene, outstanding winner of the postponed National, ridden by Tony Dobbin.

Two legends of broadcasting: *Top* The Voice of Racing Peter O'Sullevan: he completed fifty years of television commentary on the Grand National; and *above* Peter Bromley, who brought more than forty Grand Nationals to life for BBC radio listeners.

Opposite page The new century saw a resurgence of Irish winners, including Monty's Pass (Barry Geraghty) 2003, Hedgehunter (Ruby Walsh) 2005 and Silver Birch (Robbie Power) 2007.

This page There have been just five 100-1 winners of the National, including Caughoo in 1947, Foinavon in 1967, and Mon Mome in 2009.

In 2014 Leighton Aspell came back from retirement and won on Pineau De Re trained by Dr Richard Newland, beating Balthazaar King – and won again in 2015 on Many Clouds, trained by Oliver Sherwood, giving owner Trevor Hemmings his third win in the race.

Above The first Scottish-trained winner Rubstic, 1979, ridden by Maurice Barnes (centre).

Right The Two Golf Widows, Belinda McClung and Deborah Thomson, with their 2017 Scottish hero, One For Arthur.

Below One for Arthur's trainer Lucinda Russell with jockey Derek Fox.

Cooling water is poured over 2018 winner Tiger Roll by his jockey, Davy Russell. In 2019 Tiger Roll did it again, seen alongside the mare, Magic Of Light, who blundered at the last.

when he persuaded the 'Beeb' to put out a daily racing bulletin and this in due course became famous for 'Wogan's Wager' from Radio 2 presenter Terry Wogan.

His career took him abroad, too, giving race commentaries in France, Ireland, America, Hong Kong and South Africa.

Peter Bromley died from cancer at the age of seventy-four, only two years after giving his last radio broadcast of the 2001 Derby won by Galileo; he had called home 202 Classic races, missing only two St Legers in all that time, and more than ten thousand horse races in all.

Both Sir Peter O'Sullevan and Peter Bromley were masters of their craft, at the top of their respective games in racecourse commentary – and always with time for other people.

The Irish are traditionally as good with people as horses, and their turn in the limelight was to come, mainly with the commencement of a new century.

26

The Twenty-First-Century Irish Resurgence

Ever since three of their horses contested the first Grand National at Aintree in 1839, the Irish have had a love affair with the race. Approximately 50 per cent of winners have been bred in Ireland and more than half the jockeys riding in the race each year are Irish-born, and considerably more than that in the last twenty years. The Irish first won the race in 1847 with Mathew and followed with dual winner Abd El Kader, Wanderer, The Lamb, The Liberator and Empress. Still in the nineteenth century there were the Beasley winners and Wild Man From Borneo.

Ambush II set the twentieth century rolling for them with success in 1900, followed three years later by Drumcree. Troytown and Workman completed the pre-Second World War tally, and soon after, Caughoo added to the number.

Some may still recall Vincent O'Brien's famous three of the 1950s: Early Mist, Royal Tan and Quare Times. Mr What won for the Irish in 1958, by thirty-five lengths, but that's when their regular victories ended.

Mr What hailed from County Westmeath where his unraced dam, Duchess Of Pedulas, an £18 purchase, produced a string of winners; a filly out of her produced another Grand National winner in L'Escargot.

The story of Mr What's National rider, Arthur Freeman, is less happy, although it started well. Married to a glamorous debutante, Joanna Philipson, he had ridden for Peter Cazalet in the

1950s and won the King George on Loch Roe for him, in addition to the National on Mr What for trainer Tom Taaffe. Arthur Freeman was also godfather to Michael Scudamore, who won the National the year after Mr What on Oxo.

But in 1959, Arthur Freeman took a serious fall at Plumpton and hit his head, and his life began to collapse around him (there was no Injured Jockeys Fund then). Shortly after his second son, George, was born, his marriage ended, he went bankrupt, and the bailiffs moved in, taking all his possessions including his Grand National trophy. George was made a ward of court and first met his father when he was eighteen; a year later, Arthur Freeman died.

In 2019, George Freeman, MP for Mid-Norfolk, founded the charity Bridge of Hope 'to give everyone a second chance in life'; it is one of the beneficiaries of the Sir Peter O'Sullevan Charitable Trust.

A few years ago, alerted by Marcus Armytage that it was coming up for sale, George bought back his father's Grand National trophy, for double the reserve price.

'When the auctioneer announced who had bought it, the whole room cheered,' he says.

For the four decades that followed Mr What's 1958 win, almost all National winners were English-bred. The one Irish-trained winner during that period was L'Escargot in 1975. Trained by Dan Moore, L'Escargot was a dual Cheltenham Gold Cup winner (1971–72). His jockey for the National was Tommy Carberry.

Bobbyjo

It was Tommy Carberry who trained Bobbyjo to win in 1999, a victory made all the sweeter because the rider was his son, Paul, who had been making his mark as a jockey since 1990. Always a daredevil, he swung from the rafters that day as he dismounted, and he was to continue to light up the National Hunt scene until 2016 when injury forced his retirement. Paul was without doubt one of the finest horsemen-jockeys of his day. Never one to sit still in retirement, he embarked on a show-jumping career and by his second season had won a Grand Prix.

Bobbyjo was owned by a London publican, Bobby Burke, who had been born in Mount Bellew, and that is where Bobbyjo was buried. The small County Galway town also boasts a fine statue of their celebrated equine hero.

Bobbyjo was an easy horse to look after and to ride. Paul Carberry said, 'He would settle for you in a race and you could do anything you wanted with him.' In fact, he never once fell in his forty-eight-race career.

The year before his National win, Bobbyjo won the Irish Grand National, yet his weight allotted for the National was only 9 stone; as the minimum to run is 10 stone he was a full stone 'out of the handicap'. Blue Charm ran the race of his life, but once Bobbyjo took the lead after the last, Paul knew there would be no danger; he won by ten lengths.

So the Irish were back. Probably few realised it that day, but Bobbyjo's decisive victory had kick-started the Irish resurgence.

Papillon

Papillon followed in Bobbyjo's footsteps in the 2000 Grand National in which that gallant horse made it the second father–son result in a row, for trainer Ted Walsh and jockey Ruby. Owned by American heiress Betty Moran, the biggest obstacle the Walshes faced was to persuade her to allow her horse to take part. Eventually, having flown over from America and walked the course herself, she agreed to his participation.

Ruby Walsh had missed much of the season following a badly broken leg in a supporting race on the day of the Velká

Pardubická, the Czech Republic's 'Grand National', but Ruby rode round Aintree like the master he has remained, and had a talented partner in Papillon. They had been backed down from 33-1 to 10-1 on the morning of the race.

Together, they avoided many riderless horses and cruised into a handy position over the last few fences, and landed just in front over the last fence. From here Ruby was doggedly pursued by Norman Williamson on Mely Moss but prevailed by one and a quarter lengths.

Papillon was one of two to remount in the mud-soaked 2001 National to finish fourth; he missed the next season and ran lethargically when brought back for a hurdle race in 2003, after which he was retired to see out his days in the paddocks behind Ted and Helen Walsh's home in Kill, County Kildare.

Monty's Pass

Monty's Pass was failed by the vet as a four-year-old because he had a heart murmur. A decade on from his win in the 2003 National, his County Cork trainer Jimmy Mangan said, 'If ever a horse had the greatest heart it was Monty's Pass.'

Until Monty's Pass, Jimmy Mangan's principal modus operandi was in producing young horses and selling them on. Illustrating both the skill and the judgement he has, horses that were passed on once they had completed their education with him included 2002 Grand National winner Bindaree. Jimmy also foaled the 2004 winner Amberleigh House and his father, Patrick, had foaled the great mare Dawn Run. Jimmy Mangan hopes to produce another National winner one day.

From the start, Monty's Pass showed ability running in hunter chases and he was bought by the Dee Syndicate, comprised of four men from Northern Ireland led by bingo hall owner Mike

Futter. Crucially for Jimmy Mangan, the syndicate asked him to continue training Monty.

The bright bay by Montelimar soon repaid them, winning six handicap chases including the Kerry National at Listowel. He was also second in the Galway Plate, Ireland's premier summer chase, and second over the National fences in the Topham Chase from a field of twenty-eight runners.

This was enough to put the 2003 Grand National at the top of the agenda. He was kept going that summer and into the autumn, when he won the Kerry National, and then given a complete rest until the following March, only a month before the big one. His two prep runs over hurdles put him spot on for the National, for which he was allotted 10 stone 7 pounds. As usual, Barry Geraghty was booked for the ride (he rode him a total of twenty-seven times during Monty's career), and he was on a high, having ridden five winners at the Cheltenham Festival including the Queen Mother Champion Chase on Moscow Flyer. As members of his syndicate and others poured money on to him in the days before the race, Monty's price plummeted from 66-1 to 16-1.

The race went perfectly, and afterwards Barry Geraghty said, 'The ground was right, the sun was out, which he loves, and Jimmy Mangan had him spot on; everything fell into place and he gave me a dream ride, never putting a foot wrong.'

He was handy throughout, keeping out of trouble, jumped into the lead at the second last and stayed there, drawing clear to beat Supreme Glory by twelve lengths.

Amberleigh House, who was third, won the following year, when Monty's Pass, this time carrying a whopping 11 stone 8 pounds, was a gallant fourth; Hedgehunter fell at the last.

Monty's Pass ran in the National one more time. He managed to complete the course, but finished unplaced behind Hedge-hunter, after which he was retired and stayed with the Mangans.

Today, up to a dozen visitors a year still knock on Jimmy and Mary Mangan's door, asking to see him and to have their photographs taken with him. Monty's Pass is a healthy twenty-six years old and still pampered.

Hedgehunter

In the 2004 National, Hedgehunter – by Montelimar like Monty's Pass – made a gallant effort to make much of the running, jumping superbly until, clearly tiring, he fell at the last. He made amends in 2005. Far from being put off by his previous year's experience, he again rose to Aintree's unique challenge for rider Ruby Walsh and trainer Willie Mullins.

The talent wasn't quite so obvious as a young horse, when he was owned by ex-Irish Canadians Niall and Georgina Quaid: Hedgehunter finished second no fewer than nine times in his first twelve runs – he finally won on his tenth appearance – and by this time it was becoming expensive to keep on flying over from Canada to see him beaten yet again. So he was sold on to Trevor Hemmings and stayed with Willie Mullins for training.

Niall Quaid said later, 'If we had lived in Ireland we would not have sold him . . . I have tapes of all his races and never saw him give less than 100 per cent, he was honest and brave. Tears flowed as I saw Hedgehunter run them ragged at Aintree in 2005.'

Willie Mullins endorsed that view: 'Every time he jumps a fence, he's looking for the next one, and no matter what type of fence you put in front of him, he adapts to it.'

In the 2005 National a record thirty-two runners were still in the race after the first circuit. Hedgehunter was always in a handy position and when leader Clan Royal and Tony McCoy were knocked out of the race by a loose horse careering across them in front of Becher's the second time, he was left in the lead. From then on, he was always in command, and ran out an easy fourteen lengths winner over Royal Auclair.

It was owner Trevor Hemmings' first win in the National after trying with many different horses over the years; he was to win twice more in the next decade.

One year later, Hedgehunter followed a good second in the Cheltenham Gold Cup with another fine effort in the National, this time finishing runner-up to Numbersixvalverde carrying 11 pounds more than the year before, and giving 18 pounds to the winner. He ran in the National twice more, ninth behind Silver Birch and unplaced to Comply Or Die in 2008, after which he was retired to live out his days on his owner's Isle of Man estate.

Numbersixvalverde

Numbersixvalverde was named after owner Bernard Carroll's villa in Portugal. From the start, Carroll loved his new horse's outlook and step. His early career was surprisingly similar to Hedgehunter's: he finished second six times from eight runs before winning. His win in the Thyestes Chase once he began chasing finally put horse, trainer Martin Brassil and amateur teenage rider Niall 'Slippers' Madden on the map. He was entered for the Irish National, Martin Brassil's first runner in it; with Ruby Walsh in the saddle, he won that, too. The next year was geared to the Grand National and so, before the weights were out, he ran mostly in hurdle races. He was allotted 10 stone 8 pounds and, with Ruby naturally staying loyal to Hedgehunter, Niall Madden had the ride.

He couldn't wait. He had ridden his first winner just four years earlier at the age of sixteen and had turned professional at the end of the previous season when he was crowned champion amateur. The Grand National was to be his first ride in England. The horse had been schooled over an Aintree-type fence at Ted Walsh's and confidence began to mount. Niall's father, Niall 'Boots' Madden, had finished fifth in the race on Attitude Adjuster, so father and son walked the course together, watched videos, and

Boots imparted what advice he could to his twenty-year-old son, especially to 'hunt round on the first circuit'. Incidentally, Boots acquired his nickname as a youngster when his riding boots were too big; with his son also being called Niall, he became known as Slippers – and his younger brother, also a jockey, is known as Socks.

It was the first National for owner, trainer and jockey. Other winning debutants from all connections include Grittar for Dick Saunders and Frank Gilman; Rubstic for Maurice Barnes, John Leadbetter and John Douglas; and, strictly speaking, Jay Trump for Tommy Smith, Mary Stephenson and Fred Winter: Fred Winter had won the race twice as a jockey but this was his first National runner as a trainer.

For Numbersixvalverde the race went like a dream; he took to the course and jumped perfectly. Five horses fell at the first and, as planned, Slippers had his mount near the back on the first circuit. He then began to gain ground and as they turned for home six horses were left in contention. Between the last two fences, Numbersixvalverde swept into the lead past Hedgehunter and drew clear impressively on the run-in.

Bernard Carroll hugged the spectator next to him in the stands. He had given his owners'-stand tickets to his wife and two daughters and found himself on the public stands alongside four men from the Irish Midlands. As the horse was getting closer and closer to winning, he couldn't bear to watch, so his neighbour provided a running commentary for him. And when he won, he took the four men with him to the winner's enclosure; to the press conference; to the post-race party – and the following year invited them as his guests, complete with tickets and dinner the night before in a Manchester hotel.

Paddy 'Whitey' Quinn from Rhode in County Offaly said, 'We were treated like kings.'

One person who couldn't stay long at the post-race celebrations after Numbersixvalverde's 2006 victory was jockey Slippers

Madden because he was booked to ride the next day in Tramore, County Wexford – and he won there, too.

The victory did a lot of good for trainer Martin Brassil, who had once ridden in an amateurs' hurdle race on Grand National day. Within a year of the National victory, the stable's inmates had doubled to twenty-five, just as later happened for Pineau De Re's trainer Dr Newland.

Numbersixvalverde ran again the following year, carrying more weight, but was hampered at a crucial stage and did well to finish sixth.

Up front it was the turn of an even less experienced trainer . . .

Silver Birch

The winner of the 2007 Grand National was trained by twenty-nine-year-old Gordon Elliott, who had only received his full licence a few weeks before the race. He had yet to train a winner in his native Ireland but had notched two in Scotland and one in the West Country. His owner, Brian Walsh, was even younger, having made his fortune in the Celtic Tiger construction boom. The horse, a reject from one of England's largest yards, was bought at the sales for a modest sum; he had once been good enough to win a Becher Chase over the Aintree fences, and a Welsh National, but then missed a year through tendon trouble. When he returned to action in the 2006–07 season, he pulled up twice before falling at the Chair in the National. His next booking was to the sales.

Silver Birch went home to County Meath where rookie trainer and former amateur rider Gordon Elliott soon took him out hunting behind the Ward Union hounds. He found he had a horse who took to the big ditches and banks like a natural; rails, gates too, it was all the same to him. The small stable, change of scene and hunting worked wonders on him. He ran in a point-to-point in County Westmeath where he finished third of three finishers, and then concentrated on cross-country races, finishing second in two of them. His entry in the 2007 Grand National was intended as a prep for the La Touche, Ireland's premier banks race at the Punchestown Festival.

Gordon Elliott had at one time worked for Martin Pipe, for whom he rode one winner from six rides. Before that he learnt much from Tony Martin in County Meath, and originally with Martin Lynch, whose wife Suzanne taught him to ride. He also twice rode in the Maryland Hunt Cup over solid timber up to five feet high; in all, he rode some two hundred winners before a shoulder injury and rising weight saw him gaining a restricted training licence.

Owner Brian Walsh was always interested in racing, and with his windfall he bought a number of racehorses and also some twenty brood mares for both the flat and NH.

Gordon Elliott spent the night before the Grand National in the lads' hostel, before riding out on his charge early in the morning, along with other National hopefuls. He had hoped his mate Jason Maguire would take the ride but he was on another horse, and so he booked 'second string' Robbie Power, who would be having his second ride in the National. He was bred for riding: his father, Captain Con Power, represented Ireland in the show-jumping team that landed the Dublin showpiece, the Aga Khan Trophy, three times. (Robbie had himself won a silver medal for Ireland as a junior show-jumper.)

His horsemanship paid dividends as he rode Silver Birch in the National, always biding his time, establishing a rapport with his mount, and unafraid to take Becher's Brook on the inside where the drop was steeper. Two previous winners, Hedgehunter and Numbersixvalverde, ran again without troubling the judge at the finish. A mare, Liberthine, ran a cracker for Aintree amateur specialist Sam Waley-Cohen, as did Slim Pickings from Tom Taaffe's stable. He was leading into the last but that was where

Silver Birch, jumping magnificently, overtook him and headed up that long run-in. Slim Pickings kept trying and McKelvey came up with a fast, late run, but Silver Birch hung on for victory by three quarters of a length over McKelvey. Of these, only the Peter Bowen-trained McKelvey was at a shortish price, 12-1; the winner and Slim Pickings were both on 33-1, while fourth-placed Philson Run was 100-1 and the mare in fifth started at 40-1.

Today, that rookie trainer and emerging jockey are in their element. Robbie Power waited ten years before really hitting the big time again, but victories in the Cheltenham Gold Cup on Sizing John and the Irish National on Our Duke in 2017 led to him landing the role of retained jockey by owners Ann and Alan Potts Limited, who have many of their horses with Colin Tizzard in Dorset. (Mr and Mrs Potts both died in 2017 but their horses continue to run in their colours.)

As for Gordon Elliott: he now trains some two hundred horses, approximately seventy for Gigginstown House, in a modern, tailor-made and ever-growing establishment; and he has won virtually every major race there is, not least a second Grand National . . .

Rule The World

Ireland had to wait nine years until their next National win, but then it might so easily have been three, even four, in a row had not the owner of the 2016, 2018 and 2019 National winners withdrawn his best horses from the 2017 race in protest at the weights they had been allotted, believing they were unfavourably treated compared with the British horses. One of those withdrawn in 2017 was Tiger Roll, who won in 2018 and 2019. Could it have been three in a row (and four for the owners)?

No one could have deserved the 2016 win more than trainer Mouse Morris at his thirtieth attempt (double that of jockey A.P.

McCoy), but it was bitter-sweet. Less than a year before, he had lost his eldest son, Christopher, known as Tiffer, through that terrible silent killer carbon monoxide poisoning, at the age of thirty while travelling in Argentina. A chef, he was due to open a restaurant on his return. (Incidentally, I once, during a storm, woke up with a splitting headache; downstairs, my dog was unconscious – a fierce wind had forced the fumes back down the flue and into the room. The answer is to fit a carbon monoxide alarm.)

As if by divine intervention after Tiffer's death, Mouse Morris won the following Irish National with Rogue Angel and the Grand National with Rule The World.

Extraordinarily, before that the nine-year-old gelding Rule The World had never won over fences, and had been plagued by injury; he had twice fractured his pelvis. He was running in his fourteenth chase, and had placed eight times, including in Grade 1 company, and had been runner-up in the previous year's Irish National. He had also won five hurdles and, at the start of his career, a four-year-olds' maiden point-to-point in County Waterford.

His jockey in the National was the teenage David Mullins, having his first ride in the race. David, son of Tom Mullins, nephew of Willie and grandson of the splendid, hands-on ninety-year-old Mullins matriarch Maureen Mullins, was born to ride and showed a cool head at this young age, biding his time on Rule The World while up front two outsiders led from the joint favourites, The Last Samuri and Many Clouds.

Heading out on the final circuit, with a number having fallen and more pulling up before the second Becher's in the soft ground, Rule The World made steady progress, survived his only mistake four out, and approached the last fence in third place behind The Last Samuri and the thirteen-year-old veteran 100-1 shot Vics Canvas. It looked like being a close three-way finish as the trio were virtually level at the elbow, but then the maiden over fences Rule The World drew clear for a six-length victory from The Last Samuri and Vics Canvas.

Only Bruce Hobbs in 1938 has been younger than June-born David Mullins, although Pat Buckley was nineteen with a July birthday when he won on Ayala in 1963. The last novice chaser to win before Rule The World was Mr What in 1958. David Mullins kept a level head, not only in the race but also in the many post-race interviews. He said, 'That's the best ride I've ever got off a horse and it's the best feeling to come back into a place like this. It was just brilliant.'

Mouse Morris said, 'He's a class horse on his day, even though he was a maiden over fences coming into this. The last few weeks have been a bit like a Disney story. I just can't believe it. With half a mile to go I was going to be happy with third, but somebody was obviously looking down on us again.

'I didn't want to ask [Christopher] twice, having already won an Irish National. I thought we'd used up all our luck. But he must be an iron horse to win a Grand National after his injuries.

'He's fractured his pelvis twice. Before that I always thought he was the best horse I ever had, how good would he be with a proper rear end on him? [meaning his pelvis problems] He had a nice weight and he's a class horse on his day.'

After the National, Rule The World ran in a novice chase, as he was entitled to, and finished down the field in the Champion Novices Chase at Punchestown, and was then retired to Gigginstown House Stud in County Westmeath to graze and roam with other retired horses in the same ownership.

Gigginstown House Stud, at the time dominant as owners in Irish racing, is headed by Ryanair boss Michael O'Leary and his racing manager and brother Eddie, a bloodstock supremo when it comes to buying at the sales, and who is also owner of his own stud at Killucan, not far from Gigginstown in County Westmeath.

Perhaps surprisingly, this was only the second time Gigginstown had runners in the race, following Hear The Echo in 2009, and they fielded three: First Lieutenant and Sir Des Champs, who both fell, along with Rule The World. They had fourteen horses entered for the 2019 race, nine of whom were guaranteed a run should they be declared.

Rule The World's win came straight after Gigginstown won the Cheltenham Gold Cup with Don Cossack.

Michael O'Leary hailed Mouse Morris a genius of a trainer, and added that the young jockey had shown great maturity, had kept his cool and given the horse a masterful ride.

In 2017 Gigginstown fielded five runners for the great race in spite of having withdrawn a number in protest at the weights they were allotted, but they were a second XI: four failed to complete and the fifth was eighteenth of nineteen finishers. In 2018 they again started five, and three of these finished eighth, sixth – and first.

Tiger Roll

Tiger Roll is the sort of horse that it's easy to love. On the small side at 15.3 hh., but neat and well put together with a big white star, he has 'character' written all over him. He is also exceptionally talented: it is hard to imagine any other horse winning three such divergent Cheltenham Festival races as the JCB Triumph Hurdle (2014); the four-mile National Hunt Chase for amateur riders (2017); and the Glenfarclas Cross-Country Chase of 2018 – and a month later the Grand National at Aintree.

In the year that Authorised won the Derby, 2007, the Grand National was won by Silver Birch, trained by one Gordon Elliott. Wind the clock forward eleven years, and he trains another Grand National winner, Tiger Roll, whose sire is none other than Authorised. Back in 1863 and 1864 the full sisters Emblem and Emblematic were by the 1851 Derby winner, Teddington; the

1884 National winner, Voluptuary, had actually run in the Derby three years earlier, finishing sixth under Fred Archer. When he won the National as a six-year-old it was his first ever run in a steeplechase.

Tiger Roll was also bred for the flat, and was bought as a foal by Godolphin for 70,000 guineas but never ran; at almost three he was gelded, and sold to the astute Nigel Hawke for £10,000. Nigel won a Grand National himself on board Seagram in 1991; two years later in a modest selling hurdle race, he suffered a head injury so severe that his riding career was over; he was not allowed to drive a car for four years, but he turned his hand to training from his Devon farm with considerable success.

Tiger Roll won his one and only start for Nigel Hawke; it was a modest juvenile hurdle for three-year-olds at Market Rasen with a prize worth less than £4,000 to the winner. His price was 10-1, and he ran a bit green, like the novice he was, in the closing stages but won by three and three quarter lengths. It would not appear to have been either a world-shattering or an eye-catching performance, but he was promptly sold to Gigginstown House Stud for a reported £80,000.

In January 2014 he travelled over to begin a famed life in Gordon Elliott's County Meath yard. The next month he finished second at 16-1 to Guitar Pete in a Grade 1 juvenile hurdle in Leopardstown earning €14,800, and in March, on only the third run of his life, he won the Triumph Hurdle at 10-1, the championship race for four-year-olds at the Cheltenham Festival. In the hands of Davy Russell, he led approaching the last and drew clear on the run-in to earn £68,340 for his connections – just about his purchase price from his initial two runs for them.

Davy Russell, one of the most senior Irish jockeys after Ruby Walsh (they are a month apart in age), had been stable jockey for Gigginstown, but by this time he was a 'spare' rider for them, and apart from having the next ride on him, at Punchestown in 2014,

Davy Russell did not renew his acquaintance with Tiger Roll for almost four years, at the 2018 Grand National. By this time Tiger Roll, known as Tiger at home, was becoming a favourite of punters and press alike, following his Cheltenham Festival exploits. He had also won a Midlands National at his owner's local course, Kilbeggan, where Michael O'Leary sponsored the race. In the same year, 2016, Tiger Roll went on to win the Munster National at Limerick, and so he was proving an out-and-out stayer.

Tiger Roll's win at the 2017 Cheltenham Festival came at 16-1 in the National Hunt Chase for amateur riders – at four miles, twice the distance of his JCB Triumph Hurdle win three years earlier. He was ridden by Lisa O'Neill, the daughter of former Irish jockey and trainer Tommy O'Neill, and a stalwart of Gordon Elliott's yard for the previous five years, both with the horses and in the office.

'It keeps me quiet, and I love riding different horses every day,' she says.

At the start of her career, Lisa had ridden Vintage Fabric to win handicap hurdles for Nigel Hawke in Devon in June 2010 and again in April 2011, and in Ireland she won the Ladies Derby on the Curragh in July 2010. Her connection with Nigel Hawke, who sold Tiger Roll to Gigginstown via the sales, is purely coincidental: Lisa had been invited to take part in an Ireland v GB lady amateur riders handicap hurdle race; lots were drawn, and she drew the winning horse trained by Nigel.

It was only six months before her Cheltenham Festival victory that she had ridden her first chase winner after ninety-five attempts, in the 2016 Kerry National at Listowel, a race she was to win a second time in 2018, when she was also Ireland's leading lady rider with twenty wins. She remains amateur, and lost her claim by landing a double on the sands of Laytown beach in September 2018 for English trainer Jamie Osborne.

But Cheltenham was the cream – 'absolutely fabulous'. Lisa had survived several jumping mistakes from Tiger Roll, too.

Interestingly, his first three Cheltenham Festival wins, up to his first Cross-Country success four years after his Triumph Hurdle victory, fell on his actual birthday, 14 March (officially, all registered thoroughbreds have a 1 January birthday).

He was entered for the 2017 Grand National but was one of those to be pulled out immediately after the weights were announced.

It was different in 2018.

The race proved a thriller. Leading for much of the way was Pleasant Company; Milansbar and Double Ross were among those in a handy position, and Tiger Roll was bowling along in mid-division. He improved to be closing in on the second circuit until he cruised up to share the lead with Pleasant Company two out; approaching the last he was on a tight rein, and on that long run-in Tiger Roll drew so well clear that the result looked over, bar the shouting. But yet again that infamous stretch of turf nearly produced a turnaround. The tiger began to roll and David Mullins, victor in 2016, was drawing ever closer on Pleasant Company. Both jockeys, with nearly two decades of age separating them, rode brilliantly, but the Tiger had just enough left in his tank to win by a head in a photo finish. For Davy Russell, who hails from County Cork, it was victory at his fourteenth attempt; it came shortly after the death of his mother, and the birth of his fourth child.

Tiger Roll's win brought his total earnings to almost £802,000 – ten times the sum paid for him.

The main aim for 2019 was to win the Cheltenham Festival Cross-Country race again, but before that Tiger Roll gave notice of other ideas. In February, as a portly outsider at 25-1, he hacked up in the Grade 2 Boyne Hurdle in Navan, and was promptly installed as the new favourite for the Grand National. For good measure, he also cruised to the smoothest success in the Cheltenham Festival Glenfarclas Cross-Country race, winning by 'a country mile'.

After his Navan win, Gordon Elliott told the press, 'He's a special horse, he's a favourite around the yard and everyone loves him.'

His weekend lass is Louise Magee, mother of two sets of twin boys, aged eight and six. She was the one who travelled with Tiger Roll to Aintree, plaited his mane, polished his coat until the bright bay with black points shone, and oiled his hooves. At home, he is 'a sweetheart' who loves nothing more than treats and cuddles, and has an exceptionally calm demeanour, but come race day he grows in stature, looking more than his 15.3 hands, and begins to sweat and shake with anticipation and excitement.

His outstanding performance in 2019, when he became the first back-to-back winner for forty-five years, is told in the final chapter.

The only certainty about the Grand National is its uncertainty; occasionally the favourite will win: Tiger Roll in 2019 was just the eleventh favourite, along with three joint favourites, to win since 1900, and over the nearly two centuries of the race there have always been surprise winners, five of them at 100-1.

27

100-1 Winners

The Grand National has often been referred to as a lottery – and how apt that that was the name of the first winner – but there have only been five 100-1 winners of the Grand National throughout its history. At least two and probably three of those won on merit rather than luck but had 'fallen under the radar' with the press, and punters plunged on other horses.

In 1928 the tubed 'no-hoper' Tipperary Tim was a 100-1 rank outsider. This was followed a year later by Gregalach (see chapter 8), also on 100-1 in the mammoth field of sixty-six. The Irish horse Caughoo started at the same price in 1947, and twenty years later Foinavon's win after the famous melee, when only he managed to negotiate the twenty-third fence at the first attempt, was so extraordinary that the fence was named after him (see chapter 12). Forty-two years after that Mon Mome became the latest longest-priced winner when, like Gregalach and Caughoo, his obvious credentials had been largely ignored. Tipperary Tim and Foinavon should also, along with those three, be given credit for having negotiated the fences without falling.

Tipperary Tim

In 1928 the eight-year-old Easter Hero, on top weight of 12 stone 5 pounds, led the field jumping well until the Canal Turn, which in those days was an open ditch. He got no further, but landed straddled on top of the fence as the rest of the field bore down on him; only a handful got over safely, and by the second Becher's just five runners remained, and this had been reduced to two as Billy Barton (33-1) and Tipperary Tim approached the last fence. Here, Billy Barton fell (and remounted) leaving Tipperary Tim, owned by Mr Harold Kenyon and ridden by amateur and newly articled solicitor Mr Bill Parker Dutton, to a distance victory.

Caughoo

Rumour had it from the jockey of the runner-up in the 1947 Grand National, run in thick fog, that the 100-1 winner, Caughoo, had pulled up and then rejoined as a fresh horse to win; original photographs show indisputably that he jumped Becher's twice, completely repudiating the accusation.

The Big Freeze of 1946–47 meant that the Grand National would, most unusually, be run before Cheltenham, as the NH Festival had been postponed to April from mid-March. The Liverpool date was 29 March and, with owners and trainers doubtless as keen as the jockeys to get a run at last, fifty-seven horses were declared, the second biggest field ever in the National's history (after a field of sixty-six in 1929).

In 1947 there were without doubt a number of no-hopers; twenty-six started at 100-1, virtually half the field. After all, how could they be taken seriously against the all-conquering Prince Regent and a host of other horses with promise, including Sheila's Cottage who was to win the next year, and Silver Fame who was to win twenty-four races including a Cheltenham Gold Cup. Previous winner Bogskar (1940), now fourteen years old, was among those priced at 100-1. Others with fair credentials were also overlooked in such a large, competitive field, including Irish eight-year-old Caughoo.

This horse, trained on Sutton Strand, north of Dublin, had already won two Ulster Nationals round the switchback course of Downpatrick. That sandy coastline north of Dublin was a crucial factor in his Grand National success, as he was able to continue working while the majority of horses were confined to straw circles laid down in the snow.

Caughoo had been so useless in flat races, finishing unplaced every time, that his jockey, Morney Wing, advised his owner John McDowell to shoot him, but he was sent jumping and finished third in the Galway Hurdle. Chasing followed, and after he won the Ulster National of 1945 a good offer for him was turned down.

Caughoo enjoyed striding out on the beach, and he loved it at the end when, stripped of his saddle, he was allowed to roll, while 'lad' Ted Wright, who looked after him 'night and day', hung on to the reins.

After winning back-to-back Ulster Nationals in 1945 and 1946, the McDowell family debated whether to tackle the Grand National at Aintree or to bid for a hat-trick in Ulster. The brothers John and Herbert had faith in their horse and though small he might be, he had stature, so off to Aintree he travelled. He was supported by an anonymous eighty-three-year-old farmer from Ennis in County Clare who had such a vivid dream that he placed £30 on the horse. When Caughoo won he felt so guilty at having 'taken' £3,000 when he 'knew' the result in advance, that he sent £1,000 to the Pope to aid starving children.

It was the days before live TV broadcasts of the Grand National, let alone the internet – or all-weather gallops, for that matter. To see the race, you had to go to it, and so the crowds flocked in to Liverpool in spite of the miserable rain and fog. Spectators began arriving at daybreak and, travelling by whatever means they could in the pouring rain, they were soon said to be numbering 100,000 per hour; newspapers variously reported the crowd as being 300,000, 400,000, even half a million. There were 600 policemen and 30 patrol cars marshalling them on to the course; and a plane circled overhead issuing directions.

When Caughoo's jockey Eddie Dempsey arrived at the course, not only were the huge fences strange to him, but it was also the first time he had ever set foot in England. What's more, at thirty-five years old, he hadn't ridden a winner for three years. Nevertheless, he rode a remarkably cool, intelligent race. Nine horses travelled over from Ireland, including the favourite – of punters and the general public – Prince Regent, even though he was now twelve years old and set to shoulder 12 stone 7 pounds.

By the first Becher's half a dozen were riderless, and Caughoo was nearly one of them; he pitched on his nose over the first three fences but then got the hang of those unfamiliar obstacles and remained foot-perfect thereafter, one of those to adapt to and then relish the experience.

Caughoo was being given a patient ride by Eddie Dempsey and was among the second group, along with Prince Regent, as they literally disappeared into the fog and out into the country. Lough Conn, another Irish horse, led by ten lengths and by the time they reached Valentine's both Prince Regent and Caughoo were improving rapidly.

When the remaining runners re-emerged out of the mist, Lough Conn was hampered by a loose horse and it was Caughoo who swept into the lead. Very few of the hundreds of thousands of spectators could identify his green and blue colours as he put twenty lengths between him and Lough Conn at the line in the slowest time for twenty years. Kami overtook Prince Regent for the minor places, which meant that three unusually small horses had performed best in the atrocious underfoot conditions.

Caughoo came home to a splendid Irish reception with crowds lining the Quays and O'Connell Street, some climbing statues for a better view. The parade was led by the Emerald Girl Pipers Band and the James Stephens Pipers Band.

Caughoo ran in the 1948 Grand National but was pulled up early on.

The current McDowells have plenty of Caughoo memorabilia in their home overlooking the River Boyne in County Meath where they keep a few brood mares – and where they bred 1991 Cheltenham Gold Cup winner Garrison Savannah, who was second to Seagram in the 1991 Grand National.

Mon Mome

'I don't fuss, so Venetia doesn't worry' – words to make any trainer envious when it comes to engaging with owners; and all the more reason for the trainer to run that owner's horse as close to her home as possible. In this case that is a tiny hamlet in East Sussex; Plumpton is, not surprisingly, Mrs Vida Bingham's favourite course as well as being her nearest. The French-bred Mon Mome was also taken to other south-eastern tracks like Fontwell and the now defunct Folkestone, and placed several times over hurdles without winning. Chasing was to be his forte.

Mrs Bingham remembers her first win in February 2003 with her first horse, Heron's Ghyll, named after her home. It was at Hereford, trainer Venetia Williams' nearest course, and it looked like a dead-heat but her horse had hung on by a short head. Mrs Bingham, small of frame and stout of heart, was a former athlete and the owner of the runner-up was a man she was well acquainted with, Olympic runner and founder of the London Marathon, Chris Brasher; he died just a few days after this race.

Venetia's French agent, Guy Petit, sourced Mon Mome and Mrs Bingham was happy to purchase the bay gelding. Just six years later, in 2009, Vida Bingham found herself leading in Mon Mome, the winner of the world's most famous horse race, ridden by Liam Treadwell, trained of course by Venetia Williams, and looked after in the King's Caple, Herefordshire stable by Sarah McQueen.

Venetia Williams grew up in lovely Scorrier House, Cornwall, which is still the Williams' family home, and became an amateur rider, well-known in the point-to-point field riding a number of winners in the West Country, and won and placed in hunter chases. In 1988 she rode Marcolo in the Grand National. Unfortunately, the 200-1 shot fell at Becher's Brook first time round and Venetia was knocked out. On her next ride two weeks later, she suffered another fall and this time broke a bone in her neck. She called time, and set about learning the training craft by working for some of the best in Britain and around the world.

When Venetia Williams started training with just six horses in 1995, she soon showed she had what it takes. Within three years she had a favourite for the Cheltenham Gold Cup, Teeton Mill, who was on the back of eight almost straight wins interrupted by one second; his wins were of the highest class, including the Hennessy Gold Cup and the King George in 1998. Unfortunately, he pulled up lame in the 1999 Gold Cup.

The popular but tiny £400 purchase Lady Rebecca became a Cheltenham specialist, with seven of her thirteen wins coming at the Cotswolds course. At such an early stage Venetia Williams' embryonic training career was on a roll and she has been near the top of the UK training tree ever since, concentrating on the winter game. One only has to watch Venetia at work to recognise that it is an all-consuming passion, not just in the care and training of the hundred-plus horses, but also with her staff and her owners. She is invariably among the best-dressed exponents of her profession both at home and at the races, in breeches or at Cheltenham, and her grounds and stables are kept immaculately; young horses soon learn not to be afraid of peacocks flying up on to a walled garden beside them.

Of Mon Mome's early career, Vida Bingham says, 'He was

hopeless over hurdles but after falling early in his first chase he showed promise.'

In fact, the rest of his novice chase season was highly successful: second by a neck, followed by his first win; another second and two more wins, the last two at her local tracks of Plumpton and Fontwell.

She particularly remembers the Richard Davies memorial race at Worcester. 'Venetia never tells owners if a horse will or won't win, but when they were turned for home she suddenly said, "If Sam Thomas [his jockey] hurries him, I think he'll win this." They were beaten by a neck.'

He won next time at Plumpton, and then again, odds-on at Fontwell. Here, Venetia was bolder at the start. 'You know, I think he'll win this.'

Mrs Bingham habitually placed a £5 bet on any horse of hers, but admits, 'Now that inflation has taken place, I sometimes put on £10.'

At the conclusion of his successful novice chase season, Mon Mome took his chance in the Scottish Grand National, but unseated at the seventeenth fence. He then went through the 2006–07 season placing in the first four in all six runs but without winning. For 2007–08, he did not appear until February 2008, but staying was clearly his game and, although placed no better than third in his five runs, he tackled the Grand National for the first time, completing the course in tenth behind Comply Or Die, ridden by stable jockey Aidan Coleman.

'Tony McCoy and Butler's Cabin fell immediately in front of him and Mon Mome jumped over both him and the horse. Mon Mome always jumped the National fences well, he didn't find them difficult,' Mrs Bingham recalls.

The race left her full of hope for 2009, and after finishing unplaced in the 2008 Scottish National, that's what he was aimed at. 'But you never think you're going to win it, you're just hoping for a place.'

The season that was to end so gloriously went well from the start: a neck second in an established big-race trial, the Betfair handicap chase at Haydock; a Listed chase win at Cheltenham's December meeting; eighth in the Welsh National; and reverting to hurdles he finished a good second. Seventh in a Grade 3 at Haydock and a disappointing eighth in the Midlands Grand National followed, after which his jockey Sam Thomas told the owner that wasn't the horse's true showing. He added he wished he could ride him in the National; he could not, as he was contracted to his boss, Paul Nicholls.

In the build-up to the race, Vida Bingham was interviewed by a TV crew and she told them she was 'not without hope'.

Venetia's number one jockey Aidan Coleman opted to ride Stan and so Liam Treadwell came in for the ride on Mon Mome, who was led up as usual by Sarah McQueen.

Liam Treadwell rode an intelligent race, 'hunting round' in the old tradition on the first circuit, then gradually improving his position until jumping into the lead at the last; he drew clear from the previous year's winner, Comply Or Die, on the run-in.

As Venetia is quick to point out, the form was there. His weight of 11 stone shows that the handicapper thought sufficiently well of him, too.

Vida Bingham says, 'I wasn't surprised, I knew he could do those fences,' and adds, 'Sam Thomas found me afterwards and threw his arms around me.' Sam had pulled up his horse at the seventeenth.

In 2010 Mon Mome fell at the twenty-sixth when still in touch (under Aidan Coleman), and in 2012 he pulled up behind Neptune Collonges when out of contention.

Today, aged nineteen and retired to his devoted groom Sarah McQueen, Mon Mome takes pride of place in the annual parade of Venetia's horses at her owners' day at Aramstone (originally owned by her grandparents), overlooking the lush pastures leading down to the River Wye.

Mrs Bingham still has a couple of staying chasers, Achille and Nesterenko, with Venetia and apart from racing she also enjoys playing bridge, having been of national standard.

The horses in this chapter all won at 100-1 – but what odds for a jockey making a comeback from retirement and promptly winning two Grand Nationals in a row?

28

Leighton Aspell

Back-to-back wins, 2014 and 2015

Jockey retires. Has been successful enough – a journeyman who was once second in the Grand National and is still in demand – but the hunger has gone. Tries something else for a couple of years. Gets a few niggles in his head. Begins to wonder if he'll regret his decision in ten years' time. Decides to make a comeback.

Wins the Grand National. And then wins it again on a different horse the very next year.

No, not a Dick Francis novel. Even he couldn't have made this up.

Leighton Aspell, modest, polite, helpful, joined a small band of jockeys who have won back-to-back Grand Nationals, but only Tom Olliver, in 1842 and 1843, and Leighton, in 2014 and 2015, have done so on different horses for different trainers and different owners. The others have all had at least one common denominator: George Stevens, J.M. Richardson, Tommy Beasley and Ted Wilson in the nineteenth century; Bryan Marshall and Brian Fletcher in the twentieth; and now Davy Russell in the twenty-first.

Born and bred in County Kildare, where his father Patrick worked on a stud, Leighton began riding from the age of ten, and in time worked on Saturdays riding the stud's yearlings; summer holidays were spent riding out for local trainers, but it was when the stud started keeping a few of their progeny that, at fifteen and still at school, Leighton had about a dozen rides on the flat. He was hooked, left school without doing his final exams, and became apprenticed to Reg Hollinshead in Staffordshire. He has remained in England ever since.

Leighton loved his time with Hollinshead, riding and travelling all over the country, and notching ten wins before, at seventeen, his weight began rising and jump racing beckoned. He wrote to three of the country's top National Hunt trainers, of whom the first to reply was Josh Gifford; Leighton became a conditional jockey for him.

'Josh threw me in at the deep end; I did a lot of schooling and had my first ride over jumps in January 1995.' His first winner was for Richard Rowe, formerly a jockey for Josh Gifford, followed by several more for his guvnor. Leighton was building up contacts so that when he lost his claim, he still got plenty of race-rides, after riding out for Josh at Findon in the mornings. One of the trainers to spot his talent was Oliver Sherwood, and Leighton became a regular choice for him.

Oliver says today, 'He's a horseman with long legs, but he had always gone under the radar. He's a man of few words but when he does tell you something you take note of what he says, and learn a lot about a horse.' He added, 'A lot of jockeys look up to him.'

Pineau De Re

The top yards in England generally house a hundred or more horses – and in Ireland a couple are on two hundred – so that when a horse wins the Grand National, which is a feat in itself, from a yard that houses just twelve horses it is not only remarkable but also a wonderful illustration of what the National is all about: hope, dreams, and in this case beating the big boys.

Not that the sporting Dr Richard Newland would see it that way.

For Dr Newland, the horses are a fascinating and fun sideline to his successful medical healthcare businesses and after his win he vowed to remain as small. Almost inevitably, he actually doubled his yard, although a casual daytime visitor will only see empty boxes because every horse spends the whole day out in the steep, neatly railed fields of Linacres Farm after morning exercise finishes at 10 a.m. They stay out regardless of the weather until 4 p.m. when all except four return for their evening feed; those four are trained entirely from the field – all the time with the main yard gate securely locked.

The original yard has a traditional courtyard design, and what were once the tack- and feed-rooms, hay barn and lorry barn have all been turned into extra stables. A purpose-built self-contained tack-room, office, canteen sits attractively to one side and another yard of new stables is beyond that. An all-weather gallop is up the side of another steep hill.

In August 2019, and with more time to spend away from his businesses, Dr Newland moved into a forty-box yard about ten miles away.

The Grand National has always drawn him, since the days of sitting down as a family and watching Red Rum. He did not learn to ride until in his thirties, with three young pony-mad daughters.

He loves the 'brain puzzle' of racing, taking it from all angles, 'as well as the magnificence of the animals' and the challenge of bringing them to peak fitness for a certain day – as he did with Pineau De Re for the 2014 Grand National.

Dr Newland's number one member of staff is Caroline White. It is no understatement to say she lives and breathes for horses and none could be under better care. It was she who drove the lorry to Aintree that early April day in 2014 and she who led up Pineau De Re before the race, and washed him off afterwards.

Officials wanted her to be present for the prize-giving but it was Pineau De Re who came first, and only once he was comfortably settled did she return to join in the celebrations.

Caroline White describes Pineau as a straightforward horse, with a penchant for apples, although he was also always a bit of a worrier and had to travel loose in the lorry to stop him sweating.

Caroline hails from Wiltshire, where her first job, lasting twelve years, was for leading flat trainer Richard Hannon Senior, after which she spent fifteen years in Devon working for Rod Millman. She also had a break for two years when she had her two children (she now has three grandchildren), and then returned to work part-time. She moved to Worcestershire and Dr Newland in about 2012.

Pineau De Re's early racing career was in Ireland, trained by Philip Fenton for Barry Connell for whom he won and placed a good many times. He moved to Dr Newland for owner Mr John Provan in June 2013 and went summer racing, placing a couple of times. That autumn saw his first taste of the Aintree fences in the Becher Chase, where he fell, but he won a three-mile chase at Exeter in January 2014; his next race was the three-mile Pertemps Hurdle Final at the Cheltenham Festival, in which in a three-way photo finish he was beaten a nose and a neck. Next stop, Aintree, for which his weight was 10 stone 6 pounds.

At 6 a.m. on Saturday, 11 April 2014, Caroline and her partner Mick Turner, who works for the British Horseracing Authority, set off in the lorry with their precious cargo loose inside it, along tiny, narrow Egg Lane that within a mile took them on to the main road heading for Worcester, past the layby with coffee and flower stalls, and barely half a mile from there turned north on to the M5 motorway. Once at Aintree they asked for a quiet box for their charge and were allocated box 96 – where the last National winner to be trained in Worcestershire, West Tip, had been installed in 1986.

'I didn't expect Pineau to win but I thought he would run well,' Caroline recalls.

But once on the course there was a pre-race scare about him running at all, for he failed the compulsory veterinary trot-up. Eventually the vet agreed that it was not lameness but the horse's natural gait, and he was thereafter put on the 'bad movers' list.*

Leighton Aspell had been getting 'some juicy' rides for Dr Newland but it was Sam Twiston-Davies who had ridden Pineau De Re to a good third in the Pertemps Final three-mile hurdle, his prep race for the National. Twiston-Davies, however, was booked to ride top-weight Tidal Bay for Paul Nicholls in the National. Leighton Aspell then saw a paragraph in the *Racing Post* saying that the doctor was looking for a rider for the big race.

Leighton sent him a text offering his services, and within ten minutes he received a reply of acceptance. He had one schooling session on the little bay, who stands barely 16 hands, over the replica Aintree fences at Lambourn and found the eleven-year-old showed no fear and had a good, economic technique and was 'really well trained' for the big day.

He says he saw the race itself through several viewpoints, firstly with his mount jumping well near the back of the field; by the second Canal Turn he was picking off other runners, one, two, three, until, with a high tempo, he kept on catching up.

Watching from the lads' stand, Caroline thought Pineau had fallen at the second fence but it turned out to be a horse with similar colours. Pineau De Re's only serious mistake came at the thirteenth.

By the time he was over the second last and sharing the lead with Rocky Creek, Caroline was jumping up and down with excitement shouting for her charge; little Balthazar King gave

* List of horses with poor gait, which could be taken for lameness but is not.

chase, ridden by Richard Johnson, but brave as he was, Balthazar King, on 10 stone 13 pounds, couldn't haul in the 25-1 winner.

Pineau De Re galloped further ahead to an unchallenged five-length victory.

'It was surreal,' Caroline remembers, 'an amazing day, I couldn't quite believe it.' Next day, while celebrations continued at the nearby Mug House pub, it was business as usual for Caroline, with three runners to convey to Market Rasen. Two of the horses won, including one for Pineau's owner, John Provan.

Pineau De Re ran in the following year's National, in which he finished unplaced behind Many Clouds; he won one more race, a three-mile-one-furlong hurdle, but retired in 2016. He turned his hand to eventing with Lizzie Doolittle, and he is part of the parade of previous winners before the National every year. Lizzie rides out at Dr Newland's, and of Pineau De Re, she says he is 'intelligent, honest, loyal and great fun to ride'.

Leighton Aspell naturally thought Pineau De Re was the cherry on top of the cake in terms of his career. Little could he have guessed what lay ahead . . .

Many Clouds

It is rare indeed for only one jockey to be the rider of a given horse throughout a long career. Three bumpers, six hurdles, eighteen chases, spanning six seasons. To nurse it as a baby, to begin to dream those dreams, to win the Grand National, arguably to top even that by beating the most exciting Gold Cup prospects in decades – and to be with him to the end.

From the start there was something about the gawky, gangly youngster out in the field that caught Oliver Sherwood's eye; he looked a nice individual.

Every summer, like Trevor Hemmings' other trainers, Oliver would visit Gleadhill House Stud near Chorley, Lancashire, to view his current crop of youngsters and to see if he could pick out one and ask for that to be allocated to him.

Competition is fierce – Trevor Hemmings uses some twenty or so trainers in the UK and Ireland – but the dark bay was by Cloudings, a stallion not yet fashionable at that time, and so the four-year-old Many Clouds came to Rhonehurst, Upper Lambourn for the rest of his life – to the yard, in fact, from which Battleship had been sent out to win the 1938 National.

To begin with, Many Clouds was the baby in the class; another four-year-old new boy, Puffing Billy, owned by Tim Syder, was way ahead of him both mentally and physically. Many Clouds was timid and easily spooked by the most mundane of sights that other horses took in their stride; he was also a pernickety feeder. In time, he would become King Kong,* but not then.

One of his first work riders was Rose Osborne and one day Many Clouds 'tanked off' with her up the gallops. Perhaps he was turning into a 'proper horse'. It's easy for geese to look like swans at home, and only the racecourse will tell the difference.

Leighton Aspell schooled him, and rode him in his first bumper. So began their long and extraordinary association. That first bumper was in Wetherby, and Oliver Sherwood was not there. Many Clouds won by an impressive twelve lengths. He was a swan – or more correctly at this stage, a cygnet.

Leighton reported to Oliver Sherwood that the horse was 'a bit out of the ordinary'.

Bumpers at the Cheltenham Festival, where the owner loves to have a runner, and Aintree saw him unplaced but several of the horses ahead of him were to become racing household names:

---

* Someone or something of outstanding size or strength, from the film of the same name.

Champagne Fever, The New One and Jezki at Cheltenham and The New One again and My Tent Or Yours at Aintree. It was all part of his education, as was his season over hurdles, where he had moved on from nursery to primary school with even more encouraging results: second, first, second, first, second and, finally, pulled up when tried over three miles for the first time – ironic, given he was in time to win over the ultimate distance.

For the next season it was moving up to secondary school, starting at the bottom again in novice chases. Swiftly he showed he was the 'real deal', beating Knock A Hand and Holywell first time out at Carlisle. He was also beginning to take a keen hold in his races – gone was the gawky schoolboy, he was relishing his role as a racehorse.

Leighton, not one to go over the moon about a horse, reported to the trainer, 'This is a proper horse.'

Dreams could begin: the Hennessy Gold Cup at Newbury became the target for the following season. Meanwhile, Many Clouds had to complete his novice season; after a second at Haydock and another win at Wetherby, it was off to Ascot for the Reynoldstown Chase.

That he was both beaten in this and brought down in the RSA Chase at Cheltenham was, Oliver Sherwood believes, a blessing in disguise, for had he won either he would have been 'handicapped out' of the Hennessy – that is, would have been allotted too big a weight.

Even so, he won at Carlisle and Oliver had the same fear.

But the race brought him on, there were no hiccups en route to Newbury, and as Many Clouds strode up the finishing straight, Oliver began 'shouting and screaming like a fishwife – and that's not like me!'

His stable had been out of the big time for a number of years. There was a flow of winners, of course, but Cenkos winning the Sandeman Maghull Grade 1 Novices Chase over the Mildmay course at Aintree in 2000 was the last really big win – and Many Clouds ended that fourteen-year lean-ish spell. It was also a very popular win, as Newbury is the local track for Lambourn.

'From day one, Many Clouds put everything into every race and would die for you – which of course in the end he did,' says Oliver.

In fact, in due course the horse was put on the BHA (British Horseracing Authority) dehydration 'watch list' so that staff could be on hand with buckets of water at the end of a race. (Today, that has become the norm for all horses.)

Oliver Sherwood, thirty-four years a trainer, is a former champion amateur rider (1979–80); he rode a number of Cheltenham Festival winners, including Venture To Cognac in the 1979 Sun Alliance Novices Hurdle and five years later the Foxhunters Chase on the same horse. He also won the 1980 Foxhunters with Rolls Rambler, and he rode Venture To Cognac in the 1983 Grand National (eighth to Corbiere). His wife, Tarnya, also rode in the National (as Tarnya Davis) on Numerate in 1989 (100-1, pulled up in Little Polveir's race).

In 2015 he was convinced the eight-year-old Many Clouds was not only a year too young for the National but he also feared that he was 'over the top' and had done enough for the season. He had run disappointingly in the Cheltenham Gold Cup and Leighton told the trainer that the horse 'just hadn't turned up'. At home, his work rider Nathan Horrocks also felt the spark wasn't there. His elderly owner, however, was keen for him to run, and so Oliver, out of courtesy, rang Dr Newland to say that Leighton might be needed for Many Clouds and so would be unavailable to ride the previous year's winner in the National (because Leighton was Oliver's number one jockey, a system well understood in racing. On occasion, a stable jockey will be 'let go' when he has been offered a ride elsewhere that is better than his own stable can provide.)

Trevor Hemmings

The prospective purchaser peered over the stable door and was attracted to its occupant. There was something about the bay foal with a white star by Cloudings that he liked. He wasn't on the list of foals to look at, but Trevor Hemmings decided to buy him anyway. It was Tattersalls Foals Sales in Fairyhouse, Ireland, and as usual Trevor was accompanied by 'my man in Ireland' Jerry O'Leary. Jerry sources much more than prospective race-horses for Trevor Hemmings: in addition to finding him ponies and shire horses to mingle with his thoroughbreds on his Isle of Man estate, or on his property in County Cork, or his stud in Lancashire, he also finds him footballers for his Preston North End Football Club.

Trevor Hemmings could be described as an elder statesman of NH racing in the UK. Quietly spoken, he has a passion for the sport. He was not born to riches but he used his brain and worked hard, very hard. His family moved from London to Lancashire during the Second World War, and Trevor Hemmings was still little more than a boy when he became a builder's apprentice and attended night school to gain necessary qualifications. His first development deal cost him £12. He built it up and sold it on for a profit, bought another, worked when other people were at play and steadily built himself a fortune, in later years buying and selling a number of leisure centres. At one time he owned Blackpool Tower.

Besides becoming friends with Fred Pontin of Pontin's, he also met and became friends with Ginger McCain and Noel Le Mare (Red Rum) and resolved that he, too, would one day win the National. He had always loved horses right from his young days of driving a horse and cart to the local market and selling goods from it. Now, he loves nothing more than to have them around him, to glance out of his windows and see them grazing – young, old, thoroughbreds, ponies and heavy horses.

It was 1984 when he first became a racehorse owner and from there he built up a string to carry his white and green quartered colours. Every horse he buys is with chasing in mind, with the Grand National always the long-term aim.

His first National runner was Rubika trained by Stan Mellor in 1992 (it finished fourteenth); he next tried in 2000 with two runners (The Last Fling finished seventh) and up until 2005 he had a further nine runners, until at last he achieved success in the world's greatest steeplechase with Hedgehunter.

Trevor Hemmings, with his trademark flat cap and quiet demeanour, lives on the Isle of Man and generally keeps himself to himself, enjoying close friends, family, football, and always his racing. He also keeps his hand in with his business – it would be hard to imagine him otherwise. At eighty-four, his work ethic has not diminished; he still works longer hours than others a quarter of his age. He still puts in a seven-day week – bar the Cheltenham Festival in March and Aintree in April. He gets up early, walks his dogs, makes his breakfast – and sets about work.

Trevor Hemmings' Ballaseyr Stud on his beautiful Ballavodden estate is home to some of the young potential chasers. They roam the lush fields, undergoing breaking and initial training by his capable staff, before moving to his Gleadhill Stud near Chorley, under the care of Irishman and former jockey and trainer Mick Meagher. Ballavodden is also home to his retired stars, Ballabriggs and Hedgehunter among them. Ballabriggs was named after a property on his estate in the north of the Isle of Man.

He clearly loves the island and its people, not least because it reminds him of his youth when 'neighbours talked to neighbours. The Manx people are lovely.'

His other great passion besides racing is football; he has always followed Preston North End Football Club and became its owner in 2010, bringing it back from the brink. Even as an octogenarian, he still employs about two thousand people. On the quiet, he is a generous donor to various charities close to his heart.

*

Oliver Sherwood remained not keen to run Many Clouds in the National but a telephone from Mick Meagher relayed that 'the boss wants to run, and we've both backed him each way before making the news public'.

So that was it. Leighton Aspell, unlike the previous year, chose not to school him over the replica Aintree fences at Lambourn for fear that he might over-react to the bigger fences and leave a mental scar when it came to Aintree.

A fairly relaxed Sherwood party set off for Aintree without high expectations, only the hope that their horse would return safely and learn from the experience for the next year. Oliver and Tarnya stayed as usual with friends Richard and Sally Aston about forty minutes from the course.

From the moment Leighton Aspell was legged-up on to Many Clouds he felt a different horse from Cheltenham. He 'grew a foot' in stature, and soaked up the atmosphere in spite of wearing ear plugs (a relic from his nervous younger days). He felt fantastic, and maintained that feeling in the race, relishing the challenge. After four fences Oliver could see he had taken to it. He prayed he could keep out of trouble.

Leighton Aspell rode beautifully, tucked in behind the leaders, close to the inside. At one stage, Aspell took a pull to fill his mount up with oxygen. He jumped into the lead five out where leader Druid's Nephew fell, and there he stayed; A.P. McCoy on Shutthefrontdoor looked the eye-catching danger but he ran out of stamina from the last and it was left to Saint Are to try and catch Many Clouds, but the winner was too good for him.

Many Clouds staggered, struggling for breath, after the race. He looked as though he was going to collapse but copious quantities of water were quickly on hand to restore him. Leighton Aspell had to take off his saddle and walk without his brave horse back to the winner's enclosure, accompanied by the normal police horse escort, a strange sight.

In time, Many Clouds was sufficiently recovered to walk in to the cheering crowds himself.

His was the third win in a decade for Trevor Hemmings, following Hedgehunter in 2005 trained by Willie Mullins and ridden by Ruby Walsh, and Ballabriggs in 2011 trained by Donald McCain and ridden by Jason Maguire. This put Trevor Hemmings in the select band of owners to have won the race three times. The others are James Machell in the nineteenth century, Charles Duff, later Sir Charles Assheton-Smith, nineteenth–twentieth century, and Noel Le Mare twentieth century (the only one to have achieved that with one horse, Red Rum). (Another three-time winning owner was to follow.) In fact, Trevor Hemmings is proud owner of four Grand National trophies because his friend and source of his love of racing, Fred Pontin, stuck by his promise to leave him Specify's 1971 trophy in his will 'because you'll never win it yourself!' Sir Fred Pontin died in 2000, aged ninety-three, before Trevor's first win. And his remaining ambition? To win a record-breaking fourth National.

Many Clouds' win took a while to sink in for Oliver Sherwood. The first phone call he received was from Richard Hannon Senior, and after that the phone 'just went bisbo'. After numerous interviews it was time to start the celebrations: the Astons put on a party in their Shropshire home; Oliver rang through to the landlord of the George pub in Lambourn to arrange for drinks to be laid on there.

After partying until late, Oliver went up to bed. He woke at 5 a.m. and asked Tarnya, 'Did that really happen?'

They were home by eight, to find a 'pig's ear' had been made of their house by their children Sabrina and Archie, helped by assistant trainer Andy Llewellyn and, doubtless, many other revellers. By the time Many Clouds returned home at 9 a.m. the yard was heaving with press and well-wishers. Trevor Hemmings flew in by helicopter – 'the best owner one could ask for,' Oliver says. 'Half the fun is plotting and planning with an owner.'

*

Of the changes to the National fences, Oliver says simply, 'Without them there would no longer be a National, it would have been banned. Peter Greenall [Lord Daresbury] and the whole Aintree team deserve a hundred out of a hundred for what they have done.'

And, of course, both Oliver and Tarnya can reminisce on their rides in the great race before the modifications to the fences.

Like many a National winner before, the main aim for Many Clouds for the next two seasons was the National. In 2016, after running prominently and leading at the 26th where he made a mistake, he faded into last place, being virtually pulled up, behind Rule The World. The 2017 National was once again the target. It was not to be.

The titan battle between Many Clouds and 'the new Messiah' Thistlecrack in the Cotswold Chase at Cheltenham in January 2017 was not just the jump race of the season but possibly of the century.

Thistlecrack, trained by Colin Tizzard for John and Heather Snook, had won his last nine races; among his hurdle wins were the Grade 1 Stayers Hurdle, one of the big four, at the Cheltenham Festival. Most recently, he had won all four of his starts over fences, including the King George at Kempton on Boxing Day; as a result, he was heavily fancied for the Gold Cup, and this was to be his prep run. Leighton Aspell figured the only way to beat him would be to test his stamina, especially as the staying chases at Cheltenham are nearly two furlongs longer than three miles, and the run-in is a stamina-sapping incline.

Off he and Many Clouds set in a close-up position until four out they swept into the lead and stayed there until two out when Thistlecrack, as expected, came to challenge. The pair took off and landed together as one over the last fence and set off up the run-in. Thistlecrack had the younger legs. For most viewers it looked all over bar the shouting. But that was without taking into account the tenacity and determination of Many Clouds. The winning post came and he thrust his brave face in front to win by a head. After he passed the post, he pricked his ears and felt 'as bright as a button' with no hint of anything untoward. But then as they began circling prior to walking back in Leighton felt his back legs wobble and he collapsed to the ground.

Leighton says, 'I knew at once he wasn't going to get up this time. It was a different feeling to previously.' The brave horse had given his all.

No one would wish such a scenario, but that Leighton Aspell was there with his great partner, Many Clouds, as he died is somehow fitting.

The saddle had to be taken off the prostrate body of his faithful partner in order to weigh in. In all his twenty-seven races, Leighton Aspell had been his only jockey, a truly remarkable record, never off injured or called upon to be on another horse in all that time. (Likewise, Charlie Swan was on board triple Champion Hurdle winner Istabraq in all twenty-nine of his races.)

After the obligatory weigh in, Leighton simply got in his car and drove home to Sussex, alone with his thoughts.

For Oliver, it was the end of an era. He recalls, 'I'd never felt such an eeriness, the whole course went silent.'

He added, 'Cheltenham were very good to us, they really looked after us.'

Alice Plunkett, a friend, wanted to interview him for *Channel 4 Racing*.

'Give me twenty minutes,' he said. It was a tough task, but he composed himself, and then, remaining a true professional throughout, paid a moving tribute to his staunch ally. At home, Tarnya, assisted by Emma Chubb, answered every single message of sympathy that arrived at Rhonehurst, all of them still kept in a large box.

At his owner's request, Many Clouds was cremated and his

ashes scattered in the grounds of his Isle of Man home. Like at Oliver's, Trevor Hemmings' home is filled with memorabilia of an extraordinary horse.

Leighton Aspell and his wife, Nicola, have three little daughters, Lucy, Niamh and Kitty, all passionate about riding, trail-hunting and taking part in the Shetland pony Grand Nationals at the Christmas Show at Olympia.

Leighton lives in Pulborough, West Sussex, not far from Findon where he first worked for Josh Gifford, and he runs a successful rehab and pre-training business from a yard he rents from Amanda Perrett. He works in this most mornings, unless he is schooling at Oliver Sherwood's, and rides in races in the afternoons. That two-year retirement spell, when he thought his hunger for racing had gone, seems a long time ago now.

Two Grand National victories and some two hundred other winners since then sees Leighton Aspell still nurturing a burning ambition: to win a third Grand National.

As a nation, Scotland was hungry for victory, too . . .

29

One For Arthur, Two for Scotland

And some Welsh wizardry

Utterly charming, with an effervescent personality and winning smile, Lucinda Russell always has time to talk to people and welcome them to her yard at Alary House just outside Milnathort at the top of Loch Leven. She and her partner, Scu – eight times former champion jockey Peter Scudamore – maintain a happy ship, which is evident from the moment one sets foot there – a hard-work ethic that also shows plenty of humour.

Up the drive from the yard is the fine Georgian Alary House built in the pink stone of the area and lived in by her parents, Peter and Edith. The family hailed from Edinburgh where Peter Russell was a whisky broker who became very good at his job. Lucinda's first memory of the Grand National is of Red Rum and she vaguely thought it would be a great race to win, but at that time she had only one wish in life: to own a pony, to ride, to dream of being an Olympic Show Jumper, or was it Bending Pole Champion, and of being presented with a gold medal by Princess Anne.

When Lucinda was thirteen and her father was doing 'rather well' in the whisky business they bought Alary House, and a pony called Magic came her way. He was a 'little sh*t and I used to fall off him all the time', but nothing was going to deter her. She went on to reach 4* level at eventing.

The original two stables for Lucinda's ponies have steadily multiplied, including converting former cattle sheds, until now there are some fifty stables dotted around in groups of varying sizes. Each horse spends some time out in one of the various paddocks every day, and one member of staff is employed solely for turning out and bringing them in. After winning the National, Lucinda splashed out on special 'horse-rails' for each paddock. There is a sand gallop and the ubiquitous horse-walker. Among the many dedicated staff is the Spanish vet Eugenio Cillán-Garcia who graduated from the Veterinary School at Edinburgh University, longest-serving staff member, assistant trainer and travelling head girl Jaimie Duff, and assistant trainer James Turnbull. Scu, of course, is hands-on partner in the whole operation, and mentor to the stable jockey, originally Peter Buchanan and currently Derek Fox.

The Lomond Hills encompass the property gently to the east and the main 'magic' woodchip gallop is a mile and a half away – the hack there and back is a regular part of the incumbents' exercise. Lucinda herself rides out anything from two to six lots a day, depending on the number of riders available, and has 'about fifteen' favourite horses.

But she hasn't been aboard stable star One For Arthur since *that* day – the day he brought home the Grand National trophy. She does spend a lot of time minding him, though, for now there is a camera permanently recording his every moment in his spacious, airy corner box. It was installed for added security but Lucinda finds herself fascinated to watch how often he lies down, to listen to him giving little whinnies, like a sleeping dog gives tongue when dreaming, to observe his traits and habits. A dark bay with long white blaze and somewhat angular frame, he stands all of 16.3 hh.

Although Bel McClung and Debs Thomson attended the same weekly boarding school, a convent called St Mary's, Berwick, they were in different years; they got to know each other better through the Buccleuch Pony Club and teenage parties before life moved on. Bel's parents had horses in training and her great-uncle, Donald Wares, won the Topham Chase over the National fences in the 1950s. They had a horse in training with John Leadbetter, of whom more later, and after he trained Rubstic to win the National Mr and Mrs Wares gave a big party – and the young Bel became obsessed with the National.

'I always loved *National Velvet*,' she says, 'and my mum always gave parties on National day. Winning the National was a dream.'

As a child of four or five she and her younger brother Jeremy used to go hunting all day with the Jedforest whether they wanted to or not – their parents were chairman and secretary and didn't have babysitters.

Debs is a farmer's daughter and she always loved anything to do with horses. As a family they always used to watch the National, and her father, Bill, used to take their bets.

It was at an owners' lunch at Alary that Bel and Debs met up again in 2012; both their 'other halves', Fraser and Colin, already had a horse with Lucinda Russell. What impressed them most was that there was no 'hard sell' to prospective owners, as a result of which it was to Lucinda they turned when the idea of sharing a horse was espoused – they wanted something to do together at the weekends while Colin and Fraser were away playing golf.

Bel and Fraser had made plans to go to the Cheltenham Sales and, after a few gin and tonics, Debs and Colin said they would, too. A shortlist of possible horses was drawn up and when they looked round them, both Bel and Debs independently picked out One For Arthur as their choice. There was something about the four-year-old, his presence and kind eye, that let them imagine how he might look when no longer a gangly youth.

It resulted in One For Arthur heading for a life in Scotland – but only after the two menfolk in the story had been persuaded to part with half as much again of the original £40,000 budget. Peter Scudamore, acting on their behalf, immediately feared he had made a mistake in spending £60,000 for them when he was asked by someone in the know 'What on earth did you buy that for?' The horse had been well tried in Ireland, and only won a point-to-point on his fifth attempt. However, in that, at Lingstown in County Wexford, he made all the running and ran on well to score impressively.

The backward, immature frame of One For Arthur needed that magic tonic, Time; time to fill out and grow into his young frame. Bel and Debs had a bit of fun in registering as owners, too, when they came up with the tongue-in-cheek name of Two Golf Widows. Debs already had the consistent Big River under the ownership name of Two Black Labs, after Colin felt sorry for his girls (Debs and her two black Labrador bitches), with colours sporting two black Labradors on a white background.

One For Arthur finished second in his only bumper and was second and third twice in his first three novice hurdles. Staying was soon his game, and he won his next three novice hurdles in succession over distances from two miles three furlongs to three miles – and the co-owners 'got very excited', although next time out, tried in a Grade 1, he was pulled up behind Thistlecrack at Aintree, before being turned away for a summer at grass at Di Walton's in the Borders, and more time to mature. The autumn of 2016 saw him straight into staying novice chases and he quickly showed his aptitude, winning first time out. He was still big and weak and did not win again that season, although he placed almost every time he ran.

Until this point, he had always been ridden by stable jockey Peter Buchanan who hailed originally from Northern Ireland. In his thirteen years at Lucinda Russell's he earned a name in staying chases, winning the Grand Sefton over the National fences on Forest Gunner, the Grand National Trial at Haydock twice on Silver By Nature, and the four-mile Eider Chase on Companero. He hung up his racing boots just a year before One For Arthur's National and in his fifteen rides on the horse, he finished out of the first four just twice.

Derek Fox became an able stable substitute and quickly

established a rapport with the big horse by winning first time out at Kelso. He then sampled the Aintree fences in which he showed stamina by putting in his best work near the finish, staying on to take fifth place in the three-mile-two-furlong Becher Chase, only two and a half lengths behind the winner, Vieux Lion Rouge, in a pulsating finish.

Arthur started the race by ballooning over the strange fences in novicey fashion, but then he got into a rhythm, adroitly side-stepping fallers. That was the day he 'manned up' and afterwards thoughts of the Grand National were entertained. He was only seven and his handicap mark was still low.

But it was next time out in a three-mile-five-furlong handicap chase at Warwick that those with an eye on the National could detect the next winner, for Arthur scored an impressive victory.

That was January 2017, and Arthur was officially eight years old. Now it was next stop Aintree for the big one on 8 April.

The day began with some problems for connections, but not for the horse. Debs and Bel had travelled down the day before, but at 4 a.m. received a phone call from the booked driver for Colin and Fraser asking, 'Where are the boys?' They had been at a dinner, missed their intended flight, then got lost and eventually took a much later flight – by which time the two women weren't talking to them . . .

It was a long day from that 4 a.m. start until the race more than thirteen hours later. Time hung, tension was high, nerves were abundant, and Bel lost her mobile phone.

It must have been with mixed feelings that Peter Buchanan watched number 22, One For Arthur, canter down to the start shortly after 5 p.m. for the 2017 Grand National. Did anyone notice the significance of the horse's number as being the same as Rubstic way back in 1979 who was, until then, the only previous Scottish-trained winner of the Grand National? Certainly, all Debs, Bel and Lucinda hoped for at this stage was the safe return of their special horse.

The three of them stood together on the owners and trainers steps watching the race unfold.

Arthur, jumping well, was intelligently ridden by Derek Fox having his first ride in the National; to the women he seemed quite far back but he was biding his time, staying out of trouble, steadily moving up – and suddenly the friends realised every other jockey was 'rowing away'.

Lucinda turned to them and said, 'I think he's going to win.' A bump at the second last, where he jumped left and collided with Blaklion, made them hold their breaths but, recovering quickly, he took the lead, and although Cause Of Causes tried to go with him, from the elbow it was Arthur's race.

'My legs turned to jelly,' Bel recalls, 'it all went in a bit of a blur for me.'

Debs adds, 'I couldn't believe it.'

They are full of praise for Arthur's Sligo-born jockey, Derek Fox, who was twenty-four at the time of his National win, saying he has 'a clock in his head' and doesn't panic. After cheering their hero into the winner's enclosure and enjoying the trophy presentation, they found themselves 'pulled from pillar to post' giving interviews. For the press room interview the assembled journalists all had water provided for them, while the girls, facing them at the front, were given champagne.

They stayed on the course drinking more champagne until about 9 p.m. and then headed off to the Malmaison Hotel, Liverpool, where the celebrations continued – until they hit a brick wall at about midnight and went to bed.

The following day, One For Arthur was paraded in front of well-wishers at Alary stables and the party continued at the Grouse and Parrot in Kinross.

It was the next day that they received one of many congratulatory phone calls. It was from the PA to Nicola Sturgeon, Scotland's First Minister and devout campaigner for Scottish independence. She had got wind that One For Arthur was to parade at Kelso racecourse the following day. Could she meet him in the paddock, she asked Belinda who had taken her call.

'Hold on,' said Bel, 'I'll ask the others.'

The 'others' were rolling around in laughter, believing the call to be a wind-up.

Quick-wittedly, Bel went back to the caller and said, 'No, sorry, we don't feel politics and racing make good bedfellows,' or words to that effect, adding they wanted to stay in the Union.

The owners don't court the limelight, they go racing in winter for the social life, the fun not the money, but they do enjoy what the victory has brought them, including being able to buy a special piece of jewellery as a memento.

'We have met lovely people, and we were invited to lunch at Jack Berry House [the Injured Jockeys Fund northern rehab centre], and racing with Lord Daresbury.'

Lucinda had vowed that winning the National wouldn't change her life but now admits it has. 'It's opened up so many things, especially in social life, and the three of us are such good friends.'

She was also awarded an OBE in the June 2018 Queen's Birthday Honours list for services to horse racing. She and Scu travelled to Buckingham Palace, where the Queen presented the award to her, so in a way her childhood wish had come true.

One For Arthur was the second Scottish-trained winner of the Grand National. The first, thirty-eight years earlier in 1979, was Rubstic, trained at Bedrule, between Jedburgh and Denholm, by John Leadbetter, a man still held in high regard throughout Scotland and further afield.

Rubstic was the first National runner for John Leadbetter, for owner, former international rugby player John Douglas, and for jockey Maurice Barnes, whose father, Tommy, had finished second on Wyndburgh in 1962. Rubstic carried 10 stone and started at odds of 25-1. He had been a bargain basement buy at only £1,200 as a three-year-old from Tattersalls Horses in Training Sales, Newmarket, but he won Sedgefield's Durham National in 1978 (and twice more carrying top weight of 12 stone 7 pounds) and was second twice in the Scottish National at Ayr in 1978; he also won a prep race for the National at Kelso, and he was steadily backed down from 120-1 to 25-1 before the 1979 Grand National – enough to clean out local bookies. From the previous September right up to the race, John put £5 each way on Rubstic every week.

John Leadbetter told the *Daily Record* in 2010, 'I was ever hopeful that he might do it but I didn't go with great expectations. He was only £1,200 to buy and you pay your money and take your chances.

'I've been buying and selling horses all my life and I don't believe you can predict X, Y and Z. Some you win and some you lose. It really is a lottery, and we won it that day.'

It was a race full of incident. Rubstic made a mistake at the second but seemed to learn from it. At the Chair, the fifteenth and biggest fence, two loose horses ran amok, causing eight runners to come down in the biggest pile-up since Foinavon's race twelve years earlier. Unfortunately, seven fences later, at Becher's for the second time, the race was marred when the then Cheltenham Gold Cup hero and race favourite Alverton, ridden by Jonjo O'Neill, fell fatally, breaking his neck and being killed instantly.

The depleted field saw three horses rise to the last fence in line abreast, Rubstic, Zongalero and Rough And Tumble, with Rubstic prevailing by one and a half lengths. The Pilgarlic finished fourth and only seven of the original thirty-four completed.

John Leadbetter found there was a tremendous atmosphere at Aintree but admitted that afterwards was a bit of a blur – and for the whole of the next week. Rubstic returned to a huge reception in Denholm, with church bells ringing, bagpipes playing and crowds cheering – and drinking. John Leadbetter recalled, 'We came back from Liverpool that night and the scenes in Denholm were amazing. Everyone was determined to party hard and the pubs were open all night. It seemed like nobody would go to bed. I didn't get to the pub until around midnight and it was jam-packed.

'I stayed for a few drinks, then headed to Jedburgh to meet friends and associates. I never felt tired. Adrenaline was sky-high.'

The following day was even busier. John paraded Rubstic around Denholm and was bowled over by the generosity of well-wishers. He said: 'It seemed the world and his wife turned up. It was a scene I will never forget.'

Owner John Douglas, who had been capped twelve times as number 8 for Scotland, and jockey Maurice Barnes were carried shoulder-high round the village green by cheering locals, and John Leadbetter had people coming to visit his yard for months afterwards.

Years later, he admitted that win had been 'one of life's better days, a magical moment, and an amazing feeling. To achieve and produce a winner of the Grand National is a remarkable thing but then Rubstic was a remarkable horse.'

Rubstic was favourite for the following year's National having won his two prep races but took the only fall of his life at the Chair when in second place. The race was won by Ben Nevis, who with his partner Charlie Fenwick had won the Maryland Hunt Cup and American Grand National twice each over timber fences. Bred in England, his form in point-to-points before his export to America was decidedly indistinct: a moderate win and two falls, and a pithy comment in the annual form book, 'speedy, a bad jumper and only able to stay a bare three miles'. Didn't sound too much like a future Grand National winner back then.

John Leadbetter had been apprenticed to Harry Blackshaw in Middleham, and then became head lad to him. He took out a training licence in 1975, just four years before winning the world's most famous steeplechase. He also became a hands-on supporter for MS sufferers, and in retirement would take groups of them to

Aintree and show them round the great course – and doubtless plied them with many tales.

After retirement from racing, Rubstic spent the rest of his life with John Leadbetter. The pair enjoyed hunting together for many years with the Jedforest. This much-loved equine hero, by then well-retired, died in 1995, aged twenty-nine.

John Leadbetter paid tribute to his friend in *The Herald:* 'The horse enjoyed a great life and is being buried here at Ladykirk in a field next to the yard where he lived in retirement. He was part of the family – you get to know horses like friends in the same way they get to know you.

'Although he may not have been top class, at least he won a proper National before they modified the fences. It is a modern race now, with speed and Gold Cup class horses taking part. Rubstic was a horse who had a first-class attitude to racing and must have been one of the most consistent staying chasers in Britain since the war. He'll remain in my memory forever.'

He still holds the two-mile-five-furlong course record at Haydock Park.

The name Rubstic, incidentally, is said to be Swedish for the rough equivalent of a Brillo pad.

Scotland had so nearly produced a winner before. The remarkable Wyndburgh was runner-up three times in the years 1957–62, the second two when trained by Ken Oliver in Hawick; between the first time in 1957 (to Sundew) and the following year, Ken had married the unofficial trainer of the horse, Rhona Wilkinson (at the time, women were not allowed to train). Ken Oliver, a leading amateur rider, held a permit in 1959 when Wyndburgh's jockey, Tim Brookshaw, had a stirrup iron break at the second Becher's and he rode the rest of the way home, over the remaining eight massive fences, with no irons – and still finished second, this time to Oxo. Five years later Tim Brookshaw was paralysed in a fall.

Wyndburgh was second yet again in 1962, behind Kilmore. He was also fourth in 1958, making him the only horse in the race's history to have finished in the first four four times without winning. The Irish mare Frigate was second in 1884, '85 and '88 before winning in 1889. West Tip a century later won once, was second once and was twice placed fourth.

Freddie, owned and trained by Reg Tweedie in Berwickshire and ridden by Pat McCarron, had tried so hard to bring the trophy home to Scotland in the 1960s. He was a close second in 1965 to the American horse Jay Trump, beaten only three quarters of a length, and second again the following year behind Anglo, well beaten in heavy ground. Like all the others bar Foinavon in 1967, he was caught up in the melee at the twenty-third fence, but got over at the third attempt to finish.

While Scotland now has two Grand National winners to its name, Wales is still stuck on the one that Kirkland brought home in 1905. One hundred and two years later Peter Bowen from Haverfordwest trained McKelvey to finish second behind Silver Birch; and in 2013 Welsh-trained horses finished second and third, via Cappa Bleu, trained by Evan Williams in the Vale of Glamorgan, and Teaforthree in third, trained by Rebecca Curtis in Pembrokeshire.

Bred in County Limerick by the Reverend E. Clifford and then owned by T.A. Hartigan, Kirkland won his first race at Kilmallock as a four-year-old and was promptly sold to Frank Bibby, a Liverpool businessman, and sent to the Pembrokeshire coastal village of Lawrenny for training.

The big, strong chestnut sired by the Australian-bred stallion Kirkham won over hurdles as a four-year-old in Ely, Cardiff, and in 1902 he won at both Carmarthen and Tenby, before finishing second in the Welsh Grand National at Cardiff and winning the Grand Sefton at Aintree.

Kirkland made his National debut in 1903, and although the

seven-year-old was making up quantities of ground on the run-in, he failed by a head to deprive the mighty Manifesto, at fifteen more than twice his age, of third place; the winner was Sir Charles Nugent's Drumcree.

The King's Ambush II, winner in 1900, was favourite for the 1904 race but fell at the third fence. The race belonged to Moifaa but it was again near the finish that Kirkland put in his best work, fending off The Gunner by a neck to secure the runner-up berth eight lengths behind Moifaa.

Before the 1905 National, Kirkland's owner, Frank Bibby, paid £300 to his jockey Frank 'Tich' Mason, booked for the third consecutive year, not to take any rides in the two weeks leading up to the race. He regarded his jockey so highly that he did not wish to risk him being injured beforehand.

The now nine-year-old Kirkland had done enough to start second favourite, carrying 11 stone 5 pounds behind the holder, Moifaa, who was top weight on 11 stone 12 pounds, and started 4-1 favourite. He was the King's new purchase, his 1900 victor Ambush II having died in training.

An incident-packed race was run on good ground and in clear weather; Timothy Titus, another Welsh-trained horse, led the field for a long way until falling. Altogether, more than half of the twenty-seven runners fell, the most significant being Moifaa at the second Becher's. Frank Mason, meanwhile, waited until three fences from home before moving smoothly into the lead on Kirkland with two fences left to negotiate, and then fending off the challenge of Napper Tandy on the long run-in to win by three lengths.

Kirkland's owner and jockey were fellow Liverpudlians, and so it was not just the Adelphi Hotel that lit up that night, but the whole of Liverpool.

Journalist Brian Lee did a great job in unravelling who actually trained the winner: although Colonel Frederick Lort-Phillips trained a large string from his castle home at Lawrenny, he allowed the trainer's name to go as that of his stud groom, Edward Thomas, on this occasion.

When he had come to Lawrenny, Thomas's only horse knowledge was of one hunter and a pony trap – and it was said that his ambition was to work as a porter on the Great Western Railway – but, recommended to him by local farmers, Colonel Lort-Phillips is said to have written, 'I would rather have a Pembrokeshire farmer's opinion of anything to do with horses than that of almost anyone else.'

And so the trophy was taken home to Lawrenny to great acclaim. Better known for fishing, boat building and yachting, Lawrenny is also where racing thriller writer Dick Francis was born.

Evan Williams began his racing career as a highly successful point-to-point rider, being champion in 2002, and he rode in the Aintree Foxhunters several times. As a trainer he had runners finish in the first four for five consecutive years from 2009–13 in the Grand National, a remarkable record.

Evan grew up on a typical small Welsh dairy farm at Llancarfan in the Vale of Glamorgan, along narrow sunken lanes and at the top of a hill. Today, the hill makes an excellent woodchip gallop; the old dairy and buildings were converted to house the point-to-pointers and now house youngsters and a sick bay, and across the lane are several purpose-built stable blocks housing eighty-one horses and a house designed to look like a barn, with the interior planned by Evan's wife, Cath, home to their three daughters – one of whom, Zoe, is a successful amateur rider.

Although giving the appearance of being remote, Cardiff Airport is only two and a half miles from the farm, and to the north, the M4 is just seven miles, making routes countrywide easily accessible.

In State Of Play and Cappa Bleu, Evan had two contrasting horses who nevertheless relished the challenge of Aintree. Both were owned by William and Angela Rucker; Angela's mother is Pat Tollit who was a seriously able point-to-point rider in the Midlands, long before women could ride against men, let alone under NH Rules, and yet she notched up 171 wins and was leading lady rider six times in the 1950s, '60s and into the early '70s. Angela also rode in point-to-points, as do some of the third generation.

State Of Play did much to put comparatively new trainer Evan Williams on the map, and was a model of consistency. He was small – barely 16 hh. – but brave, athletic and much like a rubber ball. As a six-year-old in 2006 he won the prestigious Hennessy Gold Cup at Newbury off 11 stone 4 pounds with Paul Moloney in the saddle.

He first ran in the National two and a half years later for the 2009 renewal, after Evan persuaded Angela Rucker to let him run. 'I have never gone to Aintree for the sake of it but with some sort of chance,' he says.

And so it proved. Crossing the Melling Road with two fences left, Evan thought his horse might win, but State Of Play had been hampered at the second Becher's and although he rallied the mistake had taken its toll, and he finished an honourable fourth behind Mon Mome.

State Of Play ran in the National a further three times, from a total of just four races in all that time. The next year, in 2010, he finished third behind A.P. McCoy on Don't Push It when again he was staying on at the finish. In 2011, he finished fourth behind Ballabriggs, ridden as in the previous two Nationals by Paul Moloney, and once more he was staying on at the finish; and in 2012 he unseated early on.

Cappa Bleu was an altogether different model to State Of Play, being bigger and stronger, yet he was elegant and 'floated over the ground', barely seeming to touch the turf. While not timid, he was a little delicate and needed careful handling. Evan learnt to give him a gallop less than most horses, or he would run the risk of 'leaving his race at home'.

He took his racing well and after winning two Irish point-to-points and two more in England as well as the Cheltenham Foxhunters, he went to Evan for his professional career. In November 2011 he took the Betfair Multiples Handicap Chase at Haydock by a head from Tamarinbleu, was third in the Welsh National behind Le Beau Baie, and third again at Ascot in February 2012, leaving him spot-on for an attempt at the National.

This meant Evan had two runners, but Paul Moloney chose the ten-year-old Cappa Bleu over his old friend State Of Play, who was now twelve.

Cappa Bleu was hampered at the first Foinavon but by the end, with Neptune Collonges, Sunnyhill Boy and Seabass gone clear, Cappa Bleu was nevertheless eating up the ground and was, in vain, catching those ahead of him with every stride, to finish fourth only twelve lengths behind the winner.

His target was clearly now the 2013 National, before which he ran second twice in both two prep races. In an exciting race, he was to be bridesmaid, finishing nine lengths second to Auroras Encore (trained by Sue Smith and ridden by National debutante Ryan Mania) and just chinning his Welsh compatriot Teaforthree in third.

Of his jockey Paul Moloney on those horses, Evan Williams says, 'You've got to have the horse and the right guy for the horse. Paul Moloney was magic round Aintree, he had the touch.'

In fact, apart from those five placings for Evan Williams, Paul Moloney also finished fourth in the next two years on Alvarado – meaning he finished in the first four in the National an incredible seven years in succession, before injury forced his retirement in 2017. One of many to post tributes was champion jockey Richard Johnson who noted 'we will miss him in the weigh room and watching him win on horses that never should have'.

With a number of top-class trainers in Wales, a second Welsh winner should soon come about, following Kirkland way back in 1905.

Although there has been only one Welsh-trained horse to win the Grand National, a number of Welsh-born jockeys have been successful.

Henry Potts of Glan-yr-Afon, Mold, Flintshire, west of Chester, won the forerunner of the Grand National, the Grand Liverpool Steeplechase, on The Duke at Maghull in 1837.

Montgomery-born Roddy Owen won on Father O'Flynn in 1892. Jack Anthony, from West Wales, is one of the elite band of riders to have won the race three times, on the one-eyed Glenside in 1911, on Ally Sloper in 1915 and on Troytown in 1920.

Frederick Brychan Rees, better known as Dick Rees, from Tenby, won on Shaun Spadah in 1921, and the following year his elder brother, Lewis Bilby Rees, won on Music Hall, while Carmarthen's Dudley Williams won on Kellsboro Jack in 1933.

Wrexham-born Fulke Walwyn won the 1936 race on Reynoldstown (see Chapter 9) beating Ego, ridden by another Welshman Harry Llewellyn, later Sir Harry of show-jumping's Foxhunter fame. The next year was the turn of the Vale of Glamorgan's Evan Williams on Royal Mail; the jockey lived in the Bear Hotel at Cowbridge, close to current trainer Evan Williams (no relation). Royal Mail was trained by Welshman Ivor Anthony at Wroughton in Wiltshire (so, as with horses trained by Irishmen living in England, does not go down as a win from their country of birth).

Royal Air Force Flight Sergeant Mervyn Jones, a nephew of Ivor Anthony, had special leave to ride in the 1940 race and won on Bogskar. Sadly, he was later killed on a flying mission.

Barry-born John Cook won in 1971 on the fast-finishing Specify, and Neale Doughty, from Kenfig Hill near Bridgend and a graduate of the Llangeinor Hunt Pony Club, took the 1984 race on Hallo Dandy. The following year, 1985, Carmarthen's Hywel Davies won on Last Suspect after persuading Anne, Duchess of Westminster to let the horse take its chance.

In 1992 Pembroke-born Carl Llewellyn won on probably the tallest winner of the race, Party Politics, and he made it two when winning the race again in 1998 on Earth Summit.

Wales remains waiting, as female jockeys do, too; either could soon be in the winner's enclosure.

30

Twenty-First-Century Women on the Brink

Talk about racing royalty – a Walsh and a Carberry rode in the National eleven times between them and then both retired after riding winners at the 2018 Punchestown Festival. No, not one of their illustrious brothers, but sisters-in-law Katie Walsh and Nina Carberry; they dominated the first part of the twenty-first century as far as women riders in the National were concerned. More than that, between them they did so much to enhance the reputation of female riders, never more so than in the Grand National itself, as well as at home in Ireland and also at the Cheltenham Festival.

Just before their era, another female rider had covered herself in glory when Carrie Ford and Forest Gunner came fifth of twenty-one to finish in Hedgehunter's 2005 National. Remarkably, the horse was sent off 8-1 second favourite, a far cry from the list of long-priced no-hopers ridden by women in the previous century. Carrie took the lead four fences from home and a female winner appeared distinctly possible, but the horse could only plug on at one pace. Married to trainer Richard Ford, Carrie had won the previous year's Aintree Foxhunters only ten weeks after giving birth to a daughter, Hannah. This qualified Forest Gunner for the Grand National, and it meant both horse and rider had experience of the unique course before they tackled the big race.

Before that the best placing had been Rosemary Henderson, also fifth, on 100-1 shot Fiddler's Pike in 1994.

Nina Carberry rode in the National six times, completing in four; she married Ted Walsh Junior, and in May 2017 gave birth to a daughter; in October that year she resumed race-riding, and retired on a winner, Josies Orders, at the Punchestown Festival the following April. She won the 2011 Irish Grand National on Organisedconfusion, trained by her uncle, Arthur Moore.

She and her sister-in-law Katie Walsh, married to trainer Ross Sullivan, were outstanding horsewomen and jockeys, and always seemed to be smiling.

Katie Walsh also rode in the National six times, completing in five and memorably becoming the first, and so far only, female jockey to place when finishing third on Seabass in 2012, a remarkable record. Seabass started at 8-1 joint favourite (with Shakalakaboomboom). Trained by Katie's father Ted Walsh, Seabass took the lead four out and only relinquished it at the elbow.

What a race that was! Jim McGrath's commentary for the BBC captured the excitement: 'As they come to the elbow, Seabass is not done with, Katie Walsh is coming back and Neptune Collonges is joining in as well. It's Sunnyhillboy with 100 yards left to go, Neptune Collonges digging deep on the nearside. Sunnyhillboy in front – he's shortening his stride, he's a half-length in front! Neptune Collonges is diving in and – oh, it's tight! It's very tight between Sunnyhillboy and Neptune Collonges – a photo in the Grand National!'

Only a nose separated the first two, and Katie Walsh and Seabass were five lengths back in third; they were seven lengths ahead of fourth-placed Cappa Bleu. Katie's brother, Ruby, one of the all-time great jockeys, was unable to take his intended mount in the race, having suffered concussion in an earlier race.

In Katie's next National ride the following year, she teamed up again with Seabass but could only finish thirteenth behind Auroras Encore; Seabass had started as outright favourite at 11-2.

In 2018 Katie's mount was the 16-1 shot Baie Des Iles. 'National

Punters Plunge on Katie' roared one headline; 'More Support for Monster Gamble on Baie Des Iles' was another. In the end, the mud-loving grey could only finish last behind the victorious Tiger Roll.

Katie hung up her racing boots later that month after riding a particularly good winner at the Punchestown Festival on Antey, beating Barry Geraghty's mount by a nose in a three-way photo finish. She had won the Grade 1 Bumper at the Cheltenham Festival the previous month. Her biggest success was in the 2015 Irish National on Thunder And Roses.

This was a far cry from the early years of women riding in the National when the starting odds of most of their horses were around 100-1, representing a true reflection of their hopes; three were at 200-1 and one at 500-1. Of the first fourteen female-ridden horses, only one got round, and that was in last place. The fifteenth was Rosemary Henderson whose creditable fifth was described earlier.

Whereas the first female rider, Charlotte Brew, suffered vilification in the press, from male riders and even from other women, women are now securing rides that have much better chances, and in the twenty-first century we have twice seen one go off as favourite. Of the seventeen up until 2019, twelve completed the course, in addition to the third place of Seabass.

In 2018, for only the second time in the history of the race, three of the runners were ridden by women, but the difference this time was that all three were genuine contenders. In the end it was Milansbar, 'Mars Bar' to his stable, ridden by Bryony Frost, who came out not just best of them but of Britain: the four horses who finished ahead of her, led by Tiger Roll, were all trained in Ireland.

Only two years before, at windswept Larkhill in Wiltshire, I had presented Bryony with the trophy for winning the ladies point-to-point race; a few weeks later she went on to win the

Foxhunters at Cheltenham. A year later, the same point-to-point presentation went to another Paul Nicholls protégé, Harriet Tuckey, and while there, phone clapped to ear, Paul exclaimed, 'I've had an unexpected winner at Cheltenham.' It was Bryony Frost on Frodon – and Bryony was on her 'Saturday roll', the day when the feature races are televised and the winning rider receives welcome exposure of his or her prowess. Since then, Bryony Frost has taken the sport to the front pages by winning the Grade 1 Ryanair Chase at the 2019 Cheltenham Festival on Frodon. Her loquacious interviews are a joy to listen to: the rapport with the noble horse, the thrill of the partnership as they fight back from being seemingly beaten, her sheer joy at race-riding – and even the mundane mucking out of stables and other routine chores.

Frodon is her star horse, but Bryony is much more than a one-horse wonder. The way she booted home Present Man in the Badger Beer Chase at Wincanton, for the second year running, was jockeyship and riding ability as good as it gets. She also won the Peter O'Sullevan Memorial Chase at Newbury, in the colours of J.P. McManus on Kapcorse – and these are just a few of her successes.

Racing, of course, is a great leveller. On a modest Monday meeting at Southwell, only four days after victory in the Ryanair Chase, she took a fall and broke her collarbone – probably the most common bone to break for jockeys, and very painful – and so her chance of a ride in the 2019 National was gone. Like all jockeys and riders in general, she is no stranger to injury.

Bryony Frost grew up with stories of the Grand National in her West Country home. Her father, Jimmy, won the race in 1989 on Little Polveir, giving trainer Toby Balding success for a second time, twenty years after Highland Wedding, and her older brothers Dan and Hadden were good jockeys.

'I would be lost without my father, and the whole family – all my grandparents were involved in racing; he gave me the inspiration, and my grandmother was a walking dictionary; I was a complete sponge, soaking up stories of their mistakes and triumphs.'

Missing the 2019 National – she was due to ride one of Gordon Elliott's eleven – was 'not easy' and she would rather have been riding than behind a microphone (for ITV Racing).

Much of Bryony's childhood was spent mucking about on ponies with her brothers. She sat on a racehorse for the first time at the age of nine, progressed to pony racing and then point-to-point circuits, along with some top-level show-jumping, and in 2017 found herself partnering Pacha Du Polder, a stalwart of the Paul Nicholls yard, in the Cheltenham Foxhunters – 'the amateurs' Gold Cup' – and winning it by a neck at 16-1. She then had her first taste of the Aintree fences when finishing fourth in the Foxhunters on the same horse.

Pacha Du Polder repeated his Cheltenham Foxhunters win the following year, 2018, for Harriet Tuckey, but was pulled up in 2019 and retired.

Bryony turned professional, becoming a conditional jockey in Paul Nicholls' stable, in the summer of 2017. (A conditional jockey is the equivalent of an apprentice on the flat: a young jockey attached to a particular stable and able to claim a weight allowance in most races contested by full-blown professionals, the Grand National being one of the exceptions.) By December of that year she had ridden her first Grade 1 winner on Black Corton in the Kauto Star Novices Chase at Kempton. It was her fifth win on the horse and, now riding as a professional, pundits and plaudits alike were awakening to a star in the making.

One thing about Bryony, in addition to her work ethic and riding ability, is that she imparts her enthusiasm to her horses. As a result, they get into a rhythm and will do their best for her in a tight finish.

By the end of 2018 she had ridden out her claim, but the rides kept coming. The 2018–19 season saw her crowned the season's champion conditional jockey with fifty winners on the finale day at Sandown, where the presentations were made. She also made a winning comeback ride from her injury, winning the bet365 Oaksey Chase on the horse that did so much to put her on the map: Black Corton.

Between races, in her quieter moments, Bryony likes nothing better than to roam across Dartmoor, soaking up the solitude and beauty, alone with her thoughts – and reflecting on how she can improve on her race-riding.

It is only a matter of time until a female jockey wins the Grand National, whoever she may be. The resulting media coverage will no doubt match the volume generated by the first girl to ride in it, Charlotte Brew, back in 1977, but the tone will have improved. Instead of disparaging remarks there will be recognition of a landmark moment in the world's greatest horse race.

It was not to be in 2019, but history was nonetheless on a roll.

31

The Grand National, 2019

Two in a Row for Tiger Roll

It's 9 a.m. on Saturday, 6 April 2019. A weak sun is strengthening, unlike the relentless rain of Thursday, and I set off to walk the course. First, I bump into Richard Pitman (a little more portly than when he memorably rode Crisp forty-six years ago), and then Neptune Collonges, returning from an early stroll prior to the afternoon's parade of former winners, looking a picture and lapping up polos and attention from fans.

Out on the course, the first five fences have been re-dressed since yesterday, the divots put in, and the grass rolled in broad stripes. There is a bit of yield in the ground, perfect for jump racing's biggest test. The repair crew has reached Becher's – my, how that fence has changed on the landing side; I admire their handiwork and move on to Foinavon, met slightly on the turn, and named after the 1967 victor. These first seven fences range in height from 4 feet 6 inches (standard NH height) to two at 5 feet. The right-angled Canal Turn is then the first of five in a row at 5 feet high, including a big open ditch at the eleventh (and twenty-seventh). Re-crossing the Melling Road, there are two plain fences before the Chair – 5 feet 2 inches high with a 6-foot-wide ditch in front of it, making a total spread of 11 feet; now that is a big fence, though like all the others its inner core has been made more flexible. The Chair is followed by the smallest fence, the water, but neither of these are jumped on the last circuit, hence the ultra-long, stamina-sapping run-in. As I walk this route it is surprising how sharp and funnelled the jink – the elbow – is between the water jump and the Melling course, before coming to a running rail to guide a tiring leader, like Tiger Roll last year.

Tiger Roll: will he, can he win again? I've been fervent about him since his super-impressive Cheltenham Cross-Country following his unexpected Grade 2 hurdle win at 25-1. Some previous winners place again several times, but many others never win a race of any description after the National, let alone showing the improvement and versatility of Tiger Roll. Last Saturday, one week ago, when we visited him at Gordon Elliott's in Ireland, his lass, Louise Magee, wouldn't hear of defeat for him. The extra weight this year? Not a bother. There's still another seven hours until we can find out.

Finally, on the course walk, the winning post – and a look at Red Rum's grave, bedecked by flowers, with packets of polos strewn around, and surrounded by fans, many taking selfies.

The sun is out, the number of helicopters has increased markedly, as has the number of visitors pouring in. Hordes of them will fill the ensuing hours drinking in one of the many bars – mostly named after greats of yesteryear – perusing the form, drinking, placing bets, drinking, chatting with friends, drinking . . .

There are five races to be got through – OK, three are Grade 1 and two Grade 3, so there is nothing ordinary in this Randox Health-sponsored Grand National meeting. The sun is now gloriously warm, a perfect spring day, so the array of six-inch heels, open toes and skimpy ladies-wear of the Liver-birds is not quite so incongruous as in less clement years. They add to the colour and atmosphere of the occasion, as does the group of a dozen or so men dressed in tiger costumes and chanting for Tiger Roll on the steps around the unsaddling enclosure.

I perch on a stool by the paddock; the lady on the next one tells me proudly that her visit is an eightieth birthday present to herself. 'I've always wanted to come,' she says. She is clearly enjoying every minute of her first visit to the great race.

Bryony Frost, long hair flowing and looking smart and fashionable in spite of her arm being in a sling, pops in front of a microphone in the paddock. She has joined the ITV team for the three-day Festival, adding glamour along with wise and knowledgeable words for the armchair viewers.

The parade of former winners illustrates how well cared for these old heroes are. Pineau De Re is ridden, the rest led: the chestnut Bindaree, now twenty-five years old; Silver Birch; Mon Mome, who is bucking and jigging his way round; Don't Push It; Neptune Collonges and Auroras Encore. Two other former winners are absent for the simple reason that they are running in the race again today: One For Arthur and Tiger Roll.

Out near the stands, I find myself beside a St John Ambulance volunteer. About 120 of them are scattered through the enclosures as well as at the fences. Their services are called for more frequently among the punters than the jockeys, he tells me. He has come all the way from the east of England, and his day job is train driver.

By the fourth race, the rail between the stands and course is a continuous line of yellow-coated policemen facing out to the course, all the way from the Chair to beyond the winning post. Every fifty yards or so there is also a policeman facing directly towards the crowds. I make my way to the pre-parade ring to await the Grand National runners. Before the first one arrives, a security guard checks every stall.

On through the massive crowds to the top of the stands and an excellent view of the course. Many of the ladies have given up on their shoes and are walking barefoot, some in tears, and others have swapped into flip-flops; many are clearly inebriated. But as soprano Laura Wright embarks on her rendition of the National Anthem they join everyone else in standing up and singing along.

The moment we've all waited for, come here to see live, is almost upon us. The horses have walked past the packed stands, mound and concourses, and cantered back towards the start.

They are lining up but – there is Tiger Roll, reluctant to turn and join the others, 'acting the maggot', as Davy Russell was later to say. Help is quickly at hand from another of trainer Gordon Elliott's record eleven runners in the shape of Denis O'Regan on A Toi Phil, who helps coax the little star into the line-up, Davy using his legs out of the stirrups to help, and after one false start they are soon away on their near four-and-a-half-mile journey.

Two things are clear from the start: the mare Magic Of Light is loving it, and Richard Johnson's mount Rock The Kasbah is not: he was last over the second fence, made a bad mistake at the third and never got into contention. The sharp-sighted can see Tiger Roll tucked away bang in the middle of the field.

No fallers at Becher's, and Ruby Walsh's mount Rathvinden sweeps into the lead at the Canal Turn. (Ruby retired from a sensational career the following month, immediately after winning the Punchestown Gold Cup.) At the Chair, the mare makes a bad mistake, followed at the water by Rathvinden doing likewise. And now the horse with a lot of late support, from 100-1 down to 25s, Livelovelaugh, comes on to the scene. Before the race, bemused commentators figured it must have been its name that made once-a-year punters latch on to it. It is ridden by David Mullins, too, who from three previous rides in the race has tasted victory and a photo-finish second.

There have been no fallers since the first fence, but now three go at the nineteenth, an open ditch, where one of them, Rock The Kasbah and Richard Johnson, is brought down. Some great jockeys are destined never to win the National.

As the field approaches the Foinavon fence, Tiger Roll is beautifully poised on the inside and on the heels of the leaders. Uncharacteristically, he makes two significant nods on landing at the twenty-fourth and twenty-fifth, but thereafter his jumping and economical style is pure joy to watch. Magic Of Light is also continuing to jump brilliantly and retakes the lead at the third last, where Pleasant Company, the head second last year to Tiger Roll, unseats his jockey.

At the last two fences some ten horses pull up, the Lizzie Kelly-ridden Tea For Two among them; they were behind early on in the race but had then made some progress. Valseur Lido, the other lady-ridden horse, was to place tenth of the nineteen finishers (her jockey, Rachael Blackmore, finished runner-up in the Irish champion jockeys table, a huge achievement). Also plugging on are Walk In The Mill, Anibale Fly and 2017 hero One For Arthur, who ran on well to finish sixth.

But now it is all about the last fence and the battle up front. The mare Magic Of Light is still leading, but she blunders badly and, alongside her, the Tiger is clearly on a Roll. Voices are cheering, yelling, as he draws away; hats are thrown in the air; behind him both Magic Of Light and Rathvinden are being hard ridden and Davy Russell has yet to move on his little partner. He does no more than give a shake of the reins in the final hundred yards – and gallops into the history books, the first back-to-back winner since Red Rum.

It was truly an 'I was there' moment.

Owner Michael O'Leary is talking to the press afterwards. So was Tiger Roll the best investment he ever made? A slight hesitation, and then: 'The second best; the engagement ring for my wife was my best investment,' he quips.

Gordon Elliott admits the stats were against Tiger Roll. 'I thought it was impossible. He wears his heart on his sleeve, he's special,' he says, beer in hand. 'I wasn't born with a silver spoon, and I don't even know what champagne tastes like.'

Michael O'Leary describes winning for a second time as 'an out of body experience', and adds, 'Everyone grows up hearing about the Grand National and it's the first race a kid puts a bet on; I did, without my mother knowing.'

Jockey Davy Russell pays tribute to 'a fantastic horse; he jumps really well, so quick, he was passing horses in mid-air. He loves to run and jump, he enjoys it so much.' He adds, 'And he knows his own name; when he heard it on the intercom, he rose in stature.'

In fact, for anyone under forty-five, Tiger Roll will be remembered as THE Grand National horse; you have to be middle-aged to remember Red Rum and a nonagenarian to recall Reynoldstown.

Like Red Rum, Tiger's story is pure fairy-tale. Small in size, big in heart with that all-important, intangible quality in a racehorse, the will to win.

Long may Aintree and the world's greatest horse race continue.

Postscript: Virtual Grand National, Saturday 4th April 2020

Ready for the race party with friends; check the laptop, notebook and champagne; put on the hat, and pray once more that Tiger Roll can achieve the unprecedented three consecutive Grand National victories. Now, how do I work this newfangled Zoom thing? Ah, click, wait a moment, and there is my hostess in Scotland! She is surrounded by more of her friends from Sussex, London and places all the way up to the Highlands. Far-flung we may be, but there is one thing in common – well, two actually, as all the ladies are wearing hats – and we are all holding glasses of champagne.

4 April 2020 was supposed to be Tiger Roll's legitimate attempt at three Grand National wins in a row, until Covid-19 intervened. The whole country was in lockdown and everything was cancelled. Everything. So here we were, settling down to watch a Virtual Grand National, compiled by Inspired Entertainment and produced by Carm Productions for ITV in dead secrecy. Thanks to modern technology and clever algorithms, we were able to watch its surprising realism. Bookmakers were taking bets, but only to a maximum of £10, and all proceeds were donated to NHS charities. Some 4.8 million viewers tuned in to watch.

The runners on the small screen are remarkably lifelike. Talkischeap leads them over the first few fences, closely accompanied by Walk In The Mill and Top Ville Ben, while handily close to the outside is Tiger Roll. As they approach the Chair, the tenth and largest obstacle on the course, he is just leading. There has been a scattering of fallers by the 18th where Top Ville Ben takes over the lead, and at the 21st fence Tiger Roll appears to be fading. They soar over fence 22, the second Bechers, led now by Rachel Blackmore on Burrows Saint. Could there be a famous first victory for a female rider?

Yet by the 26th fence, with only four more and the gruelling run-in to come, Tiger Roll is bouncing along in the lead again. Three fences from home and he is five or six lengths clear, but at the second-last Aso, who has always been prominent, is in the lead – only to fall. Tiger Roll was briefly in the lead once more. This is where a horse called Potters Corner was mentioned for the first time. Now they come to the last, and he wings it. Tiger Roll gives chase, but it is left to Walk In The Mill to put the wind up the leader, with Any Second Now also passing a tiring Tiger. We rush to look up the jockey: he is a seventeen-year-old called Jack Tudor, who cannot use his 7lb claim in a race of this stature. He had won the Welsh National on Potters Corner last time out, and he needed two more wins (which his trainer Christian Williams was confident he would get) before he was allowed to compete in the race. Williams too is only a little past rookie status, but as a jockey he won three novice hurdles on the great Denman, and he finished second in the 2005 Grand National on Royal Auclair. It is the only the second-ever Welsh-trained winner of the race.

We down more champagne, salute the creators of this race – and fervently look forward to the real thing in 2021.

Sources

I am grateful to the following publications and websites for their invaluable information.

Belfast Telegraph
Daily Record
Daily Telegraph
Eclipse Magazine
Evening Standard
Express
The Free Library
Gallop Magazine
Guardian
Horse and Hound
Independent
Irish Field
Lancashire Post
Racing Post
Scotsman
Scottish Sun
Sun

Online Sources

www.eclipsemagazine.co.uk
www.freewebs.com/grandnationalanorak
www.gallop-magazine.com
www.grandnational.org.uk
www.horseandhound.co.uk
www.horseracingphoto.co.uk
www.theirishfield.ie
https://sites.google.com/site/jockeypedia/
www.thejockeyclub.co.uk
www.theracingapp.co.uk
www.racingpost.com

Bibliography

Anne Alcock, *'They're Off!': The Story of the First Girl Jump Jockeys*, J.A. Allen & Co, 1978

Bobby Beasley, *Second Start*, W.H. Allen, 1976

T.H. Bird, *One Hundred Grand Nationals*, Country Life, 1937

Peter Bromley, *My Most Memorable Races*, Stanley Paul & Co, 1988

Bob Champion and Jonathan Powell, *Champion's Story: A Great Human Triumph*, Victor Gollancz Ltd, 1981

Peter Churchill, *Horse Racing*, Blandford Press, 1981

Declan Colley, *When Bobby Met Christy: The Story of Bobby Beasley and a Wayward Horse*, The Collins Press, 2010

B.W.R. Curling, *British Racecourses*, Witherby, 1951

—— *Royal Champion: The Story of Steeplechasing's First Lady*, Michael Joseph, 1980

Richard Dunwoody, *Obsessed*, Headline, 2001

Tim Fitzgeorge-Parker, *No Secret So Close: The Biography of Bruce Hobbs*, Pelham Books, 1984

Mick Fitzgerald and Don Maclean, *Better Than Sex*, Highdown, 2009

Dick Francis, *Sport of Queens*, Michael Joseph, 1982

Clive Graham and Bill Curling, *The Grand National: An Illustrated History of the Greatest Steeplechase in the World*, Barrie and Jenkins, 1972

Reg Green, *The History of the Grand National: A Race Apart*,

Hodder & Stoughton and Marlborough Books, 1992

Ivor Herbert, *The Queen Mother's Horses*, Pelham Books, 1967

—— *Red Rum*, William Luscombe, 1974

Ivor Herbert and Patricia Smyly, *The Winter Kings*, Pelham Books, 1968

Anne Holland, *The Grand National: The Irish at Aintree*, The O'Brien Press, 2008

—— *The Grand National: The Official Celebration of 150 Years*, Macdonald Queen Anne Press, 1991

—— *In the Blood: Irish Racing Dynasties*, The O'Brien Press, 2009

—— *Stride by Stride*, Macdonald Queen Anne Press, 1989

John Hughes and Peter Watson, *Long Live the National*, Michael Joseph, 1983

Peter King, *The Grand National: Anybody's Race*, Quartet, 1969

Sean Magee (ed), *Coming to the Last: A Tribute to Peter O'Sullevan*, Partridge Press, 1997

Finch Mason, *Heroes and Heroines*, The Biographical Press, 1911

A.P. McCoy with Charlie Connelly, *Winner: My Racing Life*, Orion Books, 2015

David Hoadley Munroe, *The Grand National*, William Heinemann, 1931

Jacqueline O'Brien & Ivor Herbert, *Vincent O'Brien: The Official Biography*, Bantam Press, 2005

Peter O'Sullevan, *Calling the Horses*, Stanley Paul, 1989

Nigel Payne and Dominic Hart, *Everyone Must Leave: The Day They Stopped the National*, Mainstream, 1998

John Pinfold, *Aintree: The History of the Racecourse*, Medina Publishing Ltd, 2016

—— *Gallant Sport: The Authentic History of Liverpool Races and the Grand National*, Portway Press, 1999

Fred and Mercy Rimell, *Aintree Iron*, W.H. Allen, 1977

Joan Rimmer, *Aintree's Queen Bee: Mirabel Topham and the Grand National*, SportsBooks Ltd, 2007

John Ellis Rossell Jr, *The Maryland Hunt Cup Past and Present*,
The Sporting Press, 1975

Vian Smith, *The Grand National, A History of the World's Greatest
Steeplechase*, Stanley Paul, 1969

Directory of the Turf, various editions, Pacemaker Publications

Hunter Chasers and Point-to-Pointers, various annuals, Sale and
Mackenzie

Raceform: Up-to-Date, Sporting Chronicle Publications, various
editions

Index

Picture Credits

The author and publisher are grateful to Getty Images for permission to reproduce photographs, with the following exceptions:

p.1 (top) Topfoto
p.5 (top) Shutterstock
p.6 (below) Alan Johnson
p.8 (above) Frank Casey; (right) PAImages
p.9 (top) PAImages; (right) Shutterstock; (below) RacingFotos. com
p.11 (below) PAImages
p.15 (top and right) Shutterstock